# *ABORTION ANALYZED*

Bernard J. Ficarra, M.D., K.S.G.

President
Catholic Academy of Sciences
in the
United States of America
Washington, D.C.

Health Educator Publications, Inc.
1580 Kirkland Road
Old Town, Maine 04468
(207) 827-3633

**Library of Congress Cataloging-in-Publication Data**

Ficarra, Bernard J. (Bernard Joseph), 1914-
Abortion analyzed.

Bibliography: p.
1. Abortion — United States. 2. Abortion — Moral and ethical aspects. 3. Abortion — Religious aspects — Catholic Church. 4. Catholic Church — Doctrines. 5. Abortion — Law and legislation — United States.
I. Title. (DNLM: 1. Abortion, Induced. 2. Catholicism. 3. Ethics, Medical. 4. Public Policy — United States.
HQ767.5.U5F53  1989    363.4'6    89-80595
ISBN 0-932887-25-2 (pbk.)

**HEALTH EDUCATOR PUBLICATIONS, INC.**
1580 Kirkland Road
Old Town, Maine 04468

"Is a society redeemed if it provides massive safe-guards for accused persons and yet fails to provide elementary protection for its law-abiding citizens?"

Chief Justice Warren E. Burger
United States Supreme Court

# HIPPOCRATIC OATH *

"I swear by Apollo the physician, and Aesculapius, and Hygeia, and, Panacea, and all the gods and goddesses, that, according to my ability and judgement, I will keep this oath (vow) and this stipulation — to reckon him who taught me this art equally dear to me as my parents, to share my substance with him, and relieve his necessities if required; to look upon his offspring in the same footing as my own brothers, and to teach them this art, if they should wish to learn it, without fee or stipulation, and that by precept, lecture, and every other mode of instruction, I will impart a knowledge of the art to my own sons, and those of my teachers, and to disciples bound by a stipulation and oath according to the law of medicine, but to none others.

I will follow that system of regimen which, according to my ability and judgment, I consider for the benefit of my patients, and abstain from whatever is deleterious and mischievous. I will give no deadly medicine to anyone if asked, nor suggest any such counsel; and in like manner I WILL NOT GIVE TO A WOMAN A PESSARY TO PRODUCE ABORTION. With purity and holiness I will pass my life and practice my art. I will not cut (from Latin verb temeo, literally meaning to castrate) persons laboring under the stone, but will leave this to be done by men who are practitioners of this work (surgeons). (...I will keep apart from men engaging in this deed, which was regarded as an abomination because it was sterilization.**)

Into whatever houses I enter, I will go into them for the benefit of the sick, and will abstain from every voluntary act of mischief and corruption; and, further from the seduction of females or males, of freemen and slaves. Whatever, in connection with my professional practice, or not in connection with it, I see or hear, in the life of men, which ought not to be spoken of abroad, I will not divulge, as reckoning that all such should be kept secret. While I continue to keep this oath unviolated, may it be granted to me to enjoy life and the practice of the art, respected by all men, in all times! But should I trespass and violate this oath, may the reverse be my lot!"

* These hieratic words of Hippocrates (460 B.C. - 377 B.C.) were called an oath by subsequent healers of illnesses. It constitutes the most ancient, historically known document that codifies the ethical conduct of a professional guild.

** Dr. Savas Nittes in Bulletin of the History of Medicine, VII, 719, 1939. Published by the American Association of the History of Medicine at Johns Hopkins University School of Medicine, Baltimore, Maryland.

# CONTENTS

# PREFACE

*Each thing insofar as it is in itself,*
*endeavors to persevere in its being.*
*Benedict Spinoza*
*(1632-1677)*

On January 22, 1973, the United States Supreme Court legalized abortion in this nation. The sixteenth anniversary of this legal decision highlighted the dissolute distinction that tallied the record of more than twenty million babies destroyed. This is a Pyrrhic victory for no one.

A discussion on abortion evokes tripartite, inseparable topics that arise from the intrinsic essence of the subject matter. These components are the medical, legal, and moral attachments that are inchoate to it to the same intensive degree that they are indivisible. Not even the legalization of abortion can eradicate the immorality of the act. Neither the addition of a socioeconomic reason nor a nonmedical indication for an abortion eliminates its amoral offensiveness.

It seems that today's world has people running in every unchartered direction as it appears determined to produce even more instruments of personal destruction. The time has arrived for all those concerned with human life to redouble those efforts that strive to place in proper order first things first. There is no doubt that this troubled world needs many socioeconomic reforms. Indeed, the world needs many changes, yet there are certain things that never change. No matter how hectic life becomes, to destroy the unborn is evil and no law, social opinion, economic necessity, or personal necessity can change it.

Today's society is so lost, so in chaos, that it does not know what to do with itself or how to manage itself. The basic unit of that society is the family. Many present day families are "so torn, so disturbed, so decayed, that their needs are different and more demanding than the times of yesterday"(1). Out of these families come many women confused by life who have an unwanted pregnancy which produces a moral eclipse in the astronomy of life.

Human conscience does not allow anyone the luxury of ignoring the abortion upheaval either by sufferance or for any other reason. Any productive opportunity to cry out against it cannot be ignored. An ancient Arabian proverb tells it well: "Four things come not back the spoken word, the sped arrow, the past life, and the neglected opportunity."

As an author, I cannot present a visible provenance to satisfy all the opposing inquisitors who will criticize, either constructively or destructively, the contents of this book. All that is desired is the courtesy of a stoichiological allocution on the abortion issue.

This medicolegal, socioeconomic, moral question must be evaluated and answered without outrecuidance. A trimerous studied evaluation of abortion must be cogitative, cognitive, and salient. Our acknowledgements support ardently standard ethology that enhances modern ethnography. With this obligation is entwined the need for the elucidation of deontology that should be the conscience of abortion advocates.

The presentations in the subsequent chapters have acquired considerable importance as a study in the ethical approach to a problem that has divided modern medical practice in America. Abortions are on the increase, performed on women who, in perfect good health, argue in favor of their claims to be aborted. In 1983, New York State had the highest abortion rate, with 731 abortions for every 1000 live births; Utah had the lowest abortion rate in the nation. It must be obvious that the existence of this practice raises certain questions, both for the party directly involved, and for those whose duties as physicians, medical students, nurses, and allied personnel bring them into contact with abortion procedures as a *particeps principis*.

The many faces of the abortion problem are more than sixteen years old. Thus, it is not entirely new and much philosophical discussion has taken place in regard to the moral values involved therein. Theological necessity reiterates condemnation of abortion. Certain aspects of the subject have ceased to be controversial in the minds of Catholic theologians. "It is never permitted to perform acts wrong in themselves. No matter how legitimate their intended end may be. In one sentence, the end no matter how good in itself, can never justify the use of means, unlawful in themselves, to its attainment"(2).

As to Catholic physicians, nurses, and ancillary attendants taking part in the activities of abortion clinics or hospitals, the rules governing their participation in morally condemned operations in the operating theatre are applicable(2). They must not give active proximate cooperation to any causally related procedure that induces an abortion. Participants in abortion can neither alienate their duty to abstain and refrain from encouraging an abortion nor can they acquire any right to its performance. The natural and divine positive laws are such that the preservation of a new life is an inherent human right. "This is the divine law and not just a disciplinary measure imposed by the Catholic Church as so many non-Catholics seem to think"(2).

The adoption of a procedure such as abortion has the effect of propounding to human liberty a possibility outside the social range of life that was not imagined up to our day. An ethical problem for the human conscience is to know whether or not it is morally right or wrong to perform an immoral act made available via the mechanics of secular law. Mental reflection unfolds that this question, which may appear simple, hides another infinitely more complex one. Namely, that of knowing if, by introducing the categories of the legally permitted and the morally forbidden, does the person aborted still remain within the combined ethico-social framework when the ethical half has been left behind in the destroyed unborn child? It is somewhat puerile not to condemn the practice of abortion because it is protected by a system of legal rules from whence the act implies its fundamental existence. Social legitimacy of this act is the essential irrelevance as the protector of this inherent moral transgression.

Definitely, it seems that most people have arrived at "a moment in history when the sense of absolute prohibitions and commands of any kind whatsoever is practically lost. It is only natural that the atheist should have lost this sense. It is indeed amazing, in their turn, to see believers allowing themselves to be drawn on to that slope, without their ceasing, however, to hold on to their own particular form of belief. It is against this sort of interior defection that a group such as the right-to-life must react vigorously"(3).

While this work on abortion has been written by a Catholic, it is not primarily or exclusively a Catholic oriented text. From its incipiency, the author had in mind the many thousands of non-Catholics to whom the book might be helpful. To both the non-Catholic and Catholic physician population, this written effort may be an aid in some way. There may be many persons who refuse to accept the recommendations of their consultors, confessors, or confreres. Delays occasioned by the desire of these people not to adhere to the advice given could be morally costly or even physically fatal.

Experienced physicians have learned that what is morally proper is usually medically good. When the upright medical practitioner can satisfy his/her patients that he/she is authoritative in the advice given, the patient's mind is at rest. Thus, the reception of the physician's opinion is more likely to eventuate. There is no divisiveness between time-tried medical ethics and scientific medicine.

"The ethician seeks to discover the same truth which is sought by the conscientious physician. Truth in the science of ethics cannot contradict truth in the science of medicine. For the source of all truth is the same all-knowing, all-wise God. It is God who is the source of all truth, whether the truth in question refers to matters of religion, ethics, mathematics, physics, chemistry, or medicine. It is the study of this truth which is the objective common to every sincere scholar, be he/she a moralist or a physician"(4).

*Bernard J. Ficarra*
*Washington, D.C. 20016*
*July 4, 1989*

# CHAPTER ONE

# PHYSIOLOGY OF FERTILIZATION

*Integrity without knowledge is weak and useless, and
knowledge without integrity is dangerous and dreadful.*
Dr. Samuel Johnson (1709-1784)

One of the ten biological functions of living organisms is reproduction, which is necessary for the continuation of the specific species. Human beings are no exception to natural physiology. In order that reproduction may take place, ovulation in women is a necessity. An understanding of ovulation is inextricably bound to the menstrual cycle.

Menstruation is the result of the interworkings of a delicate mechanism operating in women's bodies. It involves the function of the pituitary gland (located in the sella turcica of the skull), the ovaries, and the uterus. Menses is the end of a physiological cycle of activities that have been ongoing during the previous month. It is an overt, tangible, normal manifestation on the part of the female human body that the reproductive cycle is active and repetitive. With the occurrence of menstruation, the pituitary gland releases (or sends) impulses as hormones (internally produced medications) into the blood stream. In this manner, the pituitary gland stimulates the ovary (one side each month alternately) to produce a single mature ovum (abnormally more than one may be produced). The ovary, in turn, secretes its own hormone called estrogen. This hormone has for its function the rebuilding of the lining of the uterus (called the endometrium). With the extrusion of a mature ovum from the ovary at the mid-cycle (ovulation), the ovary produces a second hormone (progesterone), whose special purpose is to prepare the uterus for a possible pregnancy (5).

A failure to fertilize the available ovum instigates certain alterations in the uterus. These are regressive changes in the endometrium with the expulsion of blood tinged endometrial debris. This is the terminal stage in the phenomenon of menstruation, as the cycle commences again. All the effort of the menstrual cycle with ovulation is to prepare the uterus as a future home to nourish to fulfillment another specific being for the continuation of human life.

Nature's intention is the lofty demonstration of the preservation of human life via the biological pursuit of ovulaton, with the ultimate goal of fecundation. These natural efforts are a scientific enunciation of the Christian-Judaic principles which are founded upon the laws of nature. Consistency with the biological human order coincides with those ethical dicta promulgated by Catholic, Hebraic and other theologians.

Consider in effect that there is nothing more marvelously majestic than the biological process of creating another human being. Can physical love, even at its most carnal impetus, aimed at creation, be surpassed as an inexplicable mystery? Here an analysis bearing upon the notion of the metaphysical essence of life could not answer all the inquiries pertaining to it.

Nevertheless, the unseen traditional concept of giving of self is the primordial instinct that initiates the reproductive process. A willing woman gives herself to a man. Honor, social acceptance, and moral approbation accept the relationship, recognizing it in marriage as the salve for the conscience of the partners. Between this giving of self, the incarnation within the womb, and the birth of a child, biological processes cannot be disturbed if nature is to complete its task. Imposed ethical conduct sanctions nature's duty and imposes moral behavior to protect it.

To disrupt the natural order alienates the doer from normalcy. Humanity cannot consider its own essence and the constitutive relations of its own being with nature on any factor that dehumanizes the natural order. This dictum prevails, even if the reasons against it are legitimate under laws legislated by the state. Nature is the essence of a thing. It does nothing in vain for the generation and birth of living beings. Nature is that which exists apart from and uninfluenced by humanity.

In the world of today, where practices such as abortion are accepted, it is most difficult not to forsee how the dissociation of love and pleasure from the reproductive act can fail towards becoming the rule in this biological function. The consequences of such dissociation are easy to imagine (2). Thus, the social acceptability of certain beliefs of yesterday inevitably have been called in question.

Everywhere in the universe, the narrow breach of a tolerated exception to nature's rules has a propulsion to enlarge itself. Finally, "it causes the whole of nature's structure to topple, although it was the original intention of the exception-maker that the structure should be respected" (2). Succinctly, it is to be recognized that where something sacred must be preserved, it is inevitable that such rigid negative additions as "in no circumstances" or "under no pretext" should find a place in the formulations (2). "In the secular order, these negative formulations should not have the keys to the city of uncontrolled human conduct. Indeed, that is precisely what can never be said of sacred things, because here the commandments are absolute" (2). Hence, the personal illusion cannot prevail which believes that "one can remain in a system of determined values, while one has recourse at the same time to a process which supposes the negation of these same values" (2).

## Fertilization and Migration

The mature ovum is fertilized approximately two hours after the successful meeting with an active spermatozoon. Definitive fertilization is accomplished when the sperm penetrates the ovum. Under the usual circumstances, this takes place in the lateral one-third of the fallopian tube. After the ovum has been the recipient of the sperm, it commences on its way down the tube to the uterine cavity for implantation into this organ. Between three and five days are needed for the passage of the fertilized ovum down the tube to the uterine cavity. Approximately another five days will pass before the imbedding of the ovum into the uterine wall is completed. About ten days are required for the entire process of fertilization and implantation to be completed (5).

As the fertilization of the human ovum takes place, cellular life continues with structural changes. Individually, the ovum and the sperm are considered to be excess cell units which are not amoebae, but similar to them as simple, functioning biological cells. Both the ovum and the spermatozoon are expendable cells which are created as a biological product. They are not physiologically similar to the end result of the digestive process which has residue that must be excreted.

The biological productions of the ovaries and the testes are designed for the specific definitive purpose of procreation. When each cell unites with the other, a jointly integrated dual cell is formed into one. Rapidly, the newly created duality metamorphosizes into a multiple cellular structure which geometrically increases in quantitative numbers as cellular life continues to grow as an amalgamated entity.

Legal experts recognize that fertilization becomes possible on the fourteenth day of the normal menstrual cycle, and usually takes place in the distal third of the fallopian tube. From the moment of fecundation (conception) to the time of uterine implantation, ten days usually have elapsed. If the zygote fails to be implanted into its natural physiological habitat, an ectopic pregnancy may result. An organism produced by the union of two gametes (male and female reproductive cells capable of entering into union with one another in the process of fertilization and of conjugation) is called a zygote. It is the fertilized ovum before cleavage which is cell division of the zygote. Also known as segmentation, it is an early stage in the process of development between fertilization and the blastula (a spherical mass consisting of a central cavity surrounded by a single layer of cells produced by the cleavage of the ovum), at which time the embryo consists of a mass of dividing cells, the blastomeres (6).

An ectopic pregnancy refers to the implantation of the zygote outside the uterus or in an abnormal location within the uterus. "By far the most common ectopic location is the fallopian tube. Pain is the primary symptom of tubal pregnancy. Abdominal pain is present in most patients having an ectopic pregnancy in the fallopian tube. Amenorrhea (absence of menstruation) and vaginal bleeding occur in 75 percent of these patients. Other signs of an ectopic fallopian tube pregnancy are a mass in the pelvis, shock, subnormal temperature, and decreased or falling blood pressure. Laboratory reports record a below normal hemoglobin and hematocrit reading with a leucocytosis (increase in the white blood cell count). A sonogram can verify the diagnosis. Surgical exploration of the abdominal cavity is indicated when the diagnosis of an ectopic pregnancy is made or strongly suspected (7).

"It has been stated that iatrogenic (physician-caused) damage to the uninvolved fallopian tube occurs in at least half of the patients operated upon for tubal pregnancy. This iatrogenic damage to the contralateral tube can be avoided by early operation, removal of blood clots plus all unclotted blood, conservation of the remaining tube, and testing the patency of the residual tube within a few weeks after the operation. Tubal pregnancy must be regarded as a major cause of maternal death. Appropriate obstetrical management is required to avoid maternal mortality as well as unnecessary sterilization" (7, 8).

## Uterine Implantation of the Fertilized Ovum

The possibility of the zygote not surviving is not to be discounted. From the exact moment of penetration up to the days prior to uterine implantation, the nutritional survival of the propagating cells arising out of the fertilized ovum can be in doubt. Nutritious elements for sustaining life must be obtained by internal sustenance which, in the process of consummation, may be self-destructive. Since the food supply of the increasing cells is derived from the cell protoplasm,* if the balance between cell multiplication and food consumption is not maintained cellular death due to inanition results. Thus depascent growth results in self-annihilation, if a secondary source of alimentation is not discovered.

Prior to uterine implantation, nutrients are derived from within the cell substance without an external source of nutrition supply to sustain the propagating cells. When the internal nutrients are exhausted, there is no longer any available substance which the ever-increasing, newly formed organism can call upon to supply the energy necessary to build additional cells. No other original available tissue (building material) itself is obtainable for cell growth because it has been consumed. Without nutrients, the cells diminish in size, do not multiply, become crenated, and die.

The proposition that the fertilized ovum is not a human entity is out of scientific tune with the reality of the natural biological order. The size of the objective substance does not change its intrinsic human, composite characteristics. Speculation, conjecture, hypothesis, and theory, individually or collectively, are not basic scientific dogma.

Microscopic life in a growing species is equivalent to macroscopic life in the same species. A physical diminution in the container of a

* Protoplasm is the viscid (glutinous) material constituting the essential substance of living cells upon which all the vital functions of nutrition, secretion, growth, reproductability, and motility depend.

spiritual essence does not change its fundamental invisible composite nature. Quantity is not the indicator of the life principle. A dwarf has the same spiritual life as the giant. The passage of the unborn to the born child through the anatomic birth canal is a mechanical process that neither can alter the nature of a species, nor rearrange its spiritual being. The life principle (anima) as the spiritual half of the human being cannot be measured by any yardstick as the physical half can be weighed and the height calculated.

The time has arrived for ethical people from the ranks of biological science to concern themselves with the onset of human life. It must be explained to those who look upon the fetus as a mass of protoplasm bereft of any spirituality. Scientific knowledge is not to be silenced by the juridical decisions that do not listen to the drowned out voices of those encased within human uteri. Modern abortion laws have barricaded the unborn from entering the splendid portals of childbirth that lead to life's grandeur.

What the abortionists have not considered, realized, or have purposefully ignored is that spiritually and physically the intrauterine conceptus is a member of the human democracy in which, regardless of circumstances, every one is equal. Each is entitled to the same animated benefit and physical preservation as any other member of a democratic nation. A fetus is a future postnatus adult who is imprisoned temporarily waiting only to be released from predated uterine confinement. Mere unastonished attunement to pristine vestigial instinct sustains this primordial biological premise.

### Advent of Human Life

Philosophers and theologians have stated: "It is true that science cannot establish when the soul is infused in the fetus and human personhood begins. But it is because we do not know precisely when this happens that the life process at all stages of prenatal development must be protected. In effect, we must treat the fetus as a human person from the moment of conception or risk the unjust taking of a human life" (9).

As a scientific supplement to the theological quotation, an enlightenment is proposed which may diminish the poignancy of the adverb *precisely*. Scientific research has a philosophic precedent in that it has a mediate dependency whose relationship between the subject studied and the predicate pronounced must be unaltered, pristine, truthful, transcendental, and immovable.

Medical knowledge is gained via biological science. It is founded upon ethical clinical or laboratory medicosurgical research. Investigative medical activities are *a posterior* syntheses in that conclusions are determined either by intellectual or physical experimentation. Scientists adhere to an ethical code in research as a universal obligation not only of their discipline, but as participants in the habitat of humanity.

Ethical conduct of scientists as a moral integer is applicable to them metaphysically, meaning that it excludes all exceptions. Ethical conduct does not admit to any exclusion in any order of creation, even of divine origin. An example of this dictum is that a stone is not a living, breathing, biological being. No manner of scientific research, legislative act, federal/state law, or political persiflage can justify a contradiction to this concluded physical truism.

Science in its classical interpretation or definition is knowledge (gained) by causes (10). This acquired knowledge is contrasted to opinion. The term "cause" is derived from the Greek word *aitia*. It has the hellenic meaning of anything that is responsible for change, motion, or action (10). *De facto*, opinion is a conclusion or judgment. No matter how confidently expressed, it is not founded upon positive knowledge. If it is founded upon factually determined experimental knowledge, then it ceases to be opinion, becoming a scientific conclusion. Opinion is judgment "resting on grounds insufficient for complete demonstration. It is a belief of something as probable or as seeming to one's own mind to be true or it can be what is generally thought about something" (11). It may be a majority or a minority estimation founded upon a common or prevailing sentiment expressed by a private person or as public consensus. A quantitative opinion does not, *ipso facto*, give it qualitative truth.

With these introductory comments, it is fitting to answer with biological reasoning the often asked question on the advent of human life. Embryological studies have verified that from a fertilized ovum a unified dual cell is formed. It rapidly metamorphosizes into a multiple organic cellular structure which contains a continuously advancing subdividing cell proliferation.

When the original migrating fertilized ovum finds its nidus in the uterine wall, instantaneously, upon proper implantation, it commences to receive nourishment from human maternal blood. At this point, definitive human life is animated. This belief can be realistically, scientifically, and theologically acceptable. Contradictions to this validity must be enforced with physiological proof and theological certainty before it is altered. Otherwise spurious negations are apocryphas.

If the fertilized ovum finds an ectopic location for attachment with progressive development, then animation takes place at the same time, if or when, human maternal blood commences to nourish it. The maternal blood additionally imbues into the zygote not only organic blood elements, but also antibodies, immune substances, circulating drugs taken by the mother, hormones, and vital electrolytes. The anatomic location of blood reception with physiological absorption is not necessarily a prerequisite for animation if extrauterine life is sustained. The life principle of personhood is instilled when maternal blood nourishes the fertilized ovum, becoming the source of its life energy with future continuity.

With this ensoulement, also known as homogenicity, the natural composition of singular, egregious personhood is completed. The human totality, made to the image and likeness of God, is created of a body and a soul (the anima). The time of animation does not detract from the dictum that life commences at the moment of conception. When the sperm enters the ovum the physical half of conception is formulated. At the time of ensoulement the spiritual half is instilled which supplements into fulfillment the human life entity.

Selected language in the definitive usage of the word "life" is not to be subjected to the semantic license of multivariegated definitions. Post uterine life and fetal life are equal *ad valorem*. Although each may differ from the other in external appearance with an apparent disparity in size, shape, stability, and self-ambulation, nevertheless, the attollent, fundamental life principle remains identical.

Pertinently the attorney for the Reproductive Health Services of St. Louis, Missouri, in the Webster hearing, made a statement before the Supreme Court of the United States on April 6, 1989 (255). To wit: "...if states are allowed to declare when life begins, each (state) could choose a different point, such as viability or birth. He argued that 'procreational interests' are encompassed in the 'concept of ordered liberty' protected by the Constitution." Chief Justic William Rehnquist and Associate Justice Antonin Scalia with magistral, mutual deference disputed this contention (which followed) that abortion historically was not criminalized in the common law. This was an interpolated judicial response to the attorney's statement "to declare when life begins" by the individual states. Acceptance of this legal mutation with variable flexibility leads to the deniability of fetal life as a legally fixed human organism. This elimination as to the onset of life's beginning theoretically eradicates the criminalness of abortion. If the origin of life is uncanonically cribriform the criminality of abortion becomes apocrustically deniable.

A composite, unified, sacrosanct, unanimity of thought as to when life begins can be determined by studying embryologic physiology. Scientifically acknowledged pronouncements should be more acceptable in determining the onset of human life than legal opinion. A pronouncement of this magnitude should not be attorned to, or allowed to be the assumed provincial prerogative of unscientific selected sages, legal legislators, or non-medical judicial jurisdictions of whatever caliber.

Scientific deduction is persuasive evidence that substantiates the time of human ensoulement which is postulated to be when the fertilized ovum becomes implanted in a maternal organ. This ensoulement concept applies even if the fertilized egg is implanted ectopically either in the fallopian tube, elsewhere in the pelvis, or in the abdominal cavity. At the time of implantation hormonal activity is aroused that gives a positive reaction to tests for pregnancy. The presence of hormones indicative of pregnancy confirms the human nature of the conceptus. It is this human hormonal indicator that is additional proof that animation has occurred and prevails. Only human responses attributed to human physiology can take place in a human person.

In extremely early pregnancy or in some instances of ectopic pregnancy, the active principle for the pregnancy test to be positive is human chorionic gonadotropin hormone (abbreviated as HCG). In order to achieve a positive reaction when utilizing Sprague-Dawley weanling female rodents, twenty-one to twenty-eight days old (40 to 65 gms in weight), for pregnancy tests five rodents must be used. The urine of the future mother must be concentrated to secure the hyperemic result in the ovaries of the rats. Positive proof of pregnancy is based upon *post mortem* examination of the rodent ovaries when four or more of the ten ovaries examined have a pink to red color.

Scientifically the fundamental basic evaluation of the female urine based upon ovarian changes in rodents is an all or none test for the presence of a given level of HCG. This level is approximately 1000 international units of HCG contained in a 24 hours sample of urine. During early pregnancy, as the titer* rises from zero to 1000 international units (I.U.) per 24 hours, results of pregnancy tests can be negative which are in reality "false negatives" although conception has taken place. It must be remembered that the time it takes for a fertilized ovum to be implanted completely in the uterus is about five days. When the titer reaches 1000 I.U. with a continuous rise the results of the test will be positive (254). The over-all accuracy of the rodent hyperemia test is close to 100 per cent. Falsely positive results in postmenopausal women do not occur because the test does not respond to the increased human pituitary gonadotropin present in 2 ml. of urine. This is the amount of urine injected subcutaneously into the nape of the neck of each of the five rodents. "The only provision needed to avoid falsely positive results in general is to be certain that the ovaries of control rodents are pale yellow. This is accomplished by using a suitable diet for the rats" (254).

Medicolegalists have postulated a hypothetical question to which speculative answers have been given. In view of the gynecological information presented, it becomes necessary not to avoid the topic of frozen embryos. This subject is one of many that medical engineering has created for legal and ethical solution. It exemplifies the disparity in which the law does not keep pace with newer scientific accomplishments. Not even the proceleusmatic imagination of fu-

---

* Titer is an expression of the strength of a volumetric solution, usually grams of active constituent per cubic centimeter of solution.

turistic, cosmic, fiction writers or H.G. Wells' modern imitators could author a captivating, conjectured scenario with a conjunctioned plausibility as that which is to be related. It is an O'Henry-like short story.

Much publicity in the professional journals and the electronic media focused attention on a young married couple who were without children. "Mr. R and his wife died in 1983 in an airplane crash, leaving the physicians at Queen Victoria Medical center in Melbourne, Australia, in a medical, legal, and ethical quandary. The couple had applied originally to Australia's well known test-tube baby doctors when they learned that Mrs. R was unable to conceive by normal pregnancy. In 1981, they flew to Australia and several of Mrs. R's ova were fertilized with her husband's sperm in the laboratory. One was implanted in her womb. However, ten days later her pregnancy failed. Two other embryos fertilized at the same time were frozen and retained. According to the London newspaper, *The Mail*, Mrs. R stated 'you must keep them for me. I will be back for another attempt when I feel emotionally ready.' Two years later (1983), the couple perished in an airplane accident near Santiago, Chile.

"The two test-tube embryos, believed orphaned by their dead multimillionaire American parents, presently are in a deep freeze and await a life or death decision by the physicians. They may choose between implanting the embryos into a surrogate, destroying them, or leaving them in suspended animation. One of the legal issues involved is the right of the infants, if they were to survive, to inherit an estate worth millions of dollars. Complicating features include the fact that in Australia, and in most other jurisdictions, not excluding the United States, laws hold that the surrogate mother and the man to whom she is married are regarded as the legal parents of any infant born to her. This question may become moot for two reasons. According to the head of the Australian medical center's in vitro fertilization team, the embryos would probably not survive the attempt to implant them because the techniques used for freezing at that time were not sufficiently effective. The second reason is that there is information from the couple's attorney that the sperm was not from Mr. R" (12).

Test-tube fertilization and frozen embryos give rise to the same question as to when does an embryo become a human person? Associated with the primary question are the ancillary questions as to what are the medical, legal, and ethical obligations of the physicians involved. What is equally cogent is who has the right or power to arrive at these decisions. In response to these inquiries, it is stated that the time of animation is the *sine qua non* upon which the answer is to be given. Fundamentally, the person who performs the original medical engineering has the responsibility to decide questions of major moral gravity which are not mitigated by any paucity of legal sanctions.

## Animation

Living things are classified as animate, non-living things are inanimate. Animism is derived from the Latin word *anima*, translated as soul (the spirit). The philosophical doctrine of the reality of souls is known as animism. Anthropology propounds the viewpoint that animism maintains that souls are attached to all things either as their inner principle of spontaneity or activity, or as their dwellers. To this belief is added the anthropological doctrine that nature is inhabited by various grades of spirits which is labeled as spiritism (10).

Psychobiologists contrast immaterial versus material existence. They believe, holding to the tenet that the ground of life is immaterial (not substance) soul rather than the material body. Metaphysics advances the theory that "being" is animate, living, ensouled. Synonyms for which are hylozoism (life is a property of matter, that matter and life are inseparable, that life is derived from matter, or that matter has spiritual properties), personalism (term applied to any philosophy which considers personality the supreme value and the key to the meaning of reality), and monadism (a metaphysical unit, a soul, self, in Greek usage number one, concerned as possessing an autonomous life, and irrespective of the nature of its relations to beings beyond it) (10).

Much philosophic thought and biological investigation have been given to proving the existence of a life principle called the soul. The crux of life destruction rests upon a realistic understanding of animation. Some biomedical experts experienced in philosophy, attested to by their acquisition of doctorate degrees in both biology and philosophy, have expressed themselves with the following words. "If anyone out there can define when life begins, I urge them to write a research paper and send it . They would be assured of a Nobel Prize" (13). Other biophysicists affirm that a new, individual, and distinctive human life comes into existence at fertilization (14). What is often disputed is the value (quality of life) to be given to the new human life at the various stages of its development before birth.

Medical concentration on the embryological progress of the implanted fertilized ovum gives proof that during the first trimester of pregnancy a living human being is *in situ*. Even before the distribution of the audiovisual presentation known as "The Silent Scream", anatomic certainty verified this truth. An unborn child in the first trimester sucks its thumb and swims in the amniotic fluid. If the instruments of death approach the infant, a sonogram records the scream of pain and the cringe away from the destructive force. All this can be seen on the film called "The Silent Scream".

This pictorial presentation is powerful proof of life's early existence. Scientific studies by anatomists antedate sonography, but with the attainment of similar conclusions. Certain identifying anatomic characteristics are determinable during the first three months (trimester) of pregnancy. A description of the unborn child will be defined as it appears at the end of four weeks, at the end of eight weeks, and at the end of twelve weeks.

When the fetus has been nourished for four weeks, it reaches 3/4 of an inch in height. The heart is pulsating (beating) and blood is being pumped. The vertebral column with the spinal canal is forming. No eyes, nose, or external ears are visible. The gastrointestinal (digestive) system is beginning to form. Four small projections (buds) are present which eventually become two upper and two lower extremities (5).

At the end of eight weeks, the unborn child is about 1-1/8 inches long, weighing about 1/30 of an ounce. The face and other anatomic features are forming with discernibility. The eyelids are fused. Upper and lower limbs are beginning to demonstrate distinct division into arms, elbows, forearms, hands, thighs, knees, legs, and feet. An identifiable umbilical cord is formed. The long bones and the internal organs are developing as the tail-like process in the caudal area disappears (5).

As the twelfth week expires, the unborn infant is 3 inches long, weighing about one ounce. The arms, forearms, hands, fingers, thighs, legs, feet, and toes are formed fully. Fingernails and toenails on the phalanges are visibly developing. External ears are seen. Sockets and teeth buds are present in the maxilla and in the mandible with jawbone outlines clearly discernible. The eyes are almost fully developed, although the eyelids remain adherently fused. The heartbeat can be detected and counted with special instruments (5).

There has been a dispute among specialist members of a national obstetrics and gynecology society. It arose when some experts raised the question as to whether or not a fetus feels pain during the early stages of pregnancy. No one contradicted the fact that a fetus feels pain at some point before birth.

A statement signed by anesthesiologists, obstetricians and gynecologists is quoted. "Over the last eighteen years real time ultrasonography, fetoscopy, study of fetal electrocardiograms, and fetal electroencephalography have demonstrated the remarkable responsiveness of the fetus to pain, touch, and sound" (22). The debate over when exactly a fetus feels pain was rekindled when President Reagan, in a speech to the National Religious Broadcasters on January 30, 1984, said "that when the lives of the unborn are snuffed out, they feel pain — pain that is long and agonizing" (22).

It has been expressed by experts that a fetus can feel pain after ten weeks. This belief is founded upon the anatomic development of the nervous system that allows pain stimuli to be accepted in the first trimester of pregnancy (22). Reflexive action in the fetus has been determined at four to six weeks after conception. Histologic studies identify nerve endings in aborted fetuses after eight weeks. At ten weeks, there are chemical substances present that transmit pain stimuli to the brain. Pain receptor activity is identifiable when the unborn is twelve weeks old (22).

Biological science has substantiated the anatomicophysiological fact that within the first trimester of pregnancy there is an intra-uterine human life. Thus, science bolsters theology in the establishment that the unborn is a properly identifiable human person. This is another manifestation that science, religion, and faith are not in opposition, but are synergistically entwined under the aura of human munificence.

Scientists, knowingly, electively, or unwittingly, are persons of faith. Their daily lives rest upon faith even as they are motivated by faith. This truth is revealed in the causes of all science which rest on a faith that assumes not only the permanency but the uniformity of natural laws. Scientists believe that there exists somewhere in the cosmos a solution, amelioration, or cure for every disease and problem that besets mankind (15).

"Each experiment a scientist conducts is an act of faith. One may find men/women of uncertain faith in church pews, but rarely in laboratories. Thomas Alva Edison expressed it well when he said, 'I know this world is ruled by infinite intelligence. It required infinite intelligence to create it and it required infinite intelligence to keep it on its course. Everything that surrounds us — everything that exists — proves that there are infinite laws behind it. There can be no denying this fact. It is mathematical in its precision'" (15). Scientists have proven by their thoughts, words, and deeds that they can accept on faith that God exists.

# CHAPTER TWO

# THE RIGHTS OF THE UNBORN

*Cassius, "The fault, dear Brutus, is not in our stars
But in ourselves, that we are underlings."
Shakespeare's Julius Caesar.
Act I, Sc. 2, Line 140.*

Right and wrong are at the extremes of each other. Of the two words, wrong is more easily defined. Essentially, a wrong action is one that is not right. Hence, a great weight is given to the definition of right, which makes the definition of it quite complex. In an ethical sense, a right action is one that conforms to the moral law. Immanuel Kant (1724-1804), in his ethical pronouncements, defined the moral law as "that formula which expresses the necessity of an action done from duty in terms of one's own reflection." Hence, a *right* is the correlative of *duty*.

Certain adjectives are intrinsic to a *right*. Among the primary of these is *natural* which, when appended to *right*, equals *natural rights*. They are claims or liberties which are not derived from positive law, but from a "higher law", the law of nature. "The right to live, the right to work, the 'pursuit of happiness', the right to self development are natural rights" (16).

In considering legal rights, a broader spectrum is encompassed because it may be any claim against others as recognized by law. *Right* "as a noun, and taken in an abstract sense, is justice, ethical correctness, or consonance with the rules of law or the principles of morals. In this signification, it answers to one meaning of the Latin *jus,* and serves to indicate law in the abstract, considered as the foundation of all rights, or the complex of underlying moral principles which impart the character of justice to all positive law and gives it an ethical content" (17).

Rights are defined, generally, as "powers of free action." The primal rights pertaining to men/women are enjoyed by human beings purely as such, having been grounded in personality and existing antecedently to their recognition by positive law (18). When used with the abstract word substantive, the term *substantive right* is synonymous with *substantive justice* (19).

Rights may be described as perfect or imperfect, according as their action or scope is clear, settled, and determinate, or is vague and unfixed. Rights are either *"in personam"* or *"in rem"*. A right *"in personam"* is one which imposes an obligation on a definite person. A right *"in rem"* is one which imposes an obligation on persons generally; i.e, either on all the world or on all the world except certain determinate persons (20).

"Another applicable classification is primary or secondary rights. Primary rights are those which can be created without reference to rights already existing. Secondary rights can only arise for the purpose of protecting or enforcing primary rights. They are either preventive (protective) or remedial (reparative)" in nature (20).

On the basis of these criteria, general principles are evoked that are guides in solving some of the special problems concerning the rights of the unborn. Initially, it must be remembered that every human being has a right to life. Deliberate murder is, therefore, wrong. It violates four important, primary human rights. These are "God's right over human life, the right of the murdered person to his/ her own life, the right of society to public peace and civil order, and the right of the relatives and friends of the murdered person to his/ her love and service" (4).

The right to life applies to life in its full essence. Not only is murder wrong, but mutilation and physical injury to another are likewise wrong. Grave mutilation may be defined as one that results either from the removal of a distinct member of the human body, or in "the inhibition of the function of a distinct organ through a wound" (21).

Until recently, the majority of the United States did not allow a child, or his guardian or parent, to sue for prenatal injuries to an infant. This legal tendency is no longer steadfast, although there is no uniformity of opinion on this subject. Many states have legislated or have had judicial decisions favoring the protection of the unborn child. As early as the fourth and fifth decades of this century, the change in legal thinking was apparent (23).

In two states, Minnesota in 1949 and Mississippi in 1954, the court decision allowed a lawsuit to be maintained on behalf of a child who died before birth from prenatal injuries inflicted after it reached the age wherein separation from the mother did not also mean the end of the child's life (24, 25).

Modern scientific studies and medicolegal authorities recognize the unborn infant as a human being. Even without scientific conclusions as to the exact time at which the unborn baby becomes a human being, present day legal thinking favors protecting the rights of the conceptus within the uterus when negligence is the basis for litigation.

Scientific embryologic evidence has established the fact that the human fetus grows and develops internally from the moment of conception not by static progression, but by a purposeful, even, steady growth to the time of its birth. The human fetus is to be construed as a medicolegal human being. No other rational explanation can be given in the light of the scientific evidence which has been proven over and over again.

"Because the unborn child, viable or not, was considered historically to have no separate legal identity until birth, at common law no action would lie on his/her behalf for prenatal injury. The entire concept of tort law is predicated on the theory of some breach of a duty of care to the person who is harmed. Since the unborn child was not a legal person, no duty of care to him/her existed. Since no care was owed to him/her, no damages could be collected by the 'unperson', until after birth, when he/she was considered finally to be a legal entity. Therefore, until 1946, no jurisdiction in this country appeared to allow the child to recover damages for any prenatal injuries inflicted" (26).

Beginning in 1946, with a decision of the District of Columbia District Court allowing financial recovery, almost all states have reversed their former positions (27, 28, 29). The general rule appears to be that once the child is born alive, he/she has a cause of action for negligence against anyone who harmed him/her prior to birth. This right of action exists in addition to and independent of any legal rights the mother has against the negligent party for any damages done to her (29, 30, 31).

If the child is born alive, but dies as a result of its injuries, an action for wrongful death will lie (32). However, if a child is born dead, no wrongful death action can be maintained (33). Of course, the mother has her own cause of action for negligence. In this situation, her pain, suffering, and mental anguish as a result of losing her child are proper legal elements for awarding pecuniary damages (34).

## Prenatal Exemplary Citations

Prior to the present day era of legalistic enlightened cogitation harm occurring to a child *"en ventre sa mere"* was held to be not actionable.* No right of recovery was recognized against one wrongfully inflicting prenatal injuries (35). Even with this change in judicial attitudinal interpretations, many decisions are rendered that do not favor the infant *in utero*. Some illustrative cases in precise format are recounted to demonstrate some decisions that favored the unborn and others that denied legal relief.

### Case One

A legal action was brought on behalf of a child born mentally retarded and physically underdeveloped. The plaintiff alleged that the defendant's negligent operation of her automobile caused injury to the child who, at the time of the alleged injury, was in the first month of gestation. The appellate court reversed the trial court's dismissal of the action, holding that an infant who survives birth can maintain an action to recover for prenatal injuries, medically provable as resulting from the negligence of another, even if the child has not reached the state of a viable fetus at the time of the injury (36).

Precedent was reversed when Minnesota became the first state to allow a wrongful death proceeding for a stillborn infant. After noting that no issue of viability was involved because the infant died during delivery, the court concluded: "A cause of action arises when death is caused by the wrongful act or omission of another, and the personal representative of the decedent may maintain such action on behalf of the next of kin of decedent. It seems too plain for argument that where independent existence is possible and life is

---

* A French term descriptive of an unborn child, defined as "in the mother's womb." See reference 17.

destroyed through a wrongful act, a cause of action arises under the statutes cited" (24). Seven years later, a viable child killed in an automobile accident was deemed a person within the meaning of the wrongful death statute in Kentucky (37).

The viability rule continues to remain an adversarial issue in wrongful death actions. Even in jurisdictions allowing proceedings on behalf of stillborn infants, the viability necessity continues to be resurrected. It is an applicable contention that requires, as an indispensable prerequisite to the lawsuit, that the fetus be viable when the injury causing fetal death, or initiating the pathological process ultimately causing fetal death, occurs. Rare indeed is the recorded case awarding damages against a tortfeasor for causing death before birth of a nonviable fetus (35).

Viability is the ability to live after birth. Both the medical and legal disciplines define the word identically as "capable of living, especially capable of living outside of the uterus; said of a fetus that has reached such a stage of development it can live outside of the uterus" (6). Law dictionary definition does not deviate from its medical counterpart. Viability is defined as "capability of living. A term used to denote the power a newborn child possesses of continuing its independent existence" (17). Medicolegally, it is generally accepted that a fetus is not capable of independent extrauterine existence until the twenty-sixth/twenty-seventh week of gestation. It is acknowledged legally that modern neonatology can sustain life in premature infants born before this period of time.

Legal currents are going in the direction that eventually will witness all jurisdictions allowing recovery for prenatal injuries, eliminating the viability requirements. Although the change may not be complete or immediate, "the wrongful death statutes will be construed to sustain a cause of action for deaths occurring as a result of prenatal injuries, abrogating the viability rule and eliminating the necessity for live birth. As medical science discovers new causal relationships or negates those previously accepted, litigation may be expected to incorporate these medicolegal advances" (35).

## Case Two

In a precedent landmark decision, a Canadian provincial appeals court ruled that a child unborn at the time of her father's death can receive a death benefit from his automobile liability policy. The father was killed in a traffic accident in June 1978, eight months before his daughter's birth. The man's common-law wife sued on behalf of her daughter for the $10,200 death benefit. The lower court dismissed the lawsuit, ruling that a fetus was not a person. The Alberta Court of Appeals unanimously overturned the decision by stating that the unborn child was just as much a survivor as a child born at the time of the accident (38).

## Case Three

The Rhode Island Supreme Court said the parents of a stillborn child could sue for wrongful death. The parents had sued the physician and hospital, complaining that the doctor had negligently prescribed drugs to induce labor and failed to supervise the induction of labor. The trial court granted summary judgment to the defendants on the grounds that the plaintiff had not stated a claim for relief. However, the state supreme court said an unborn fetus, whether viable or not, was a person within the meaning of the Rhode Island wrongful death act.

The court said there was no reason to recognize a legal difference between a death that occurred immediately before birth and one that occurred immediately after it. The court also said it was illogical and arbitrary to cut off a right of action at birth.

The court recognized that many claims might be highly speculative if not totally without merit. The court held that the fact that there may be difficulties in proof was not sufficient reason to block all attempts to prove a case. The court noted that the parents had to establish that there was a causal relationship between the alleged negligence and the child's death (39).

## Case Four

A child who is born alive and survives may recover damages for injuries sustained at any prenatal level, a Texas appellate court ruled. The child was born six and one-half months after his mother was involved in an auto accident. The child's father brought suit against the other driver for the child's injuries, but the court granted summary judgment for the driver on the theory that the fetus was not viable at the time of the mishap and a cause of action did not exist for injuries to a nonviable fetus. On appeal by the father, the court cited a case in which a child born six months after his father's death was allowed to recover damages for the death of his father. The court said the same reasoning that entitled a child to recover damages for his father's death would be more persuasive in granting him the right to recover damages for his own personal injuries. The reason for adopting a rule favoring an unborn child was stronger when it concerned the child's health and ability after birth to seek complete happiness and perform his full duty as a member of society than when it concerned merely property rights and rights of inheritance, according to the court. The court held that a cause of action existed for injuries sustained at any prenatal stage if the child was born alive and survived. The judgment of the trial court was reversed and the case remanded for trial on the merits (41).

## Case Five

An action for the wrongful death of an eight and one-half month fetus killed in an automobile accident should not have been dismissed by the trial court, the highest court of Massachusetts ruled.

The fetus was injured in a collision between a car in which his mother was riding and a Greyhound bus. During the course of emergency surgery on the mother, the fetus was found dead, and the mother later died. The death certificate of the child specified the cause of death as multiple maternal traumatic injuries.

Seeking to recover for wrongful death, the administrator of the estate brought an action against the bus driver and his employer. Based on an earlier Massachusetts case, the trial court dismissed the case and the administrator appealed.

The higher court reversed the trial court's decision and said the action should be allowed. Recent developments caused it to overrule its 1972 decision in which it said that no cause of action existed for prenatal injury or death.

A majority of states now permit recovery for death or injury to a viable fetus, the court added. It was not inappropriate for the court to change the rule denying such a right of action. Since the cause of action was considered a part of the common law, it was not necessary to wait for the legislature to act. Moreover, the dangers of speculation as to the amount of damage and double recovery were no greater than in the case of an action brought after a live birth.

The former rule of permitting an action only if the child were born alive was an artificial and unreasonable demarcation, more an aid to the judiciary than to justice, the high court concluded (41).

What has been written, legally illustrated, and emphasized medically in this chapter, recapitulates that in the name of distributive justice, substantive justice, and social justice, it must be recognized that unborn infants have both primary, natural, preventive rights and secondary, remedial, legal rights *in personam*.

# CHAPTER THREE

# ABORTION DEFINED

*And the child I now go with do miscarry, thou wert better*
*thou hadst struck thy mother, thou paper-faced villain.*
*Shakespeare's II Henry IV. Act V, Sc. 4, Line 10.*

Many times in the use of language, an often-used single word or expression has a more complex connotation with profound significant meaning than appears superficially. To the usage of abortion this thought is most appropriate. This word has been laisized without an exact understanding of its etymological, grammatical, legal, medical, or moral definitions.

Most English dictionaries will describe abortion in one or more phrases. Among these definitions are an untimely birth, an arrest of development, failure in anything during progress and before maturity. All lexicographers agree that the word abortion is derived from the Latin preposition *ab* meaning from and the verb *orior* which is translated as to grow. The noun *abortio* in Latin means abortion (11).

Medical dictionaries are more specific in defining abortion. It is the expulsion of the product of conception before the child is viable. When this occurs during the first three months, it is termed an abortion. From this time (three months) to viability, the terms immature delivery or miscarriage have been applied. Expulsion of the product of conception from the period of viability to full term is referred to as premature delivery.

Although in general the premature expulsion from the uterus of the conceptus, of the embryo, or of the nonviable fetus is termed abortion, medically it is not entirely complete. An artificial abortion should be called an induced abortion, which is one brought on intentionally with full consent of the will. Thus, an artificial/induced abortion is one that is brought on purposefully.

Induction is contrasted to a natural abortion, which results from some pathophysiological deficiency. Often, natural abortion is referred to as any abortion except one which has been produced artificially. Repeated natural abortions may be habitual. The expulsion of a dead or unviable fetus at about the same period of development in at least three successive pregnancies is called habitual abortion. The expelled fetus is called an abortus when it weighs less than 500 grams (17 ounces) at the time of expulsion from the uterus (6).

Law dictionaries have definitions similar to those found in their medical equivalents. These descriptions are based upon actual legal cases which have established the definition via expert medical testimony. Thus, abortion in law is "the expulsion of the fetus at a period of uterogestation so early that it has not acquired the power of sustaining an independent life" (17). Certain citations have labeled abortion as "the destruction, or the bringing forth prematurely, of the human fetus before the natural time of birth" (42). "The act of bringing forth what is yet imperfect, also the thing prematurely brought forth, or product of an untimely process. Sometimes loosely used for the offense of procuring a premature delivery; but strictly, the early delivering is the abortion; causing or procuring abortion is the full name of the offense"(17, 43). Under the law, abortion and a miscarriage produced by unlawful means are synonymous (44).

*De facto*, abortion in modern parlance means the intentional expulsion of a nonviable, living fetus from the mother's uterus. In this context, abortion, unless otherwise specifically noted, is used in the sense of direct abortion. Among the laity, in legal discussion, and in some theological treatises, abortion is not employed universally in this meaning. In order to constitute abortion, the act must be intended directly. By this is meant that the abortion must be attempted either as the end to be accomplished or as a means to achieve some desired purpose (4, 21).

From the descriptive definitions, it can be realized that conflicts may arise between medical acts permissible under the law and ethical conduct that professionalism augments. "The very sciences and technology that allot an increasingly greater understanding of human biology also provide the medical community with increasing control over life and death issues . . . New advances in medical technology that allow scientists to keep fetuses alive outside the womb at increasingly earlier growth stages, may alter radically the current notions about legalized abortion" (45).

"The day may arrive when a woman who wants to terminate a pregnancy would do so by going through delivery and having the newborn infant taken to an intensive care facility where it would be treated, managed, fed, and permitted to grow until an adoption could be arranged" (45). This advancement in neonatology is consistent with the Hippocratic *noblesse oblige* of the medical discipline which states: "I will not perform an abortion."

With or without the largesse of scientific technology, no social, personal, or legal reason can be advanced to justify direct abortion. It is a denial of the sacred, inviolate, and unalienable right to life of an innocent human being. Therefore, it is willful murder. The act of murder is prohibited by the natural law and is expressed in God's commandment, "Thou shalt not kill." Neither the attending physician nor those participating in the performance of an abortion can exculpate themselves under the guise that it is legal. No civil authority can alter the truism that abortion is the killing of a preborn human being. "In the doctor's profession, the principal rules of right and wrong are based on the sublime truth that every human being possesses a spiritual, immortal soul endowed with certain rights that may never be violated for some material benefit" (46). An abortion performed in the operating room as observed by a trained, board certified surgeon is divested of all professional radiance even as it is a devenustated technological, skilless, manual modality.

Both the professional journals and science commentators of the news media have recorded the tragic experiences of physicians caught in the abortion maelstrom, one of the earliest examples of which occurred in New England in the 1970s. The Massachusetts Supreme Judicial Court heard the arguments on the case of a resident gynecologist who was charged with manslaughter. He was convicted on criminal charges related to a hysterotomy-abortion performed on a patient at a municipal hospital. Although there were many abortion issues related to the legal action, the Commonwealth's attorney brought forth the argument that the Boston physician terminated the life of an infant who was born, and that therefore the legality of abortion was not the issue but rather it was manslaughter.

In September 1984, a doctor was charged with murder after police authorities said he had illegally tried to perform an abortion and denied care to the baby, which died. The mother was 32 weeks pregnant when the doctor performed the operation. "The three pound, nine ounce baby died about 90 minutes after birth because she lacked oxygen and the normal care given after birth" (47).

The Philadelphia obstetrician who aborted this 32-weeks-old unborn child alive on September 12, 1984, allegedly left the infant to die. He directed others in attendance not to give her any medical assistance. Although in January 1985 he escaped murder and involuntary manslaughter charges, the accusations of infanticide and/or for abortion after viability are in the offering. If this had taken place, it would have been the first time that a physician in Pennsylvania would have to face a criminal trial since the Roe v. Wade decision sixteen years ago (48). "What did the doctor intend to do to that unborn child? Answer: he intended to kill him or her. He probably thought the unborn child to be much younger. In any case, his objective was to kill a child at age 12 weeks, 16 weeks or, as it turned out, 32 weeks in the womb . . . The United States Center for Disease Control in Atlanta, Georgia informs us that about 500 such 'live-birth' abortions occur each year. In virtually all of these cases, the innocent babies die soon after their abortion-births" (48).

More recently, a District of Columbia appeals court has ruled that a fetus is a person under the law. At the risk of reading too much into the case (it did not concern abortion directly), it is noted as to its potential significance as part of a (legal) trend (49).

"In a case of vehicular manslaughter involving the death of an unborn child, the Supreme Court of Massachusetts ruled in August 1984 that a fetus was a person and that the question of viability had no legal effect. A dissenting opinion made prochoicers nervous, even though the majority opinion went their way. It occurred when Justice Sandra O'Connor in 1984 declared that Roe v. Wade, which legalized abortion in 1973, was doomed because scientific advances have rendered irrelevant its arbitrary division of pregnancy into trimesters" (49).

"Roe v. Wade was handed down at a time of moral counter-culturalism and before advances in fetology made even less tenable notions of 'the non-human fetus.' Today withholding legal 'person-hood' from preborn persons reeks of the kind of rationalization found in the Dred Scott Decision. The unborn children in both the District of Columbia and Massachusetts cases were eight months old. Many flourishing premature babies are no older than that, and preborns at that age are entirely capable of great pain during abortion" (49).

The question of pain and suffering by the intrauterine infant has been demonstrated by the movie "The Silent Scream" which can educate the doubters who believe that abortion is not murder. Many people are interested in viewing this film. It is obtainable in 16 mm and video cassette formats, including half- inch VHS and PAL, as well as three-quarter inch broadcast quality cassettes.* This film will reawaken the knowledge that where there is life, there is sensation which includes the reception of pain. If anyone respects human dignity, then it follows like the night the day, that no one should make other people suffer who are our brothers and sisters.

Does not the Bible tell the story well? Where is your brother Abel?

Cain brought some of the produce of the soil as an offering for the Lord, while Abel for his part brought the first-born of his flock and some of their fat as well. The Lord looked with favor on Abel and his offering. But he did not look with favor on Cain and his offering, and Cain was very angry and downcast.

The Lord asked Cain, "Why are you angry and downcast? If you are well disposed, ought you not to lift up your head? But if you are ill disposed, is not sin at the door like a crouching beast hungering for you, which you must master?"

Cain said to his brother Abel, "Let us go out"; and while they were in the open country, Cain set on his brother Abel and killed him.

The Lord asked Cain, "Where is your brother Abel?" "I do not know," he replied. "Am I my brother's guardian?" "What have you done?" the Lord asked. "Listen to the sound of your brother's blood, crying out to me from the ground. Now be accursed and driven from

* Available from American Portrait Films, Suite 500, California Federal Building, Anaheim, California 92801. Telephone 714-535-2189.

the ground that has opened its mouth to receive your brother's blood at your hands. When you till the ground it shall no longer yield you any of its produce. You shall be a fugitive and wanderer over the earth." Then Cain said to the Lord, "My punishment is greater than I can bear. See! Today you drive me from this ground. I must hide from you, and be a fugitive and a wanderer over the earth. Why, whoever comes across me will kill me!" "Very well then," the Lord replied, "If anyone kills Cain, sevenfold vengeance shall be taken for him."

So the Lord put a mark on Cain, to prevent whoever might come across him from striking him down. Cain left the presence of the Lord (50).

The gift of life at any stage is intended for growth and not premature death. "The reality of eternity gives utmost seriousness to life. Believers really choose their future. If anyone clearly and definitely turns his/her back on the light (truth); if anyone chooses darkness (error) rather than light (truth) that is his/her decision. Even a God of love does not override the choice because human beings have free will which is a God-like attribute of the soul" (51).

This is not addressed "to those moments of inadvertence when anyone may succumb to an uncontrollable impulse which is regretted later, or to those choices made in good faith which may later prove to be wrong" (51). Specific reference is made to deliberate, positive, adult choice to misuse the gifts of free will and intelligence by placing them in the service of greed, selfishness, ambition, or for any other purpose without regard for the harm it causes others. Some of us may even neglect our spiritual gifts or misuse them for evil rather than good as we walk through life refusing to give of ourselves, to sacrifice for another, to relinquish any comfort, or to share our talents in the name of distributive justice. For the Christian or Judaic, life is a serious responsibility with sobriety and moderation in all things as a laudable motto (51).

Cogitative meditation will disclose that the stormy clouds of immorality which encompass the earth can be tempered to quiescence or disspelled into oblivion by persistent ethical vigilance without inflexion. Eternal moral excellence is the antidote against proabortion advocacy as it continues to be the fomes of infamous iniquity that entices profluent profligateness.

## Legal Decision on Abortion

When confronted with the socioeconomic complexities of pastoral medicine, which resurrects the ethical conundrum of abortion, the law itself is confused. Thus, it is anticipated that more and more juridical decisions will be forthcoming on abortion. Legal decisions have been made and are being rendered which elucidate specific segments on abortion. Other dicta restrict those items defined, described, or decried. So it is now and will continue to be until proabortion laws are eradicated from the American legal scene.

In an interview, a former president of the National Organization of Women said, regarding the antiabortion laws, that "these laws were taken off the books as much because they were unenforceable as because of concern for women's rights" (52). A newspaper reader became irate at the statement to the degree that he wrote a letter to the editor which is quoted. "Since when does enforceability determine whether or not a law is to be made? By this reasoning, we should also legalize drug sales, rape, child abuse, extortion, and espionage, since these laws also require extensive undercover operations and are similarly difficult to enforce. In fact, what laws, if any, are not both difficult and dangerous to enforce?" (52).

"The contention that enforceability should be a prerequisite for antiabortion laws is totally misguided. Rather than give up on our laws, we must strive harder and seek newer means to enforce them. Our country was founded on the premise that our laws would protect, above all, the right to life of all our citizens, especially the most innocent and defenseless among us" (52).

The subject of abortion has been the basis of several important decisions by the United States Supreme Court that were necessary to unify conflicting legal restrictions. Some of these are enumerated as examples of the allied implications that have arisen from abortion because its intrinsic definition that it is the equivalent to murder had not been accepted throughout the fifty states of this nation.

1. One significant argument arose out of the Missouri abortion statute which has a number of conditions on the medical procedure of abortion. Among the restrictions required by the statute are consent of the husband of a married woman, parental consent for a minor female, written consent by the woman, termination of paren-

tal rights when the aborted fetus survives, and an absolute prohibition of a saline amniocentesis-abortion after twelve weeks gestational age of the fetus. The Missouri Attorney General urged the Supreme Court to consider that the state has a legitimate interest in safeguarding the family unit and the marriage (53).

2. The United States Supreme Court heard arguments on an appeal from Massachusetts. The contention was a determination on the constitutionality of the Massachusetts General Law Chapter 112, Section 12P, which forbids the performance of an abortion on a minor without the consent of both parents. A United States District Court in April 1975 enjoined enforcement of the statute and found nothing about abortions that requires the minor's interest to be treated differently from other medical and surgical procedures to which, customarily, only one parent is required to give legal consent (54).

The benchmark decision on Roe v. Wade did not solve the abortion melee (55). "A sweeping, all-embracing action like that of the United States Supreme Court in the Roe case tempts to speculation. In a matter of such wide concern as the legality or illegality of abortion, it is only natural to ask what the results of the decision will be. There are many questions which are of legal interest and medical concern that may be answered by legislative or judicial action. The court alludes to the matter of paternal right. The court emphasizes the 'right of the physician to administer medical treatment.' The court says that it is a medically established fact that in the first trimester mortality in abortion is less than mortality in normal childbirth. If this is so, will the decision compel physicians themselves to perform the procedure? Will it deny delegation of the procedure in the first trimester to a well-trained technician to reduce costs?" (56).

Now that the magic word "pill" has acquired the additional meaning of "abortion inducer," the unanswered question is, "who is to administer it?" Will the law allow it to become a non-prescription, over-the-counter purchase? What legal safeguards will be needed to ensure its safety? One fact is known, the pill will find acceptance by the cost-containment disciples who are magnetized by economic parsimony.

This abortifacient chemical known as RU-486 was compounded by a French research pharmaceutical firm under its initiating developer Roussel Uclef. The manufacturer claims that RU-486 is 85 percent effective without inducing any side-effects or complications. Facility of usage in a physician's office has increased the enthusiastic reception of the abortion pill.

Currently it is being administered to women in France and China. The French company that holds the patent rights is not exporting the drug to the United States. However, the uproar about the chemical is so intense that the restricted sales will not deter illicit marketeers from seizing the propitious opportunity to make it available throughout the world.

"Pressure to allow its use in the United States will come from family-planning groups. In the end President Bush probably will accept the Food and Drug Administration's recommendations, whatever they are, unless the prolife movement makes RU-486 a litmus-test issue" (254 A). Pill or no pill, abortion is abortion. No matter how it is done the moral taint of abortion remains the same. Contemporaneously the courts can expect to receive future litigation quandaries to decide issues that will arise from using the pill. This includes products liability cases for anticipated lawsuits.

Mactation has destroyed more than 20 million babies up to the summer of 1989. The Roe v. Wade decision has allowed this to happen in America. The maleficent power of macaronic emotionalism is not attuned to the ultimate primordial impropriety of abortion. Hence there is a failure to recognize that the human existence of an intrauterine infant is in coexistence with the mother as two separate individual living beings with equal, sociomoral, distinctly separable legal credentials. As the summer of 1989 blossoms into flowery, vegetative life, there is discernible a waning in the former proabortion avidity. The examined, alerted conscience of Americans is being awakened to the evil of abortion. Xenophobic falsity that shrouded the innocent intrauterine inhabitant is fading away slowly, but surely, as insidiously as the stillness of the silent ending night gives way to the chiaroscuro of radiant dawn.

American citizens are looking in the mirror of morality apparently disliking the uncomeliness that is seen. An estimation of self finds a deficiency in those who have spearheaded the proabortion-prochoice movements. Accentuating with intense preoccupation the concerns of personal diurnal pursuits, a properly motivated quest for ethical knowledge can be obliterated. Under such circumstances moral forgetfulness may occur. With repetitious similar instances the chronaxie of the questioning period is prolonged with each event until the moral interrogation of self-actions lapses into the minimized nihilism of nonentity.

Most people do not look at themselves with sufficient self-scrutiny to see what they are really. This negligence often dwarfs their moral standards as it eliminates the self-examination of personal conscience. Contrariwise when people see themselves as they are, they learn to know more about themselves. To know oneself refers to the central core of the human person. When this learned state is acknowledged by the unit self then one truly knows oneself which leads to achieving the highest level of psychic activity.

To 'know thyself' means to know moral behavior that leads to persistent, elevated, ethical conduct. Ostensibly the only item that is essential material in morality is the internal (psychic) intention of the agent. The external performance is of secondary rank because without primary intention, the completed act would be accidental, excusable as non-culpable conduct, and free of contributory negligence. Self-knowledge that is knowledge of self has the added asset of intellectual intuition that lends credence to the appreciation that all human self-acquired, unguided knowledge can be fallible.

Metaphysical casuistry, sophistry, and astringent prestidigitation have been applied to the abortion eruption as to the meaning of human being, personhood, onset of life, and ensoulement. These missile-like explosions arouse many predicatives emanating from the phenomenology of variegated, disparate mentalities. Cognition requires that on this one issue of abortion a unanimity of unbiased, non-prejudicial biological fact prevail concerning the isomorphic essence of maternal life and the intrauterine fetus. The controversial debated repetition centers on "being." *What is "being?"* can be asked *ad infinitum* without tregetouring. The echolalial answer returns like a repetitious, resounding echo. It is human life.

*Ceteris paribus* the act of living *in utero* is predictatory of extrauterine life barring a pathophsiological interruption thereof. Actual life and potential life are separable in the metaphysical order. This pensive division is not tenable bioscientifically because of the factuality that an intact embryo becomes a fetus that advances to babyhood, and infancy. Chosen terms as actual life/potential life can not be allowed to be disruptive as a copula for the sequential concatenation of events that is human growth.

An intrauterine baby is not caught between the Scylla and Charybdis of two prenatal worlds in which it is powerless to be born and the other where it is looked upon as a non-living presence. Distortion of reason may mislead purposefully to justify an evil or to promote falsity for self-exculpation. By interpolating a hypothetical question this distress of rationalization is highlighted. Can it be deducted that the misidentified intrauterine infant ascends to concrete extrauterine existence or does intangible life descend into the tangible intrauterine biological being? If it is one or the other is an indifferent methodology. When does it occur? That is the crucial question. The answer has been given previously.

Reawakened teaching with receptive learning has electrified human consciousness to a renewed, reconsidered responsiveness to the inherent evil of abortion. This reconciliation of self-appraisal with moral re-evaluation has coerced legalists to appellate state courts and to the bar of the United States Supreme Court. Appropriately a case in point was heard at the state level on March 17, 1989.

"A Michigan court has upheld a state ban on Medicaid-funded abortions in the matter of a pregnant 15-year-old rape victim who sought a state-paid abortion. Lawyers for the girl have filed an appeal with the Michigan Court of Appeals. The Detroit teenager, known in court proceedings only as Jane Doe, had an abortion paid for by private donations hours after a Wayne County Circuit Court made the ruling on March 17, 1989" (257).

Ecclesiastical notice and mayoral utterances have been aggrandized with vivid publicity concerning the abortion belligerency. On March 26, 1989, the New York Times Book Review Section contained comments on the co-authored, candid written exchange between His Eminence John J. Cardinal O'Connor and Edward I. Koch, the picturesque Mayor of the City of New York. The critic of this book entitled "His Eminence and Hizzoner" terminates his critique with an excerpt from the book via the Cardinal's closing remarks on the morality of command decisions. By analogy as applied to abortion, it exemplifies the arriving at a moral decision which if left to its own course of future delay often eliminates the need for the initial decision in the first place. It is as if the force of destiny is the solvent that dissolves ethical difficulties with eventual evanescence.

"The Cardinal singles out Justice Oliver Wendell Holmes, whose 'legal bent,' he says, 'distorted our constitutional heritage in abandoning moral absolutes.' To illustrate Holmes's influence he cites a 1957 movie, *Abandon Ship*, in which the captain of a crowded lifeboat casts some people overboard to give the rest a chance to survive. But the next morning, we are told, a passing ship picks up the boat. Unfortunately the Cardinal fails to mention the heart of the film: a night-time storm in which even the lightened boat is saved only by the captain's skill" (258).

Since the Roe v. Wade decision this nation has been divided into two acrimonious, agitated camps. Each stands on its own tinderbox that may become an incendiary explosion at the slightest provocation. Hatred has filtered into families causing fulminating arguments. Zealots have aroused ire that has culminated in fomented violence against medical centers with fermenting harassment of women seeking abortions.

It would be the epitomization of political sagacity indicative of egregious statesmanship to eradicate the liberal abortion law, if for no other reason than the patriotic cause of reuniting the American people. As of 1989 these United States are not a sociomoral union. It has been disrupted by a non-military civil war that has brought forth a polarizing divisiveness contaminated by tendencies to fratricide. The prior, well-known, impeccable, elite dignity of America's respectful society cannot long endure as tranquility dissipates with half our citizens angry at the other half because of the abortion berm that separates them.

This dividing umbrage deepens when prolife advocates are marked as racketeers. Although it may appear to be a fantasy, some proabortion constituencies and the Third Circuit Court of Appeals indicate that antiabortionists demonstrating outside abortion clinics can be tried in court under a law that was passed to combat organized crime. Little consideration is given to the fact that demonstrators are protected under the Constitution's allowance of exercise of free speech rights.

"A three-judge panel of the Circuit Court ruled on March 3, 1989, that twenty-six prolife activists in Philadelphia could be charged under the 'Racketeer Influenced and Corrupt Organizations Act' (RICO). This act passed by Congress in 1970...allows, in addition to criminal prosecutions, civil lawsuits for anyone 'injured in his business or property by reason of (another's) pattern of racketeering activity.' RICO is currently the favored tool of proabortion forces against prolifers...RICO statutes also allow pretrial seizure of assets. (A prolife demonstrator in Philadelphia may lose his house because of the Court's ruling in that city.)" (259).

## Abortion Demonstration in Washington

On a cloudy Saturday, April 8, 1989, the prochoice army and the antiabortion cohort converged on the Capitol City of Washington. The resident gentry were not impressed by the panoply of the proponents of abortion. Washingtonians are not political naifs. After all, this city is also the husting capitol of the nation, where fanfares are not unusual.

Voices of the multitude bespattered the spring air with hatred that besotted some listeners who did not look upon the demonstration as hokery. Prochoice marchers had more than a soupcon that their cause was in jeopardy. Hence their quantitative presence did not reflect with exactitude the linguistic stimulation that vibrated high decibel utterances of questionable syllogistic merit.

Newspapers listed more than 300,000 men, women, and children as the number present. A more realistic estimate would be 80,000 people. The next day, April 9, 1989, a windy Sunday, the tawdry spectacle was highly visible as each state representatives alphabetically moved unceremoniously up Pennsylvania Avenue to the White House. Each group with its allies held on high many printed banners with pithy sayings. They hoped to stir public opinion in their favor. More significantly, each segregated group of disputants aimed at persuading the nine justices of the Supreme Court to act in their direction. The odd feature of this organized display of strength was the inclusion of minor children. When asked why children were included among the adults, the answer was "To show children that life allows freedom of choice." Others responded that abortion is a family matter. No secondary comment was given to explain in depth these statements.

On April 16, 1989, the proabortion devotees paraded to Capitol Hill expecting to persuade the members of Congress to bolster their position. Antiabortionists raised their voices in adamant exclamation that the abortion issue is more political than judicial. They stressed that the dispute should be heard and decided in state legislatures or in Congress. Since these bodies represent the people they are more responsive to the will of their constituencies which is an alien sentiment to nine justices of the Supreme Court of the United States of America.

The proabortionists in the majority were spurred on by their own greater numbers and the favorable public polls. Most Americans have expressed consistently that abortion should be a legal right. In a January 1989 Louis Harris Poll it was indicated that 56 percent to 42 percent with 2 percent undecided favor abortion. Another dissimilar majority stated that they believe abortion is the same act as murdering a child. In *The New York Times* poll of December, 1985, the antiabortion vote was 55 percent to 35 percent prochoice with 10 percent undecided. A Gallup poll released to the media on April 15, 1989 showed that 77 percent of American citizens queried favor legalized abortion (256). This majority consensus was publicized forcefully with the expectation of influencing the justices who heard the Webster case on April 26, 1989. The major thrust of this Missouri lawsuit was founded upon that state's denial of allocated public funds to pay physicians for performing abortions plus other anti-abortion appendices such as life begins at conception, and the right to privacy does not include the right to an abortion (255).

Each opposing side of the abortion cacophony reared on elan thrust imaginary bodkins at each other as both chivved their antagonists with rhetorical questions and exclamatory remarks. The theme of the antiabortionists was that they objected to the Supreme Court's authority to answer a non-legal abortion question. A legal mind (unless the attorney or judge has joint M.D., J.D.

degrees) lacks the practical medical experience to determine the many aspects of abortion including the ethical inherency arising out of religious teachings of the greatest number of Americans. If the Supreme Court has the power to decide the abortion controversy, there is no obstacle to bringing before the court future medicomoral questions for answers. Reference is made to euthanasia, rationing medical therapy, the administration of non-effective care, the placebo policy, etc.

As some demonstrators became rioters the participants were scrutinized — almost microscopically. Without any fond recollection, those "who came to Washington, D.C....looked familiar. Well-dressed women and a few well-dressed men, fronted by even better-dressed movie actresses supported by video trucks were there" (260). The film colony emigrants were present, not in their own interest, but on behalf of the poor. The cinema folk seemed to have a happy time as they listened to the vocal fusillades while prancing before the camera. Their misguided interpretations of the event lent a carnival atmosphere to the occasion which should have been more solemn in keeping with the serious nature of the reason for the demonstration.

"Once the poor, the people with their own pertinent and personal grievances, did the marching. It was a pictorial reminiscence of the changing wave in the dress of drummers, but the temper tantrum of the marchers remains...It is time for the American upper middle class to give protest back to folks with personal pocket-book grievances, the ones who are good at it" (260).

The internecine abortion war has become so heated that it is testing the ethical stamina of journalists. "According to the Washington Post, not a few reporters and editors participated in the April 19, 1989 'abortion rights' march on Washington, D.C." (261). Among them was a lady reporter of *The New York Times* who covers the United States Supreme Court, whose members the demonstrators tried to influence.

Ben Bradlee, the executive editor of the Washington Post wrote a memorandum to his staff when he was informed that several of the Washington Post reporters and editors had partaken in the abortion march. The executive editor wrote, "We once again remind members of the newsroom's professional staff that it is unprofessional for you (as opposed to your relatives) to take part in political or issue demonstrations, no matter on which side or how seemingly worthy the cause. It is the choice we make when we choose to work in this business and for this newspaper" (261).

When any sect, denomination, or specialized group is asked to march for or against a controversial issue, the end result is decisiveness and more decisiveness with an infinite, repetitive, plebeian continuum. This leads to avoidance of the law in compatibility with Aristotle's sentience: "The law is reason free from passion" (262).

From the observer's overview, it was blatantly discernible that the leaders of the prochoice legion found their idol in a cause and not in a hero. Those in command possessed neither outstanding character nor virtue worthy of emulation. None had sparkling, charismatic morality. Nowhere was there a scintilla resembling the enchantment of dignified armorial crusaders. A champion of heraldic chivalry could not be found in the ranks of the protesting, cynical throng.

With a visible diminished number of participants, another less dramatic, unpretentious, non-magnetic march took place in New York. Ten days after the parade in Washington, D.C., a "walk" taken by three prolife Republican State Senators "guaranteed that New York will have $15 million in its budget to facilitate abortions. An Albany Times-Union story proclaims that these senators were absent (one said he was 'getting some air') because if they were present in legislative chambers they would have to cast votes that would have derailed the budget compromise. (269).

The senators' votes would have allowed the passage of an amendment that removed Medicaid funding for abortion from the budget. "This would have put Senate and Assembly at odds. The senators are prolife but not enough to face the dislocation and loss of millions of dollars their votes would have caused" (269). Are these senators decadent legislators who lack the full courage of their conviction that abortion is murder? Does political expediency dominate ethical conduct that inflames immorality?

Elsewhere other citizens acted in a positive manner in a similar situation. "Last November (1988) Colorado, Michigan, and Arkansas voted down such funding in referenda. The United States

Supreme Court does not require funding for abortions, nor does the Federal government...If someone would overcome the inertia and risk a good fight, the State Legislature may find out New Yorkers do not want it" (269).

"Those who sit in judgment, be they judges, jurors, or professional peers, always have clear tests to apply, but they are also acutely conscious that they, too, are being judged by outsiders and that has a way of swaying the verdicts...It is a jungle in judgment land" (263). How much persuasion can be thrust at judges is difficult to evaluate. Traditionally judges are not influenceable by any individual, location, maneuver, or tactic. Politicians elected to public office are the persons who do bow to public sentiments if they desire to be re-elected.

Unmoved by outside influence, on May 15, 1989 Mr. Justice Anthony Kennedy reaffirmed a Florida law that required any woman under 18 years of age who desires an abortion must obtain parental permission or secure the consent of a judge for its performance. When asked to give this consent to a fifteen-year-old girl who was 14-15 weeks pregnant, the Supreme Court Judge said, "No." By expressing his opinion, firm support is given to this Florida law. Indirectly he released by his action an inferential preview which was an intimated prediction to some, or prognosticated interpretation by other forecasters, of his position on the Webster matter that was awaiting judicial decision.

"In the courtroom the influence of public passions is less obvious, but still felt. Law is nothing unless close behind it stands a warm, living public opinion" insisted the 19th century reformer Wendell Phillips (263). The seething emotionalism witnessed in those for and against the Webster v. Reproductive Health Services court hearing has not subsided. April 1989 will be recorded in the history of abortion as a month of bitter turmoil with a lingering tasteless aftermath. Expectations ran high on both sides in the attempts to have the Supreme Court hear and see them. Only the passage of time can disclose the rise or decline in the procacious influence of this sort of instigated ploy.

On May 15, 1989, the dictum of Mr. Justice Kennedy reopened the wounds that were healing from the lacerating experiences of the strepitous April 26, 1989 Washington, D.C. demonstrations. The dehiscence bled into sanguineous speculations as to the future effects of the Webster decision. Prolifers and prochoicers fear the loss of benefits for their respective causes. The antiabortionists cite four impediments to success in the prolife effort. These are "an unprofessional press, untrustworthy politicians, the greed with evil of those promoting abortion, and divisiveness within the prolife movement" (290). Reference to division in the ranks centers about the urgent necessity for "unity in support of a no exceptions position regarding prolife legislation" (290).

The National March for Life Committee Chairperson Nellie Gray in an address on May 2, 1989 in Garden City, N.Y. said regarding the Webster case which was pending at that time: "...the court may respond to the United States Justice Department, returning authority to the states in legislating on the abortion issue. Finally the court could concur with the preamble of the Missouri statute, which states that life begins at conception, and thus declare the unborn to be legal persons protected by the Constitution. Such a finding would in effect prohibit legalized abortion in the United States" (290).

The fermentation arising out of the morally offensive act of insensate abortion is said to be an expression of the democratic system of government. Under the aegis of a constitutional democracy life and liberty are basic social concerns. In the United States of America dynamism has spumed volcanically during our past bicentennial history. However, up to 1973, no issue has been more disruptive than the miasma of abortion when Roe v. Wade appeared on the Supreme Court docket. Since then the surreptitious immorality of abortion has infected American citizens more strongly than the contaminating AIDS virus. Like the autoimmune-disease-syndrome, a negative moral prognosis leads but to the grave.

The past and present profanity of abortion may be irrationally excusable but its demoralizing depression lingers *sub rosa* in the hearts of humanity. The *vademecum* for spiritual peace of mind and body *(mens sana in corpore sano)* remains always the same. It is adherence to the patrimonic interdependent Ten Commandments which are a prophylaxis against the evil conduct that leads to human

**41**

degradation. Until this belief is accepted by those whose free-will does not permit it to be adopted, a pervasive mental attitude favoring abortion continues to flourish. If this Mosean achievement is impossible, it may be mentally nutritious to pursue a policy of perennial pessimism. Thus the anguish of disappointment from negative performances may be assuaged. Contrariwise if a successful end result materializes, the positive delight of victory will be an enjoyable bonus.

Confidence in the ethical stamina of the American people sustains the relentless promotion of liberty for the unborn. By virtue of the concept of American freedom, intrauterine citizens have the constitutional right to be born freely to enter into the worldly sphere of earthy life. This prognostication will eventuate because no law can be sustained without the will of the people. Gradually Americans, who are moralists by nature, will realize that proabortion laws deny the freedom to live. Historically the American people react favorably to timeless truth by adhering to it. A primary truth is that microcosmic intrauterine life is definitive human life. Moreover, to take away a sinless human life is not consistent with traditional Americanism as established by our colonial ancestors and preserved by subsequent vibrant generations.

## Webster v. Reproductive Health Services

Prior to rendering the majority opinion, the pretrial question was, "Will the Supreme Court follow public opinion in deciding the Webster/Missouri abortion case?" The prolifers hoped yes, because "most Americans while not going the whole nine yards with the prolifers nonetheless are disgusted with abortion on demand. They think the political process should be allowed to reach compromises on the issue" (264).

"Different times lead to the degradation of different groups. Exemplified by slavery in America wherein the Dred Scott decision in 1858 (Dred Scott v. Sandford) the Supreme Court held that black people had 'no rights which the white man was bound to respect,' thus making black people a lot like first-trimester infants under Roe v. Wade" (264).

Roger Brooke Taney (1777-1864), pronounced "Tawney", was Chief Justice, when 48 hours into the administration of President

James Buchanan, the Dred Scott lawsuit came before the United States Supreme Court. Justice Taney's major opinion encouraged "more rancorous hate than any other judgment (decision) of a court since man first submitted disputes to the arbitrament of law." *

"The behavior of the Supreme Court in both the Dred Scott and Roe decision has striking similarity. Both were attempts to settle a political problem by removing it from politics. When the court does this, the options remaining to those on the losing side can be grouped into two general categories: efforts to reverse the decision and civil war" (264).

Fortunately the resentment against abortion has not sparked into a fighting war as happened after the Dred Scott ruling. However, with the antiabortion initiative known as Operation Rescue there may be an ugly turn of events. Many people are willing to lose their freedom by placing their physical presence between the abortionists and the destined abortion. Incrementing social tensions can occur even as the form they may assume is unpredictable. In the meantime a non-shooting civil war continues unabatedly between those who favor abortion and those who abhor it. "Such are the fruits of using constitutional adjudication to bottle up a controversy in which even partial compromise is difficult and ultimate compromise is impossible" (264).

On April 26, 1989, the abortion legal race through the corridors of state courts to the United States Supreme Court reached the finish line. The widely publicized lawsuit acclaimed as the Webster case (William Webster is the attorney general of Missouri) reached its destination. Outside the regal courthouse on that day, the scene was a slalom with fanatic, feisty, frenetic, frantic fans either for or against abortion milling about the august edifice. Vociferously opposing platoons campaigned for their objectives with each side

---

* These are the words of a 1872 Taney biographer, Samuel Tyler. Judge Taney's secondary fame resides in his romance. History confirms that he pursued successfully Anne Phoebe Charlton Key, sister of Francis Scott Key. They were married in 1806. The Chief Justice admired his brother-in-law very much. In later years he wrote that *"The Star-Spangled Banner* revealed Key's genius and taste as a poet" (268).

believing its cause to be just. The sensed sorrow is that the baryphonic animosity insidiously increased in crescendo to within a hairbreadth of truculence.

Persistent persuasion reached its zenith with the marching April scenario. This display of humanity in motion will be preserved in American archives as two days that gave filmed, cinematic presence to the promoters of infanticide that is begetting fratricide. Enhanced by television, Americans witnessed the burgeoning hatred in the facial expressions of the proabortionists who with words of anger written on banners confirmed their grimaces. No event extracted from American societal cartulary has divided Americans so perceptibly since the administration of President Abraham Lincoln.

This travesty of discord has produced an infectious animosity that has evaporated the characteristic generosity, altruism and consideration for others that has been the indigenous cynosure of Americanism. What is most startling and incomprehensible is that this social divide has been brought into concentrated focus by an emotional issue that discards embryological science as it condones a moral misadventure without any indepth authoritative biological study.

For two weeks preceding April 26, 1989, an aroused citizenry flooded the mailroom at the United States Supreme Court building with more than 40,000 letters, postal cards, packages containing photographs of dead babies, wire coat-hangers, and other similar sundries. The telephone switchboard was receiving approximately 100 calls daily. Justice Harry Blackmun received mail of condemnation. Justice Sandra O'Connor was the recipient of the largest quantity of "pleading" mail since she was thought to be the pivotal voter whose critical opinion would tip the scale of justice for or against the Webster appeal.

Rarely does public opinion sway, persuade, or dissuade judicial concepts, no matter the ponderosity of external efforts. The Supreme Court is the repository of constitutional values. It is not an hospitable host inviting public sentiment to consult with it, participate in its proceedings or thought processes. Judicial pronouncements are not alterable by extraneous influences once the justice has been appointed to the highest court of this nation. The American system of government is so constructed that the only questioning of Supreme Court Justices occurs prior to their appointment.

This truism resides in the reality that the President of the United States appoints a new judge when a vacancy exists. The appointment must be approved by the senate which can and has rejected designated appointees. Political aspects of judicial appointments are reflected in that a president invariably will suggest the name of a judge whose political philosophy is similar to his own. Hence a conservative president usually appoints an historically conservative judge who will sustain the president's political *credo*. A liberal president will do the same. This predetermined knowledge predicts the general legal pattern that will be formulated by the new appointee.

As a reflection, the administration of President Bush has its own unofficial agenda on the abortion related controversy. The non-pugnacious plans are more prolife than proabortion. President "Bush is expected to continue the former president's opposition to using federal money for abortion-related activities by Planned Parenthood and other organizations that obtain funds under Title 10 of the Public Health Service Act. Aid would be continued as long as it was not used for abortions...President Bush will stand by former President Reagan's policy opposing use of federal money for international population-control programs that pay for, perform or recommend abortions. Critics are challenging both policies in court. They have won orders temporarily suspending restrictions on Title 10 in most areas" (265).

The Bush administration has given interpretive signals on another abortion-related debate. Prolife spokesmen are not silent on the use of tissue from aborted fetuses in biomedical research. "Congress is not eager to tackle this (thorny project), so the first move could come from the Bush administration...the Secretary of Health and Human Services is expected to decide by late summer (1989) whether or not the government should fund research using such tissue, which has been helpful in developing treatment for Parkinson's disease, diabetes mellitus, and other illnesses. The Secretary of Health and Human Services has links to the biomedical community that favors such research. But he was in trouble earlier with conservatives by not expressing adamant opposition to abortion, and since taking office, he has been surrounded by prolife advocates...White House aides expect to continue the current moratorium on federal funding for such research" (265).

Boisterous protesters outside the Supreme Court building on April 26, 1989 did not disturb the calmness and circadian teflon formality of the judicial proceedings within. "Shouting, placard-waving, chants, side remarks, police lines, demonstrations, and arrests — all underscored what both factions in the throng of about 1000 people consider a mortal issue" (266). The ruction display of humanity in uproar was not an achromatic diorama, although it had no eclat, panoply, or panache. An analysis of this episode in the history of abortion will herald that Americans tolerate extravagant fancies but not anarchy.

This statement is substantiated by the actions of some picketeers who became near-rioters. The result was that "twenty-seven demonstrators were arrested for stepping over police barriers and lying prostrate on the marble steps to the court plaza. 'Keep your laws off my body!' some chanted as police carried off their apprehended comrades. All were members of two homosexual activist groups according to a spokesman for one of the organizations" (266). In the distance another segment of non-picturesque shouters were vocalizing with "Sandra Day, hear what we say: abortion's legal, we want it that way!" (Referring to Associate Justice O'Connor's probable decisive vote in the Webster case under discussion inside the colonnaded building).

Tempers were on the rise as the tempo of the crowd vacillated in its ardor. Some shouted: "People are going to die. They refuse to accept unborn babies as people. What are they, if not people when they grow up." By their clothing, protesting women believed they could be more protagonistic. "To symbolize the argument, many women wore black dresses and armbands as a eulogy for those women who died having abortions. Demonstrators against abortions agreed a threnody was appropriate, but for the more than 20 million innocents" (266). Killing is not a private matter when it is another person who is destroyed. Society's obligation is not to kill some of its members for the sake of other members. A fallacy in the abortionist's claim that abortion must remain 'a personal matter of choice.' Roe v. Wade made killing a private matter which *de facto* is contrary to the recognized social obligation of civilized nations.

In the courthouse plaza, "at one point some 30-40 reporters circled around a dispute between a black minister from Richmond, Virginia and several demonstrators provoked by his message that poverty is used as an excuse to justify abortions by black people. Many blacks as well as whites are buying the big lie that it is better for an innocent child that is black to be destroyed, rather than to face a life of uncertainty in America" (266). If poverty is the excuse, correct the poverty. Killing the unborn does not correct the underlying cause — poverty.

The president of Black Americans For Life said: "It is almost the destiny of black Americans to speak up for the unborn, because someone spoke for us 120 years ago when black people did not have a voice and were thought to be some else's property...and if we do not (speak up), it is almost a sign of ingratitude to those who spoke up for us when we were helpless (and voiceless)" (266).

Some of the disorderly crowd had arrived late Tuesday afternoon (the day before the scheduled hearing) in the hope of gaining admission for one of the 50 or so seats in the courtroom. As the spectators entered the awesome court with its crural austerity, perhaps one or more recalled the quatrain of Jonathan Swift (1667-1745).

*In points of honor to be try'd,*
*All passions must be laid aside;*
*Ask no advice, but think alone:*
*Suppose the question not your own.*

The total abortion puzzle may not be unravelled justicably but the Supreme Court has not retrenched from its assigned dutiful obligation.

Without terret "the Bush administration teamed up with Missouri's attorney general to urge the Supreme Court to overturn the landmark 1973 ruling giving women a constitutional right to abortion. In a (newer) case that could determine the continued validity of 1973's controversial Roe v. Wade, Webster v. Reproductive Health

Services is the focal site of the most volatile debate", wrangling dispute, and bitter contest over abortion to date (267). The *vis a tergo* of letting the Webster decision remain *in toto* is that the right to an abortion can be significantly altered.

The Missouri Law that was at issue bans public funding for abortions, advocates abortion counseling, requires special fetal testing for late abortions, and declares that life begins at conception (270). Arguments presented to the Supreme Court on April 26, 1989 yielded sparse indications on what was the mood of the judges. A paramount question to be answered was to what extent the Supreme Court will allow state regulation of abortion rights as they exist under the current law. From overheard prochoice conversations many expressed disappointment in that Associate Justice Sandra Day O'Connor, who was considered to have the key vote, asked very few questions.

A highlight of the pleadings raised observer attentiveness when the defendant's attorney, who represented two abortion clinics, several doctors, and nurses argued that returning abortion regulation to the states would undermine women's rights to use contraceptives because the two are interconnected. Associate Justices Antonin Scalia and Anthony Kennedy, neither of whom has voted in a decisive abortion ruling of the high court, appeared to grapple with legally distinguishing abortion from birth control in the general realm of privacy rights (267). A philosophical distinction between the two is differenced clearly.

To practice birth control is to prevent conception which is future life. Direct abortion is the wilful destruction of a life already conceived. Hence it is not a question of privacy rights but one of a duty not to destroy another human being. The compatibility of legally merging abortion with contraception into one conjointed, miscible, coequal relationship is intellectually untenable. An alliance of contraception with the abortion impasse is immediately deniable. To equalize the deprivation of privacy rights in each is an odious comparison that compels the sequestering thereof as lacking propinquity and possessing dilapidatious fallaciousness.

Concurring in that reasoned deduction is Dr. Charles DeCelles, Professor, Department of Religious Studies, Marywood College in Scranton, Pennsylvania. He expressed his thoughts in a letter to

William Webster, the Attorney General of Missouri. It was written to elucidate the non-embellished incompatibility that is the incongruity of the abortion/contraception synergism. The professor's augmented writing is recorded herewith as a personal communication to the author.

Professor De Celles's correspondence was received in the period of time between the oral arguments before the Supreme Court on the Webster case and the Court's ruling. It is included here because it provides an insightful analysis of a pivotal issue in the Webster matter, and because it offers valuable counsel to future legislators on the abortion controversy. In addition the correspondence contains bioethical opinion that constitute a meaningful prolife testimony.

*"If the majority of Americans became convinced that making abortion illegal would put in jeopardy the legal status of artificial birth control, they would presumably demand that neither the courts nor the legislative bodies of our government interfere with the present legal status of abortion. This apparently is part of the reason why the prochoice camp has recently attempted to portray abortion and birth control as intertwined and inseparable.*

*Proof of this effort to have the issues perceived as intermeshed was visible at the April 9 prochoice rally and march held in Washington, D.C. A United Press International photograph, appearing April 10 in newspapers around the country, shows a huge banner at the head of the march, behind which walked celebrities such as Jane Fonda, Whoopie Goldberg, Cybill Shepard, as well as Molly Yard, the president of the National Organization for Women. The banner read: "Keep abortion and birth control safe and legal."*

*Viewing that banner on the front page of a newspaper angered but did not surprise me. What came as somewhat of a shock, however, was discovering in the April 27 issue of the New York Times that the effort to project the issues as locked to each other and therefore inseparable had reached the hallowed halls of the Supreme Court. In Webster v. Reproductive Health Services, the pivotal abortion case, Attorney Frank Susman, lawyer for the abortion rights groups, argued that abortion and artificial birth control are inextricably intertwined, so much so that to disturb the legal status of the one would be to undermine the legal position of the other. What was even more disconcerting was Justice Antonin Scalia's reasoning that Susman's point made a lot of sense.*

*Actually the issues of abortion and birth control (contraception) are quite distinct, but the language of the antiabortion Missouri statute in the Webster case complicates matters. A section of the Missouri statute declares that "the life of each human being begins at conception." ("The general assembly of this state finds that: (1) The life of each human being begins at conception.") "Conception" in the statute is defined as "the fertilization of the ovum of a female by the sperm of a male." The statute's definition of the unborn child is consistent with this perspective. "...The term 'unborn children' or 'unborn child' shall include all unborn child or children or the offspring of human beings from the moment of conception until birth at every stage of biological development."*

*In his opening remarks, William L. Webster, the Missouri attorney general defending the statute, pointed out that Missouri's appeal involved three basic areas submitted to the Court for review. One of these was "the effect of and the facial constitutionality of legislation declaring that life begins at conception."*

*Collaborating with Mr. Webster was Charles Fried, the United States Acting Solicitor General, who spoke on behalf of the Bush administration. He asked the Court to reconsider and overrule its decision in the Roe v. Wade case which entirely prohibited the States from having laws proscribing abortion during the first two trimesters of pregnancy. (It allowed some restrictions on abortion for the last trimester only.) He specified that the request was limited. He was not asking the Court "to unravel the fabric of unenumerated and privacy rights" which they recognized and upheld in other decisions such as Griswold v. Connecticut (294).*

*In the landmark Griswold decision, the Supreme Court rejected a law that prohibited the use of contraceptives even within the context of marriage. The ruling recognized a "zone of privacy" created by various guarantees found in the Bill of Rights. In the later Roe v. Wade decision, the Court would draw heavily upon that concept of a privacy zone.*

*Mr. Fried argued that the right to abort is different from other rights inasmuch as it involves the purposeful termination of life,* potential human life in the eyes of the Court, but actually in the view of many legislators.

Speaking for the proabortion camp, Mr. Frank Susman would attempt to argue that the government really wants to eliminate the "full range of procreational rights and choices that constitute the fundamental right that has been recognized by this Court." He stated that the right to use contraceptives established by Griswold and the right to abort established by Roe are not distinct. Because of the advances in science and medicine they now overlap, coalesce, and merge.

In an attempt to establish his point before an apparently skeptical jurist, Justice Scalia, he stated: "The most common forms of what we generically in common parlance call contraception today — IUD's, low-dose birth control pills, which are the safest type of birth control pills available — act as abortifacients. They are correctly labeled as both."

In this, of course, Mr. Susman is correct. The prevailing theory regarding IUDs is that they work by interference. The low-estrogen pills work mostly by preventing release of the ovum. They cause "temporary" sterilization. But they also produce an antinidatory effect on the endometrium, that is, they "harden" the lining of the uterus. This impedes implantation if the ovum should be released and become fertilized. Low-estrogen pills allow "breakthrough" ovulation about one month in five. Released ova are fertilized about 10% of the time. Consequently, the low-estrogen pill can be viewed as sometimes working in an abortifacient manner (1 or 2% of the time).

Mr. Susman was also correct to point out that under the Missouri statute, which states that human life begins at conception but defines conception as fertilization, "those forms of contraception are also abortifacients."

Apparently Susman's point, that abortion and contraception are so enmeshed and interlocked that to pull the one thread of abortion out of the arena of privacy rights is to endanger rights regarding contraception, impressed Justice Scalia. For he interrupted Mr. Webster's later rebuttal of Susman's arguments by saying: "But he makes the very good point that it is impossible to distinguish between abortion and contraception when you define abortion as the destruc-

*tion of the first joinder of the ovum and the sperm."* When Mr. Webster complained that the issue before the Court was the state of Missouri's desire to prohibit post-viability abortions, Scalia reminded him that the issue ran deeper than that. *"Before the Court is the question of whether, as the solicitor general argues, you can overrule Roe v. Wade without endangering our law concerning contraception."*

It seems to me unfortunate from the point of view of the legal defense of human life that the state of Missouri, in declaring that *"the life of each human being begins at conception,"* chose to define conception as *"the fertilization of the ovum of a female by a sperm of a male."* The state might have done better to avoid altogether any declaration as to when human life begins. The logical consequences of this definition are twofold. In the first place, the destruction of the fertilized ovum even before implantation occurs becomes abortion. (The definition of abortion in the Missouri statute is not, however, technically consistent with this. Abortion is defined as *"the intentional destruction of the life of an embryo or fetus in his or her mother's womb or the intentional termination of the pregnancy of the mother..."* But, according to American language usage, a fertilized ovum, the zygote, is not generally designated as an embryo — much less a fetus — before implantation.) Secondly, with fertilization a new human being emerges. The statute does in fact designate as an unborn child the offspring of human parents from conception, i.e. fertilization, as mentioned earlier. Consequently, preventing implantation through mechanical means or birth control pill constitutes not only abortion, but the killing of a child. That idea would be difficult for American society to accept. That does not mean it is a false idea.

Actually, from the point of view of clinical embryology, human life is correctly designated as beginning at fertilization. Keith L. Moore, Ph.D., professor and head of the department of anatomy, University of Manitoba, in his book The Developing Human (Saunders, Philadelphia, 1974), defines the zygote as follows: *"This cell results from fertilization of an ovum by a sperm and is the beginning of a human being."*

Morally too the zygote must be regarded as a human being and treated accordingly. The largest Christian denomination in the *world, the Catholic Church, teaches this: "The fruit of human generation from the first moment the zygote has formed, demands the unconditional respect that is morally due to the human being in his bodily and spiritual totality." ("Instruction on Respect for Human Life In Its Origin and on the Dignity of Procreation," by the Vatican Congregation for the Doctrine of the Faith in Origins, Vol. 16, 1987, p. 701). The killing of a zygote is, therefore, entirely unacceptable from a moral point of view and condemnable. "Any direct deliberate attack on innocent human life, in whatsoever condition it is found from the very first moment of its existence, is wrong." (Pope Pius XII, Address to the Family Associations (November 26, 1951).*

*Not only the Catholic Church but world Christianity generally teaches that human life has to be treated reverentially from the outset, and that abortion is intolerable. The Common Catechism (Seabury, 1975), a comprehensive statement of the Christian faith, produced by an international team of forty distinguished Protestant and Catholic theologians, states that: "The Christian churches have pronounced themselves unambiguously on this point" (p.511). It quotes the Second Vatican Council as follows: "From the moment of conception life must be guarded with the greatest care, while abortion and infanticide are unspeakable crimes" (Pastoral Constitution, art. 51).*

*Nevertheless, in the interests of social justice and in the hope realistically of overturning Roe v. Wade, by isolating the abortion issue from the contraceptive issue, the Missouri Assembly might perhaps have done better to define conception as "the fertilization of the ovum of a female by the sperm of a male followed by the implantation of the fertilized ovum in the uterus of the female." This would seemingly have been a legitimate legal definition since in fact conception occurs in the two distinct stages of fertilization initially, and then implantation which begins about five days later and is completed within an additional four days. Until stage two is accomplished, conception is not definitive and pregnancy in the ordinary sense does not exist. A preamble could have indicated that the two-stage definition did not claim to be correct biologically, ethically or religiously but was a legal statement made in the practical hope of offering protection in the law to human beings from an early stage in human development.*

*If the Missouri statute contained such a definition of conception, the IUD and the low-estrogen pill, as well as the day-after pill, which also works to "harden" the endometrum and prevent implantation (as well as hold back the ovum if it has not been released), would rightfully be judged, in reference to it, simply as contraceptive, rather than both contraceptive and abortifacient. They would be viewed either as preventing fertilization (a few scholarly papers have suggested that even the IUD works this way), which is unambiguously contraceptive or as interfering with implantation, i.e. conception at stage two. That is, they would be seen as preventing the completion of conception. This would also be contraceptive. At least, it could be so viewed from the point of view of the law, since conception would not be fully accomplished nor pregnancy secured.*

*Marriage provides us with an analogy. Marriage occurs in two stages: the church or civil ceremony and later the consummation. Without consummation, there would be no complete marriage. Hence, if the union breaks up, there would be no need for divorce, only an annulment. Divorce, as a term to describe the termination of a marriage, would be inappropriate because there would have been no definitive marriage to terminate. So likewise, abortion would be inappropriate as a term to describe the termination of an incomplete conception. The pill and IUD thus would not be abortifacient, according to the language of the statute.*

*If the Missouri Assembly had defined conception as involving fertilization plus implantation, the issues of abortion and contraception would have been more sharply disentangled. Susman's point that the Supreme Court could not overturn Roe without disturbing Griswold would have been at the very least significantly weakened. Perhaps it would have fallen by the wayside completely. Of course, such a definition would have precluded the possibility of outlawing such things as the IUD, the low-estrogen pill and the day-after pill, on the basis that they were destructive of human life. But those things could not realistically be outlawed anyway, unless they posed a health hazard to the mother. Besides, the state of Missouri would probably have no desire to outlaw them.*

*But the Missouri Statute recognizes human life as beginning with fertilization, not with the completion of the twofold process of conception. Does that mean that it becomes impossible for the Supreme Court to distinguish between abortion and contraception? Hopefully not. Common sense and human experience make it abundantly clear that abortion and contraception are distinct concepts. Vis-a-vis the IUD and the low-estrogen pill, the very first stage of life, the distinction might get blurred. The two notions might get intertwined or overlap. But this is normal at the outer limits of things.*

*Because of the objection raised by Susman, the Supreme Court did not approve of that part of the Missouri statute which declares that "the life of each human being begins at conception." Nevertheless, it could overturn Roe v. Wade on other grounds, namely, that the Constitution nowhere recognizes a right to abort, nor a right to privacy that covers abortion. If it did overturn Roe, then the States would be entitled to pass laws prohibiting or curtailing abortion. If, however, a state proceeded to pass a law prohibiting the use of the IUD, the low-estrogen pill, or the morning-after pill, all regarded as contraceptive as well as abortifacient, the Court could step in and reject that law as interfering with the right of privacy established by the Griswold case, which declared laws against contraception unconstitutional. It would be difficult for the Court to do that if it accepted Missouri's declaration that human life begins at fertilization.*

*On the practical level of dealing with the courts, it seems to me, it would have been much better if Missouri had not declared that life begins at conception, in the sense of fertilization, but instead had proclaimed that human life commences with the completion of conception which includes implantation, or perhaps better still had not declared at all when life begins.*

*Nevertheless, beyond the scope of the courts, there are advantages to defining the onset of human life as being fertilization. The most obvious of these is the fact that it is scientifically correct. The second is that it makes a moral statement. The zygote, the fertilized ovum, is already a human being and therefore worthy of the respect due to members of the human family. By implication, such a definition seemingly denounces as wrong any direct attack on the zygote. Those modes of so-called "contraception" whose direct objective is to kill the fertilized ovum by interfering with its implantation into the uterus are to be viewed as unacceptable. For those people who erroneously look to secular legislation for moral guidance, the proclamation that life begins with fertilization could be very helpful, could serve as an important educative tool. Such people are given faulty signals by the status quo on abortion, which is practically one of abortion on demand. They are being told that abortion is alright. My own idea that a legislative body, at this time in history, would do better to declare that life begins with the completion of conception including implantation is not without problems. Such a declaration would also transmit a faulty signal, namely, that the life of the zygote can legitimately be taken — which of course is incorrect ethically. But the transmission of such a signal would be an undesired side effect of the honorable intent to legally protect life from the time when pregnancy is definitively established.*

*Unfortunately, the Missouri statute's clear witness to the immorality of taking human life from fertilization onward will be lost since the Supreme Court has stricken down the statement that life begins at conception-fertilization.*

*Nevertheless, a simple overturning of Roe, with no acceptance of the declaration that life begins at fertilization, would mean a major prolife victory and could result in the saving of millions of lives over the years. The partial affirmation of the Missouri statute constitutes a lesser but, nonetheless, real victory for life, and could provide a turning point in the crusade to eliminate the legal destruction of unborn human beings.*

*The effort to safeguard the false, but legally very real, right of abortion by confusing the issues of abortion and contraception is an annoying but brilliant strategy. However, it is so entirely out of tune with reality that it surely cannot provide a permanent haven for the great social sickness of legalized abortion.*

*We have every reason to hope that the Missouri case will constitute the beginning of the end of that gigantic blotch on our collective American conscience which is the present national situation of abortion on demand.*

*Whatever its future outcome, Webster v. Reproductive Health Services should constitute a learning experience for the prolife camp. When it comes to public legislation, prolife legislators should be cautious about drawing their lines too finely. They should carefully weigh the wisdom of defining human life as beginning precisely at the moment of fertilization" (270).*

Below is a continuation of Dr. De Celles correspondence received after the Webster decision:

*The Supreme Court issued its ruling in the Missouri case, Webster vs. Reproductive Health Services, July 3, 1989. As anticipated, it did not overturn Roe vs. Wade, but it did affirm the Missouri statute on all its points except the statement in its preamble that life begins at conception, i.e. fertilization. It chose not to make a decision on the question of the constitutionality of declaring that life begins at conception, the reason being that the Missouri statute did not follow through on that declaration by restricting a woman's right to abort recognized by Roe vs. Wade. "It will be time enough for Federal courts to address the meaning of the preamble should it be applied to restrict the activities of appellees, in some concrete way. ...We therefore need not pass on the constitutionality of the Act's preamble." This was also the reason the Court gave for not overturning the Roe decision, namely, that the Missouri statute could be approved without disturbing it. There was no need to decide whether to jettison it or not. "In Roe...the Texas statute criminalized the performance of all abortions, except when the mother's life was at stake...This case therefore affords us no occasion to revisit the holding of Roe, which was that the Texas statute unconstitutionally infringed the right to an abortion...and we leave it undisturbed."*

*In an opinion partly concurring with the majority ruling, Justice Sandra Day O'Connor pointed out her willingness to seriously consider overturning Roe vs. Wade if a case arose fundamentally challenging Roe and demanding its overthrow. "When the constitutional validity of a state's abortion statute actually turns on the constitutional validity of Roe vs. Wade, there will be time enough to re-examine Roe. And to do so carefully." She felt it wise and in accordance with traditional Court procedure not to decide on more than what was necessary to resolve the case at hand. "...There is no necessity to accept the state's invitation to re-examine the constitutional validity of Roe vs. Wade. Where there is no need to decide a constitutional question, it is a venerable principle of this Court's adjudicatory process not to do so..."*

Justice Antonin Scalia, in an opinion also partly concurring, pointed out that the present Court, because of its attitude of not wanting to decide issues more broadly than absolutely necessary, might end up dismantling abortion rights doorjamb by doorjamb without ever actually succeeding in totally overturning Roe, and allowing the States to produce those laws against abortion that they deem fit. He himself favors an outright repudiation of Roe.

*"...I would have examined Roe, rather than examining the contravention. Given the Court's newly contracted abstemiousness, what will it take, one must wonder, to permit us to reach that fundamental question?*

*"The result of our vote today is that we will not reconsider that prior opinion, even if most of the Justices think it is wrong, unless we have before us a statute that in fact contradicts it — and even then (under our newly discovered "no broader than necessary" requirement) only minor problematical aspects of Roe will be reconsidered, unless one expects state legislatures to adopt provisions whose compliance with Roe cannot even be argued with a straight face. It thus appears that the mansion of constitutionalized abortion law, constructed overnight in Roe vs. Wade, must be disassembled doorjamb by doorjamb and never entirely brought down, no matter how wrong it may be."*

It seems to me that one way to force the Court to directly confront the Roe vs. Wade ruling would be for a state to produce a statute in which it would declare that human life begins at conception, meaning thereby (and spelling it out) fertilization followed by the completion of implantation — so that human life would not be regarded as "begun" until implantation had definitively occurred — and then to follow through on that declaration by prohibiting all abortions, except in the case where the mother's life would be at stake and, if necessary by way of practical concession, in the cases of rape and incest. (One could perhaps simplify the declaration regarding the onset of life by stating that human life begins once implantation is secured but that might appear arbitrary and hence would not be as easy to logically defend as "conception" viewed as an extended process beginning with fertilization.) Having defined that human life begins *at conception, the state would be consistent and logical in showing an interest in proscribing abortion even at the earliest stages of life — following implantation. By not declaring that human life begins at fertilization unqualifiedly, it can avoid the inevitable clash with the Griswold decision in which the Supreme Court prohibited the states from having laws forbidding the use of contraceptives.*

*In this theologian's opinion, it would be unwise for a state to declare that human life begins at conception, in the sense of fertilization, and to proceed from there to prohibit all abortions (with the few exceptional cases mentioned) from that moment forward. Such a statute would likely be ruled unconstitutional.*

*It might be possible, however, to declare by statute that human life begins with fertilization — medically and morally such a declaration would represent a very sound position — if the statute then proceeded to prohibit abortion from the moment of secured implantation. This would make possible the avoidance of a clash with Griswold. However, it might make it difficult for the state logically to explain why it was not proscribing abortion from fertilization onward, the apparently logical thing to do.*

*It would also be possible for a state to prohibit abortion from implantation onward without declaring when human life begins. However, the state that did that would have more difficulty producing a rationale for its interest in the fate of the unborn at so early a stage in fetal development.*

*Once Roe vs. Wade is overturned, then defining human life as beginning with fertilization will not be problematic as long as perceived contraceptive rights are not taken away. Hence, it will then be advisable to do so for the obvious teaching and witnessing advantages that such a declaration would carry.*

*There may be better ways of forcing the Supreme Court to confront Roe vs. Wade head-on than the one proposed here. If so, I recommend that those approaches be employed rather than this one.*

The interpolation of the contraception attachment to abortion is a "red herring" in this legal disputation. These two items are not to be commingled. The rasping, roaring rage of denying private privilege augments the forcefulness of arguments on the secondary subject, contraception, to gain favor for abortion. In prochoice propositions there has not been an emphatic denial with scientific proof that the product of conception is a human being. The dispute always seems to question the time of life's commencement, beginning of personhood, not the zygote's future as an accepted human being.

Contraception cannot be appended to abortion either by a saprophytic union, or as a *quid pro quo* in equilibrium. Philatelists remember that several years ago the United States Postal Service issued a commemorative stamp with the motif, "America's light is filled by truth and reason." May this ornamental legend not be forgotten!

Prognosticators and oracles ran rampant with their predictions on how the Supreme Court Justices would tally on the Webster decision. Based upon previously rendered opinions, legal prophecy strongly intimated that in the counting two conceded votes against abortion would accumulate from Chief Justice William Rehnquist and Justice Byron White. Both dissented in 1973 when the Supreme Court permitted abortions under the constitutional right to privacy. Two other conservatives, Judges Antonin Scalia and Anthony Kennedy, were forecasted to be against liberal abortion. Three pro-Roe signers remain on the bench. The portention was that they would repeat their proabortion stand. These are Justices Harry Blackmun, William Brennan, and Thurgood Marshall. Mr. Justice John Paul Stevens was not appointed until 1975. Therefore he did not vote on Roe v. Wade in 1973, but he is known to be proabortion and would act accordingly.

With a middle-of-the-road policy Justice Sandra Day O'Connor does not have a firm, staunch position on abortion. Her previous utterances do not betoken a fixed direction. She has denounced the Roe's decision "unworkable scheme" of allowing abortions in the first three months of pregnancy and permitting states restrictions as the fetus gets older. She has stated that those curbs can be upheld only if they do not "impose an undue burden on the abortion decision" (271). This procataleptic phrase implies portentiously that she accepts the belief that there is some fundamental right to abortion. Neither has she explained precisely what constitutes an "undue burden" nor what her interpretation is of "appropriate state restrictions." On a previous occasion Justice O'Connor addressed one of these points. "She ruled that a Pennsylvania law requiring doctors to tell women about abortion's medical risks did not amount to such a burden" (271).

It is quoted that Justice O'Connor has said that the Roe v. Wade decision is "on a collision course with itself" (271). Her conclusion was based upon advanced neonatology that saves younger and younger babies. "One hundred sixty-seven scientists filed a brief stating that 'the outer limit of viability at 24 weeks has not changed significantly,' and many presentimenters believe that medicolegal documents "will deter the Supreme Court from changing the law radically" (271).

Although jurists are to remain unemotional, reserved, and immobile in the pressured stream of judicial propriety, nevertheless men and women are composed of organic tissues that are not static. Justice O'Connor was a mother before she was a judge. Even as she "has pondered her position in the Webster matter, she has been looking forward to the birth of her first grandchild in October of 1989. In pointing out the coincidence, the father-to-be, Scott O'Connor, says that he and his wife 'struggled for three years to get pregnant,' a struggle his mother followed closely. 'It's ironic that the issue is all the people wanting to terminate pregnancy, and we couldn't do it without trying for three years and lots of medical help,' he says. 'We spent three years trying to do something that half of America is trying to prevent" (301).

As an offensive weapon against Roe v. Wade, the Missouri statute without insolence declares unequivocally that life begins at conception. Furthermore it bans abortions in public hospitals, requires physicians who suspect a fetus to be "more than 20 weeks old to determine its age, weight, and lung maturity to decide its viability outside the womb. Critics predict women would be subjected to unnecessary, expensive tests that would discourage abortions late in pregnancy" (271).

Prediction founded upon known judicial attitudes inclines toward the preservation of the *status quo*. The Supreme Court of the United States has a record of not reversing itself on the major disputes declared before it. The High Court does not have an absolute, irrevocable commitment to *stare decisis*. "Let decided matters stand." Rarely does it go against this historical, inherited legal tradition.

*Stare decisis* is a Latin phrase meaning to abide by, or adhere to, decided cases. It is the policy of courts to stand by precedent, and not to disturb a settled point (272). An added definition is that *stare decisis* is a doctrine that, when a court has once laid down a principle of law as applicable to a certain state of facts, it will adhere to that principle, and apply it to all future cases, where the facts are substantially the same (273). Stated in other words, under the doctrine a deliberate or solemn decision of a court made after arguments on the question of law fairly arising in the case, and necessary to its determination, is an authority, or binding precedent in the same court, or in other courts of equal or lower rank in subsequent cases where the very point is again in controversy (274).

## After Webster v. Reproductive Health Services

The turmoil of abortion continues to roll on for better or for worse. The most tempestuous lawsuit on the Supreme Court's judicial calendar for 1989 was the Webster v. Reproductive Health Service case that originated in the State of Missouri. Opposite camps importune the Supreme Court with multiform verbal assaults plus acrimonious criticisms. Bold opponents to the decision will be silenced by the gentle firmness that is bolstered by the somber resolve of necessary acceptance. Always will remain parsimonious morality that breeds brevity of conscience which in turn conceals penurious integrity.

State law-makers now can whittle away at Roe v. Wade until its many areas of weakness cause it to crumble into pulverization. The Roe v. Wade law has not been dethroned but it is toppling. However, the degrading, disfiguring scars of abortion appear to be retained permanently. Division of family, discord among health care personnel, disruption of friendships, social blemishing, and sectionalism in professional circles persist.

Justices of the Supreme Court of the United States in the decision-making process are lawgivers who are by their judicial actions social persuaders who can mold public opinion while they are *perdurante munere* (as long as the position is held).

In the accounting finale the sustaining judges who voted the majority opinion were Chief Justice William Rehnquist with Associate Justices Byron White, Antonin Scalia, Anthony Kennedy, and Sandra Day O'Connor who detoured from neutrality into the anti-abortion camp. The other four were known for their views on this schismatic legal disagreement. The minor vote was gathered from the recognized liberal Justices Harry Blackmun, John Paul Stevens, Thurgood Marshall, and William Brennan. * As predicted by some attorney-soothsayers the departmentalized court opined in accordance with the conservative/traditional faction versus the liberal/avant garde assemblage. The plenum of the Supreme Court expressed itself as anticipatory intelligence had analyzed the eventual outcome.

The United States Supreme Court's majority opinion in the Webster decision may be the first disrupting, weakening, fissured defect in the legal structure that sustains abortions in this nation. Although the nine justices are not physicians, their knowledge of the multiple tentacles of the abortion polyglot is not beyond their biological comprehension. Their judicial enlightenment should enhance the ethical, moral understanding that negates abortion. Being contrary to human nature abortion is a dismaying distortion of our American heritage that loves life with the beauty that flowers from its vibrant soul. In all things attempted or performed, be they good or evil, nothing succeeds in a project like success as one successful venture begets another. In the pursuit of evil's image, as in abortion, the terminal end is self-destruction.

Sagacity has an awareness that derives from pristine, putative, sapient knowledge augmented by gainful, certified, practical, personal experience even though it may be opsimathy. Dissimilarly, reason dissipated by emotionalism does not register psychological covert turmoil correctly. Hence, unpredictable reactions arise from the frustrated realization that the anticipated progressive joy never equals the realized transient delight gained from a masqueraded, camouflaged, intractable source. This non-extinguishable reality prevails like a Shakespearean shadowy ghost. The collage of Roe v. Wade and Webster v. Reproductive Health Services falls into this category of a wicked wraith.

* See glossary at rear of text for additional data, clarification, and explanations.

On the July 4th, 1989 weekend, people commenced to gather on the wide steps of the Supreme Court building. That Friday evening, they expected to be the first to hear the response of the nine justices to the pleadings of the Missouri attorney general to let stand that state's passed legislation. No decision was forthcoming on that day. The crowd dwindled to a few excited fans by Saturday afternoon. With the advent of Sunday night the quantitative delineation between the prochoice group and the antiabortion representatives became obviously noticeable. Many devotees camped in the Supreme Court plaza from Sunday dawn to Monday morning. As the sun rose on Monday hundreds of people (200 or more) were chanting in the courtyard. Shortly after 9 a.m. a clerk of the court read the Webster decision as she stood outside the center door of the judicial edifice. Later she distributed "handouts" verifying officially what she had read.* Singing commenced again as the prolifers raised their voices in appreciation of the court's sentiment.

It may be either the fascination of coincidence or the mystique of contrivance that the Webster decision was promulgated on the eve of July 4th, 1989. This significant Independence Day marks the 213th anniversary of American colonial liberation from European oppression.

Succinctly, the pungent sentence of Chief Justice William Rehnquist said it all: "The judgment of the Eighth Circuit Court of Appeals is reversed" (308). With these words the Missouri state law was upheld. Thus the state retains the power to make decision on abortion which *de facto* returns to state government life directing authority. This momentous, benchmark decision does not void the Roe v. Wade 1973 dictum, but it has eroded it at its pinions. Legalized abortion has been wounded in its circulation. It is slowly bleeding to inevitable lethal exsanguination.

As the sustained Missouri statute prevails it reaffirms staunchly that:

1. Life begins at conception;
2. Abortions are banned in public hospitals;
3. Medicaid funding for abortions is disallowed;

* Actually, the print-outs were distributed by Toni House, spokeswoman for the United States Supreme Court.

64

4. Government professional employees are prohibited from performing abortions; and,

5. Physicians are required to determine age, weight, and lung maturity to decide viability when the age of the fetus is questionable (302).

Chief Justice William Rehnquist's majority opinion supporting the Webster case validates the argument of the State of Missouri. The basis for which dispute was that: "The Missouri General Assembly passed legislation to advance its interest in protecting the health and well-being of unborn children. One provision applying generally to the laws of the state, included findings that human life begins at conception, and that unborn children have protectable interests in life, health, and well-being. Another, applying when an abortion is considered, requires that physicians undertake tests that are necessary to make three specific findings (age, weight, and lung maturity) about the development of the unborn child" (302).

In bold black letters the presented argument was repeated that Missouri's Legislative Findings reiterate "that life begins at conception and that unborn children have protectable interests in life, health, and well-being are a constitutionally legitimate exercise of state authority" (302).

Finally, an added presented argument was: "Missouri is not constitutionally prohibited from requiring physicians to evaluate whether a fetus is viable, or from requiring physicians to make specific medical findings to determine viability, since these activities reasonably implement Missouri's constitutional interests in protecting viable unborn children" (302).

Justice Harry Blackmun's minority opinion stressed the legal injury to women's privacy rights as an invective against their constitutional inheritance. On its surface the majority opinion may appear to be a political, moral, social victory not founded upon the strict letter of the law but in accordance with the spirit of the law that complies with the *tempo* of animation. In spite of this virtue the majority viewpoint has not eradicated the abortion turmoil as this Vietnamese-like controversy continues to survive — perhaps with bated breath.

The long-awaited controversial Webster denouement may have

many unforeseen sociomedicolegal facets. Nineteen eighty-nine may be the monumental year that records the last battle of the legific lancepesades in the advocacy for or against abortion. A prognosticable opinion has been fulfilled, namely, that the American people have awakened to the reality that abortion is intrinsically evil and they are on the way to outlawing it.

Judicial intelligence without orchestration may or may not have expounded the significance of abortion from a bioethical standard via theological titration. An adiaphorous, non-prejudicial observation can find no contradiction or incompatibility with an alliance between bioethics and theophany. A biomoral code, sanctioned by law, can be founded upon theology. Bioscientists aim to preserve natural life. Theologians parallel them by preserving the natural law in its promulgated directives of pristine origin. The nominal conjunction that unites and sustains one with the other is "nature." With this coterminous, tangible, communal purpose as a bioethical goal to be achieved, a lucid meeting of the scientific mind and the theological intellect is a genuine synergism. This perception is plausible even though it is recognized that hierarchal ecclesiasticism expounding edicts in a secular society is a non-sovereign legislator.

Not until the falling sand in the hourglass of Father Time ceases to descend, can it be disclosed whether the Webster decision is the harbinger of favorable or unfavorable events to come. History will declare it as either the fountain of optimism for the antiabortion advocates or the cascading waterfall of pessimism for the prochoice devotees. As of 1989 what has resulted from the belligerency fomented by the Webster v. Reproductive Health Services case is that the Supreme Court of the United States has a new appearance — that of a battered peacemaker worthy of a Nobel laureate.

These are only a few of many questions that remain unanswered throughout our nation. Perhaps the fault lies within the fading memory of lawgivers who have forgotten the fundamental credo of our constitution that blazons forth in rubic letters that "all men are created free and equal with the right to life, liberty, and the pursuit of happiness."

# CHAPTER FOUR

# EXCUSES FOR ABORTION

*"Small ills are the fountains*
*Of most of our groans,*
*Men trip not on mountains,*
*They stumble on stones."*
Chinese Proverb

Prior to the civil legalization of abortion, there was a new baby born during each minute of every hour in these great United States. A new life in America is the indicator of its courtly greatness. The wealth of this nation is not its buildings, the gold stored in Fort Knox, or its commercial productivity, but its human population created for the benefit of all humanity. When the twentieth century sociology of human reproduction is reviewed analytically by a future historian, can we surmise what will be written about us? How will future inhabitants of this earth evaluate the medicolegal mentality that quenched the fire of life? As long as the proabortion laws remain intact, the United States of America cannot be a nation of incomparable, munificent prevenance.

Present day psychological attitudes give momentum to abortion justification, ignoring the true meaning of psychological thought. Psychology is a division of philosophy. As such, it concerns that section of philosophy that deals with life and its beginning. More specifically, it discusses the soul and its attributes.

The distortion of the true meaning of the word psychology is all too evident in the world about us. Sometimes the misuse of this word is so pronounced that it has lost completely its etiological identity. It is to be clever nowadays to adopt the standards of an iconoclastic psychology. This pattern finds its expression in varying forms and in many different social channels of our daily lives.

This avant-garde proclivity camouflages a psychological trend covering anti-democracy, anti-religion, and anti-anything that stands for orderly existence, righteousness, and many time-honored norms and institutions. The current trend of thought seems to be that if one does not wish to conform to that which is good, one should oppose it and try to destroy it (57).

In addition, there is the unconscious haste with which we all seem to be driven. In order not to be left behind in the ambitious race for success, even the philosopher leans toward molding his ideas to those of the state, and the poet, his emotions to conform to society. Both are satisfied if they can produce powerful momentary effects, rather than long-range results. "Starving in an attic" for the sake of one's art or principles has gone completely out of fashion (57).

This emphasis on transitory effects is partly the result of the modern attempt to tear down the cultural life of the past, with its standards of culture and tradition. Modern society seems to have developed what has been aptly called the commentator mentality that judges yesterday by today, and today by tomorrow (58). But, in truth, nothing analogous is more tragic to a civilization than the loss of its traditions. There is far too great a tendency to make respect for tradition synonymous with the word reactionary. Any attempt on the part of parents or teachers to inculcate respect for tradition in the younger generation is invariably met with the cry: "You're old fashioned; you don't understand."

The refusal to accept the precepts evolved from the experiences and wisdom of previous generations and from one's elders produces a restless spirit which makes it difficult to live with oneself. The person who cannot live with himself/herself cannot live with his/her fellow human beings. Those who are not at peace with themselves cannot be at peace either with their neighbors or with God.

When there is no peace of mind, the seeds that destroy truth grow into weeds that overshadow truth. This leads to continuous mental destruction. Every human being should be truthful to himself/herself, even as each human person has a right to the truth from others. The evident purpose of the power of communication is that truth should be conveyed from person to person. A lie, therefore, is wrong of its very nature because it is opposed to the rational nature of mankind. "The right to truth means that every person has a right to know those things which in justice or charity he/she should be told, and that in no case should he/she be deceived by a lie" (4). Lying is speaking deliberately against one's mind. Thus it is not an excusable error, but is an immoral attitude (4). As a reminder, the Augustinian dictum should be remembered. It states: "Wrong is wrong even if everyone is doing it and right is right even if no one is doing it."

An untruthful aspect of the abortion believers is to promote the fiction that the unborn child is an unjust aggressor. "In order to justify killing an unjust aggressor, the loss threatened must be one's life, a grave mutilation, or an object of great value either in itself or to the owner. Even under the guise of therapeutic abortion, it is evident that licitness of the abortion practice cannot be defended save on the ground that the unborn child is an unjust aggressor. The principle that a completely innocent person — in the present connection, one who is engaged in no unjust attack — may be wantonly killed in order to save the life of another is demonstrably false" (4).

The unborn child is doing nothing directly to attack the life of the mother. It is merely growing and developing according to the natural order. It possesses a right to life. If it loses its life, as perhaps it may, it must be through natural causes and not through a direct attack upon it (4, 59, 60). The unborn child finds itself where it is, not because of any act of its own, but because of the free act of one or both of its parents (4, 61). If the unborn child is a threat to the life of the mother, this is due usually not to the fetal presence but rather to the mother who, because of anatomical, physiological, or pathological conditions, is having difficulty in bringing the pregnancy to fruition. Even if the unborn child was the sole source of peril, it would nevertheless not be essentially an unjust aggressor (4, 62). Life is a serious business in humanity, with responsibility for it often a burdensome reality.

Average rational people have the facility of arriving at hard and fast distinctions among things requiring special knowledge and at least a smattering of technical information. However, when it comes "to a question of things that are most intimate to ourselves, things that are absolute bedrock in the daily experiences of our lives, then we begin to flounder, stand aghast, and make the most foolish mistakes. Youth glamorizes love, marries for the tinsel, and divorces readily when its sparkle turns to ashes" (63).

In matters of morality and religion, only a few people in compari-

son to the vast population grasp their official meaning or try to accept
their tenets. For the vast majority of the populace, moral conduct
evaporates under the rising temperature of indiscriminate broad-
mindedness. Thus, virtue fades and sin pervades. In having an
abortion, the future mother sins. In performing an abortion, the
doctor sins. Sin is the enemy of virtue, together with its allies malice
and vice.

By taking an excerpt out of biblical history, this explanation may
be made simple. "No one calls King David a malicious man. Much
less was he vicious. But he did sin. Sorrowing, he makes personal
confession to God: 'To thee have I sinned.' If he was not vicious, he
must have been virtuous. If he was not malicious, he must have been
good. And yet he did sin. How is this explained?" (64).

"Let us analyze virtue. Virtue is something; virtue does something; virtue implies something. This is to say that virtue is
essentially a quality making its subject good by reason of what it
does, i.e., good works. For the enemies of virtue, reason is too true
to play favorites, even when it comes to name calling. Vice, malice,
sin are the bad names for the foes of virtue. They are not, however,
heaped up indiscriminately, like the abuse of anger. Neatly, they fit
into an explanatory unity. If you are speaking of virtue essentially,
its enemy is vice. If you are speaking of virtue for what it does, its
enemy is sin. If you are speaking of virtue by implication, its enemy
is malice" (64).

"Vice, malice, and sin are not just a variety in names for the same
horror. In ordinary conversation, often one is used for the others.
This is of slight importance compared to a most grievous and
widespread opinion that vice is not contrary to nature. St. Augustine
flatly contradicts this terrible teaching. He says: 'Every vice, simply
because it is a vice, is contrary to nature.' St. Thomas Aquinas cooly
gives the solid reason for this belief. The vice of anything consists in
a situation of the thing out of harmony with its nature" (64).

## Individual Choice

Long before abortion became the subject that flares up like the
lights of Broadway, legal limitations were placed on individual
choice, based on the concern for others (65, 66, 67, 68, 69). These
judicial powers have not been asserted in behalf of the unborn.

Contrarily, the advocates of abortion have stressed the woman's right of choice, without being concerned for that choice of the other, the unborn child.

This is the limelight logo of Planned Parenthood. Their advertisements state: "But there are times when news of a pregnancy is met with despair. When the birth of a child would present insurmountable problems. When a woman knows her decision must be to have an abortion. Planned Parenthood, the U.S. Supreme Court, and the majority of Americans believe that this decision is best left to the woman, not to legislators or judges. We at Planned Parenthood have spent the better part of this century supporting and fighting for everyone's freedom to make their own decisions about having children" (70).

The rhetorical utterances of any group, individually or collectively, who claim abortion is a personal matter can be asked this question: "If their premise is correct, does not pushing the button to start a nuclear war also become a personal matter?" (71). "The deaths of millions of unborn lives is a public matter, and should be addressed as such ... Society has a duty to protect its members whom it encases and envelops. We who have reached embryonic fruition do not have the right to deprive another life from being born. All of us have much more power than an unborn child, but power should never be confused with rights. Should people be denied basic rights because they are powerless? Those who abuse power and take part in destroying the unborn can never expect to solve problems of the nation and the world which affect life in its latter stages. Indeed, the burdens of existing in the world today are power struggles among nations, between classes, and of adults who (even) exert their power over unborn children" (71).

Americans on both sides of the abortion controversy have a right to express their opinions, even as their adversaries have a right to disagree with them. However, one basic factor remains intransigent. It is that majority opinion does not give moral rectitude to abortion. In addition, a legal right given to an individual does not render it a moral right. In the final analysis it is known that the human conscience is educable and favors the individual who is to make the decision based on his/her own ethical matrix.

## Absence of Fetal Life

Some critics of the right-to-life bring their objections to the surface, either in writing or by the spoken word, only to negate them by their own actions. A psychiatrist writing in the New York State Journal of Medicine instigated a voluminous response from her medical colleagues when she wrote an article entitled: "Abortion: Unalienable Right." She gave twelve arguments favoring abortion. Number seven is quoted: "Let us look at the 'but-it's-taking-a-life' view. Here I assert that a non-sentient, non-independently viable, non-cognitive cell mass is not a human life; it is a potential life and so are all the ova and spermatozoa which have never had occasion to meet. When they do meet, something is furthered, healthy or diseased, and is indeed not even a definitive potential human being until the genetic code is unalterable — an occurrence at about the eighth week of embryonic life, with the closing of the neural tube" (72).

The above quotation is abounding in statements that are unacceptable either on a scientific or philosophical basis and should have been clarified by the author. Mere statements by a writer do not make them dogma, authoritative or incontrovertible. For example, the following is the quintessence of nonsyllogistic reasoning: "it is a potential life and so are all the ova and spermatozoa which have never had the occasion to meet. When they do meet, something is furthered, not started" (72).

May it be written that an ovum alone will always be an ovum, a spermatozoon alone will always be a spermatozoon. In each there is nothing resembling human life and alone each is ineffective without the other and soon dies. One cannot start life without the other and each is absorbed in solitude. It is a philosophic principle that *"Nemo dat quod non habet"* (nothing or no one can give what it does not have). However, once the ovum is impregnated by the spermatozoon a new entity commences, as discussed elsewhere in this text.

The psychiatrist author questioned calls it "non-sentient, non-independent, non-cognitive, and so forth" (72). Call it by any name, it is life, however undifferentiated it may be. Modern fetology (including the film "The Silent Scream") demonstrates a contrary conclusion as to nonsentience. The implanted conceptus has a qualitative existence. It is an entity which when allowed to pursue its natural destiny is *de facto* human life. If it was not human life from the beginning, it would not be human life nine months later. There cannot be an alteration of one species into another. A dog starts out as a dog and does not become a cat. So it is in all living things (73).

Modern scientific technology as applied to the biological studies has verified many postulates of Spallanzani expressed more than two hundred years ago. Physiologists are familiar with Spallanzani's Law which states that "the younger the individual the greater is the regenerative power of its cell." When applied to the fertilized ovum, it is this "law" that answers the immediate, progressive changes that occur which alter the histologic appearance and the physiological activity of the newly formed cells after fertilization.

Lazaro Spallanzani (1729-1799) was an Italian naturalist and physiologist who contributed greatly to the foundation of modern bacteriology. He expressed his views on spontaneous generation in determining new directions in physiology. Negating the concept of spontaneous generation, he upheld the doctrine in science that *"omne vivum ex ovo,"* i.e., everything living (animal life) comes from an egg. He experimented with animal ova in that it needed sperm to become fertilized. He did the first artificial insemination in dogs. Spallanzani disproved cross-fertilization in animals in that a dog's sperm could not impregnate a cat's ovum (74).

Fundamental embryological conceptions on the primordium or anlage further negate the propositum that the fertilized ovum is a mass of indifferent, nondescript protoplasm. "The word primordium (or its German equivalent, anlage) is a term applied to the first discernible cell or aggregation of cells which is destined to form any distinct part or organ of the embryo. In a broad sense, the fertilized ovum is the forerunner of the entire adult organism. Furthermore, in the early cleavage stages of certain embryos it is possible to recognize single cells or cell groups from which definite structures will indubitably arise. The term primordium, however, is more commonly applied to the prospective parts that differentiate from the various germ layers. Thus, the epithelial thickening over the optic vesicle is the primordium of the lens, as is the arm bud the anlage of the arm" (75).

Mechanical engineering applied gynecologically substantiates the human essence of a fertilized ovum. "The birth of the first baby born through the process of embryo transfer — which involves transferring a fertilized egg from a fertile woman to an infertile woman — was announced February 3, 1984, by physicians who developed the technique. Although the birth was heralded as a scientific breakthrough, it was met with legal concern by laws and biomedical ethicists who question how the procedure will be used" (76).

## Love as an Excuse

The fulfillment of a passionate embrace as an expression of love may culminate in pregnancy. Each of the participants exclaim to the point of echolalia that they have the right to love each other and express this love physically. However, they will not accept that the product of this anatomical love is their responsibility. Even within the bonds of matrimony, the law has intervened as it denied a husband his cause of legal action to prevent his wife from having an abortion (77).

Aldous Huxley once said, "Of all the worn, smudged, dog-eared words in our vocabulary, 'love' is surely the grubbiest, smelliest, slimiest. Brawled from a million pulpits, lasciviously crowed through hundreds of millions of loudspeakers, it has become an outrage to good taste and decent feelings, an obscenity which one hesitates to pronounce. And yet it has to be pronounced, for, after all, love is the last word!" (78).

Our awful passions can be adult entrapments. All human persons have in common their sense appetites. Physical changes do take place in the body when the senses of sight, touch, taste, etc., are contacted. "The body does move towards concrete, material things to possess them . . . We really long to possess physically the object which we know and love. If we did not have these desires for the possession of things, we would be doomed to a constant round of thumb-twiddling and doodling. Life would be very dull" (79). In brief, it would be an arsy-versy existence.

Physiological acceptance of the desire for physical possession does verify that all of us are creatures of passion. It does not mean that we should be victims of passion. As defined, "passion is nothing more than the physical change within the body which ensues when some sensible good is known and loved, or some sensible evil is known and found repugnant" (79). Men and women, because they possess a human and not entirely an animal nature, have control of their physical acts because of intelligence and free will. "Therefore, men and women are expected to exercise control over their movements of passion and ensure their subordination to reason. Passion is not acceptable as that which belongs only to the maniac, or to the person whose temper is always out of control. Nor, on the other hand, are the passions the whole story of human activity — as some would have us believe — for human beings have an immortal soul which is the source, the motor power for their distinctive acts as a man or a woman. The passions are the body's contributions to a man's or a woman's human activity" (79).

Love as a passion propels a person toward the person desired, while hate is the passion that moves one to strike out against anything that would harm the object of love. Nature, through passion as an intense or overpowering feeling, may be a trap. Nevertheless, passionate physical pleasure cannot be an excuse for an unwanted pregnancy labeled as a mistake. "Only some of us can learn from other peoples' mistakes. The rest of us have to be the other people" (80).

Anatomically, the head is above the heart and the heart is above the perineum. These structures should be used physiologically, appropriately with propriety in accordance to their scientific order of primacy. Priority of control should be in the head where nature ordained it to be. All the body organs were created for their natural designated purposes. Thus the brain is (and should be) the monitoring mechanism for all functions of the human organism. Although the cranial vagus nerves control the heartbeat, it is not the decelerator of hidden emotions. Therefore, an awareness must be given to the intellect as the auxiliary to free-will that can balance parasympathetic emotionalism. By this regulatory means spontaneous cardiac impetus will not be dissociated from reason that disallows unbridled genital arousal that results in impetuous self-gratification. Passionate desires can be tamponed in order to prevent them from excessive intrusion into the thought provoking functions of the mind.

People of each gender are beautiful to one another. God so ordained it in accordance with the Christian teaching "to love one another as I have loved you." However, some persons do not distinguish between physical and spiritual love. Too frequently persons who are loving conjure up in their minds' eye an image that is not consonant with truth. An image is not the reality. Often the fantasized image is presumed as love. Prejudicial passion is not to be in love. It is to be in lust that causes the person to fly high on wicked wings winded by wanton wishes.

Unstifled sympathy, as an *imprimatur*, is sought from friends, relatives, and others by the suppliant who seeks an abortion. Stived sorrow for having an abortion, or seeking one, is minimized by purposefully determined sought-after sympathy to the ironic state of not disengaging one from the other. Seeking sympathy for a cause or for personal comfort can have an adverse effect. "Sympathy is supposed to be a sharing — a sharing of deep feelings. It seldom is. People who really shared such feelings would be candidates for sympathy themselves" (275).

Young people who think they are in love sometimes realize they are in error. Willingly they admit making a mistake. Although empathy may be given, no moral support can accompany it if a deliberate, direct abortion is performed for a pregnancy from a mistake. Succinctly, euphemistic words with saccharine tristful attitudes do not conceal diabolic deeds. A lacrimal excuse is not a stochastic model for obscuring the disguised satanism of abortion. With each abortion that is performed another act of infamy is added to the continuous lengthening list. As long as the proabortion laws remain in any form, American cannot be a nation of munificent prevenance.

Love is not the entrance to gratifying selfishness which is a form of greed manifested in the pursuit of wanting what is wanted when "we want it". Iridescent love is giving of self. It is in giving that one receives. It is in the denial of illicit pleasure that personal character is fortified and enhanced. Contrarily it is unrestrained carnal love that injures both participants in addition to being a moral disservice to each other. Service to another is the rental fee humankind should pay for our tenancy on this earth. To have a plenary life it must contain an ardent desire to help, not injure, our fellow human beings. Without this altruism, no one can share in the beatitudes of a satisfying, satisfactory, salubrious life.

True love does not feign affection. It is all encompassing without cynical selfishness. In the face of all aridity and disenchantment, it is perennial as the grass. Under all circumstances, the anticipated enduring pleasure does not equal the transient realized delight. To love and be loved in return is part of the art of life's continuance. "The art of living is like all arts: It must be learned and practiced with incessant care." So said the German poet Johann W. Von Goethe (1749-1832).

## Psychological Excuses

A physician of the feminine gender wrote in a medical journal the following: "I speak as a psychiatrist who has witnessed in my practice of almost thirty years centered on women and their psychology, the harm that refusal of abortion has done to women and society . . . But I also speak as a woman proclaiming my indignation at the uncaring, casual, insensitive way that men have legislated women's reproductive lives, which has virtually been the sole content of their lives" (72).

"But it is the murder of the woman I am talking about, psychologic and social murder, not murder of the fetus, or rather the embryo which is what usually gets aborted. This leads me to ask: Why has the fetus got friends, while the woman has not? Why does her suffering make so few claims on the conscience of men?" (72).

Objections are made to these quoted statements. Men are blamed for "legislating women's reproductive lives". The problem of abortion is not one of male versus female. To accentuate male chauvinism in this discussion is to pronounce a smidgen. No real man worthy of his gender seeks the enfetterment of women.

When the author refers to her thirty years' practice centered on women and their psychology, she has seen harm to society from the refusal of abortion (72). What does her experience teach concerning the harm to the individual who has had repeated abortions? The psychosomatic aspects of the postabortion female have startling facets to be unravelled (73).

The psychiatrist "speaks of the psychologic murder of the woman and not murder of the fetus" (82). Any member of the house staff of a large municipal hospital in the years before the legalization of abortion had many experiences in the management of women who had abortions. These patients were admitted to the hospital because of uterine bleeding necessitating a dilatation and curettage for retained secundines. Women of all classes of society who wanted an abortion prior to the legalization thereof were not deprived of one, even if it was not under sterile technique. Many abortions were self-induced or performed by other women who were experts with slippery elm, hairpins, coathangers, ergot, and other inventive abortifacient modalities. There were available to women both professional and nonprofessional services if they were sought. Thus, the psychological reason for an abortion is nontenable and is tinged with hyperbole.

A distinguished late officer of the American Medical Association expressed his opinion on this particular argument. In an editorial "Abortion Reform", he wrote as follows: "Medical indications have become, for the most part, psychiatric. These psychiatric indications have no scientific basis, no unequivocal criteria, and no prognostica-tive reliability. The real indications are social or humanitarian and pseudopsychiatric labels are often used to mask this fact" (81). Psychical distress cannot be overcome by the subjugation of ethical virtues.

Such women who offer an irreflective psychological excuse for having an abortion do not always eliminate the mental thorn that pierces them. Following an abortion for so-called psychological stress, most aborted women rarely are relieved of their symptoms. Contrarily the primary sadness may be intensified and/or a newer more tragic one may be acquired. Many women succumb to a third guilt complex that can haunt them the remainder of their lives.

## Rape as an Excuse

Rape is defined as a sexual assault without consent which includes labial penetration by the penile organ (82). Ejaculation is not essential. It has been known — at least since the days of Queen Victoria — as the "fate worse than death" (83). "In many violent, largely urban societies, this fate apparently is befalling more and more women. FBI figures show that 51,000 rapes are reported annually. It is estimated that only one rape out of ten is recorded (82, 83).

"More than 50 percent of rapes involve the use of a weapon, generally a knife, and more than 50 percent of rape victims have, on examination, visible signs of physical violence. In more than 10 percent of these victims, the injury is severe enough to require medical attention" (82). The number of pregnancies resulting from one act of rape is miniscule. With incest situations, pregnancy can be more probable because of the repetition of the ignominy.

Rape is a legal term. Whether or not a crime has been committed is not determined by medical examination, but must be decided in a court of law. "The physician's duty is to examine the victim for corroborating evidence. Legal requirements in this regard vary from state to state and even from one judicial district to another" (83). "Amendments to criminal rape statutes by many states underline the need for emergency department personnel — often the first people contacted by a rape victim — to be acquainted with the legal, medical, and psychological aspects of properly administered appropriate therapy" (84).

Violation of chastity is not a crime of sudden uncontrollable concupiscence. Rape is a crime of aggression utilizing the reproductive organ as a weapon. It is a premeditated plan seeking a vulnerable woman for its completion. This act of assault classifies the protagonist as a nonspecific type. Intelligence, education, physical attractiveness, social standing, financial worth are no barriers to a rapacious propulsion. Most participants in this criminal disgrace are males 15 to 24 years of age. It is a crime of youthful perpetrators. Contrarily, the victim may be of any age ranging from 2 to 97 years.

Rape is physically damaging to the feminine body, associated with a psychological upheaval. This act of aggression is performed by a man who is driven by a violent, uncontrollable force that allows sexual behavior in an abnormal situation. A woman's virtue, comeliness, attractiveness or nudity are not the motivating stimuli for this aggressive act. A woman may be physically unpleasant, even disliked, by a rapist. Men can achieve erections with an orgasm even when their partner is someone who is physically or socially repulsive. This revulsion is a psychological indicator that sexual activity can be a manifestation of physical power, emotional discord, anger, or revenge (85).

A Department of Justice survey verified that more than 67,000 forcible rapes were reported in the 50 states during 1974 (86). The progressive increase in this crime rate has prompted some states to pass laws for the examination of a rape victim. An example is Ohio. "Section 2907.29 of the Ohio Revised Code (ORC) requires that every hospital which offers 'organized emergency services be available 24 hours a day for examination of persons reported to be 'victims of sexual offenses'." A standardized approach aids every victim in obtaining an equal medicolegal evaluation (87). It is the view of many that emergency physicians are competent to evaluate and treat victims of sexual assault. The basis for this belief is that "emergency physicians are trained in assessing all aspects of the patient's condition, including concomitant traumatic injuries. Emergency physicians are accustomed to managing anxious, nervous, distraught, and frightened patients. They are experienced in situations in which the legal aspects of care may be more important than the strictly medical aspects" (88).

Since the medicolegal examination of female victims of sexual assault or suspected sexual assault demands a gynecological examination in addition to physical examination of other anatomic areas, past preference has been for the examination to be performed by a specialist in obstetrics or gynecology. It is predicted that in the future almost all initial rape indicated physical examinations will be performed by emergency department physicians (88). This prognostication is based upon the fact of their diversal availability.

The majority of rape victims are taken to the emergency department of the nearest hospital. The victim is requested not to wash. If the person is a woman, she is advised not to douche. No matter the gender, the individual is asked to wear or bring to the hospital the clothing worn at the time (without washing them). In the emergency area (or private office of a physician), the police department having jurisdiction is contacted  Usually a rape squad team is dispatched immediately to the place where the victim is to be examined. The patient is escorted to a private, secluded examining room by a nurse (with or without a member of the rape team). Immediately, the nurse obtains an account of the past events, including a gynecological history, as she assembles all the necessary materials for the physical examination (87). A victim of rape falls into the category of a high triage priority.

The medical history must be as accurate as possible. Initially taken by the assigned nurse, it should be reviewed, verified, and augmented by the examining physician. The histories obtained by both the nurse and the physician must be signed individually. After the documented account of the incident is completed, a written authorization for a complete physical examination (consent) and authorization for the release of information is obtained. In the event that a minor child is involved, the parent or guardian is to sign for this permission. The obtained consent should allow the performance of a total physical examination, including a pelvic (internal) evaluation. The consent should permit the taking of necessary photographs by the hospital photographer, examining physician, or police photographer. In addition, a specified consent is to be obtained for reporting to the police that an alleged assault/rape has been committed. Other pertinent permission should be secured for maintaining the medical records of the incident in the hospital or physician's file. Consent must be obtained to collect and analyze necessary specimens for laboratory studies. Treatment cannot be administered without a signed, detailed consent (87).

The historical data should include the date and time of the incident, place of occurrence, any physical abuse other than the sexual assault. A description of the actual or attempted sexual contact is necessary, including genital, oral, or anal attempts. The time of the last bath, shower, douche, urination and defecation should be included in the history. An indepth gynecological history should record previous pregnancies, abortions, number of living children. Additional gynecologic queries to be documented are:

1. Date and physiologic notation of menstrual cycle must include any abnormality plus last menstrual period. If pregnant, how long? Any vaginal bleeding, secretions or discharge at any time should be listed.

2. The hour and day of the most recent genital experience prior to the alleged rape must be documented. Included as pertinent data should be the date of any form of sexual experience since the alleged rape.

3. Additional gynecologic information to be sought concerns the use of contraceptives, especially what kind (use of the pill). Prior pelvic surgery is important as to possibility of conception. Especially hysterectomy, tubal ligation, pelvic inflammatory disease, or venereal disease should be noted.

Before concluding the medical history taking, an inquiry should be made as to the use of drugs or the imbibing of any alcoholic beverage before or after the alleged incident. The physical examination can then be performed after the value or need for any photograph has been determined. If photographs are necessary, the use of color photographs to substantiate positive signs or significant negative evidence should be obtained.

Definitive physical examination includes the general appearance of the patient. It should also employ a Wood's Lamp or a filtered untraviolet light to detect seminal stains on the skin, clothing or elsewhere. All areas of the body must be examined for excoriations, hematoma, contusions, abrasions, fingernails or loose (pulled out) hair. Observation of blood stains, seminal fluid stains and torn clothing (including under garments) must be tabulated. Unusual skin markings from a belt, rope, shoestring or other items are to be sought. Signs of drug or alcohol abuse are discerned via needle marks, breath odor, or possession of drugs on the patient. The emotional state of the alleged victim should be written on the hospital emergency sheet.

The genital and rectal examinations are especially significant parts of the physical evaluation. A conviction for rape is fortified most often from the adequacy of the discerned signs or specimens obtained from the vagina and/or the rectum. Therefore, it is imperative to perform a total anatomic review of the perineal region. Finding of any injury is looked for in the genital and rectal tissues, including the skin surrounding them. Blood or secretions (moist or dried) may be found on the vulva, perineum, rectum, or thighs. Close scrutiny of the hymenal ring is made in order to determine whether it is present, intact, free of injury, has old scars, recently ruptured, or absent. Vaginal examination via the finger and speculum should be performed without lubrication. Water may be used. Examination of this area should include documentation of any vaginal or urethral discharge as to quantity and color. Specific notation should be made of the appearance of the vaginal mucosa, as well as any sign of trauma (hematoma, bleeding, lacerations). Manual and visual examination (when possible) results of the cervix, uterus and adnexa are essential to the written record.

Anal examination is to include inspection of the visible structures, the perianal sites with subsequent palpation of the region. Digital examination may unfold the unexpected. On one occasion, a retrieved condom brought about a fast conviction for rape. The examining finger should be inspected for blood or seminal fluid. A water moistened proctoscope inserted into the anus may be rewarding with an unsuspected finding. A *sine qua non* of this procedure is to collect suitable specimens with identifying labels. Even if the assault occurred a week previously, a crime laboratory can find substantial material for study. A physician may be reluctant to examine a person who was raped days prior to the examination. However, unless a total physical examination is performed, conclusive evidence may remain undisclosed. Factually, the older the assault, the more important is the physician's role as the expert witness giving testimony in a court of law. "To facilitate the collection and preservation of specimens taken for evidence, many scientific crime laboratories have developed standardized reliable 'Sexual Assault Evidence Kits' that are used in many states" (89). The rape evidence kit is available from most police jurisdictions without hesitancy or difficulty.

"The crime of rape requires medical evaluation and therapy concomitant with the collection of legal evidence for potential prosecution. A practical, inexpensive evidence kit has been designed that meets the needs of the local health department, police department, hospital emergency center, and district attorney personnel. Costs for the assembly kit and specimen analysis are assumed by the police department. Chain of custody is assured through tamper-proof bags, appropriate reporting forms and police involvement in specimen pick-up. Victims participate in the chain of custody by sharing in collection and authorization. The requirement for physician appearance in court is thus lessened. Standardization of examination and reporting prompts all community hospitals to share in examinations, thus preventing the overloading of a single, busy facility. Six months' experience has borne out the anticipated simplification of collection, standardization of reporting, and reduction of physician involvement in legal procedures" (90).

The following laboratory specimens are collected:

1. Loose pubic hair (obtained by gentle combing);
2. Samples of known pubic hair (about five should be pulled, not cut);
3. Foreign material on the body;
4. Samples of known head hair (pull five hairs from the root from different areas of the head);
5. Fingernail scrapings;
6. Sample of blood from victim for blood typing, pregnancy test, and venereal disease determination (VDRL);
7. Sample of vaginal secretions on a glass slide; and,
8. Sample of anal and/or oral secretions when appropriate.

By collecting these specimens, the police laboratory can determine:

1. The presence of spermatozoa;
2. The presence of seminal fluid through high concentrations of prostatic acid phosphatase;
3. Blood type of victim;
4. Blood type of the defendant through vaginal swab examination;
5. Hair color and race of victim; and,
6. Hair color and race of defendant.

The nurse and victim can assist the physician in the collection of fingernail scrapings, blood and hair samples. The treatment section on the form is completed by the physician who assumes responsibility for the examination (90).

Following the medical inquiry, the physical examination, and obtaining the specimens, treatment is rendered. In addition to the need for administering some type of sedation medication, therapy includes tetanus prophylaxis and venereal disease prevention.

Medical means may be taken to foil a possible pregnancy because the presumption exists that pregnancy has not occurred.

A venereal disease prophylactic regimen usually consists of the administration of probenicid 1.0 gm by mouth, together with 4.8 million units of procaine or Pen-G or Bensathine Penicillin G intramuscularly. Some pharmaceutical firms have manufactured an injectible solution containing penicillin with probenicid. Orally administered probenicid 1.0 gm with oral Ampicillin 3.5 gm also may be given. If penicillin sensitivity is known, then spectinomycin (trobicin) 4.0 gm is administered intramuscularly. Tetracycline 1.5 gm as an initial oral dose followed by 500 mg by mouth four times a day for four days (total dose 9.5 gm) has been prescribed for persons who cannot tolerate penicillin (87).

In order to block conception, certain preparations have been employed. The physician should try to encourage the patient with a 'wait and see' attitude regarding pregnancy. The Beta Subunit Test of HCG is an early (6 day) test for pregnancy. Victims of rape are given protection against possible pregnancy by the administration of conjugated equine estrogen. Premarin has been prescribed in doses of 2.5 mg orally four times a day for five days. Parenteral equivalent would be an intravenous bolus of 40 to 50 mg as a single dose (83). Diethylstilbesterol is to be avoided because of the potentiality of endometrial cancer. A new study suggests that a better protection against pregnancy is possible by administering ethinyl estradiol in lieu of large doses of conjugated estrogens. After 72 hours of natural copulation the results of this research demonstrated that ethinyl estradiol is more than twice as effective as conjugated estrogens as a post intercourse preventive against conception (91).

All the medical records written must be signed by the nurse in attendance, the examining physician, and whenever possible a female witness. The specimens taken must be placed in sealed containers. A label on the container should have typed on it the date, time taken and the signature of the physician or nurse (preferably both) who obtained the specimens.

The patient should not be discharged summarily from the emergency area or physician's office. It is customary to advise an immediate future consultation with the patient's own physician for a routine physical examination. Sometimes the patient prefers not to go to a physician who knows her. Under this umbrage of fear she should be referred to a gynecologist whose name is on the emergency department call list, or known by the examining physician.

All the reasons for rape are not understood. Some ideas advanced on this subject are beyond human comprehension. For example, there is a cult that believes having sexual relations with a virgin will cure venereal disease. This includes male or female virgins. With this intention, many infants and children are sought after with the end result that they are ravaged. Rape is a damaging, life altering, sad experience. It engenders fear, anxiety, guilt, shame, unworthiness, immorality, and being unclean. The victim suffers physically with pain, tension headache, fatigue, genital or low abdominal pain, nausea, even vomiting. Added to this symptomatology is the possibility of gynecological infections. Psychologically the victim may cry, laugh without cause, have a large appetite, irrationality, insomnia, nightmare, and develop a phobia to the height of paranoia (92).

Although the literature written on the sexual assault victim is quite extensive, little attention has been given to the victim's compounded emotional instability. The impact of the emotional upheavel begins with the physical act, but the continuity of the emotionalism intensifies thereafter. The mental disquietude is magnified by the intricate medicolegal procedural system that may or may not bring the rapist to court with a just punishment imposed (93). The goal of medicolegal learning, wisdom, empathy, and expertise is to achieve a lessening of this plague that nexes human frailty (94). Even though rape is an aggressive horrendous act, abortion following rape does not mitigate or militate against another evil under the guise of doing good.

When rape is claimed as an excuse for an abortion, proof that the rape has occurred must be provided. The complex medical procedure to verify that rape has occurred is rarely secured solely to document the legal rape plea. It has as a primary aim the mental/physical treatment of the victim. The mere word that a woman has been raped is a crippled excuse for an abortion in the light of modern preventive medical measures that can be instituted immediately after an alleged rape.

## Wrong Gender As Excuse

Unwanted girl fetuses are the latest victims of the monstrous abortion ogre. This moral travesty continues even when it can be documented that they are physically normal. To the fury and agony of abortion is interlaced the calescent craze of destroying babies because they are of the feminine gender. Of all the flimsy excuses given for destroying life, this is the most inane. Even an ardent abortionist can desist from placing a concinnate cachet of approval on this sparse, asinine indication for an abortion. By aborting girl babies, women are perpetuating male chauvinism, misogyny, gynecophobia, and a continual quantitative disparity in the gender gap.* This disparate hiatus may not be correctable in years to come. Where are the leaders of the Equal Rights Amendment? Why are these champions silent? Baryphony reigns in regard to this human degradation — why?

A report from Beijing in a similar critique on preference for male babies indicates that their birth score is 125 boys for every 100 girls. This disparity differs from the equality of gender births in other countries of the world. The China results are due to "the interplay of modern medical technology, ancient Chinese values, and government policies. Fancy new ultrasound equipment in city clinics demonstrates the sex of fetuses...Chinese society puts an extraordinary premium on boys...Couples now limited to one child by population control decrees are choosing to abort great number of female fetuses. Shanghai's skewed birth ratio is just one of many signs that the status of women in China, never high, is again being seriously eroded by tradition and uncodified but real official attitudes" (276).

Many children are orphaned before they are born. This is not of modern vintage but has antecedent adherents to this social human iniquity. "The Unwanted Children of Times Past" is the designation of a book written by a Yale historian. It was a highlight review in the *U.S. News & World Report* (277). As a sociotheological treatise, the subject presented reaffirms that the abandonment of children was

* Men who either agree or encourage this anti-feminine horror are equally at fault.

not alien to 18th century Europe. "Girls, over all, were abandoned slightly more than boys. Still there was the desire to have the oldest child be a boy. So if the first child or even the first several turned out to be girls, they might be abandoned until the couple had a boy. Once that happened, a family was equally likely to abandon boys and girls" (278).

Abandoning infants rather than their destruction in the 18th century is attributed to Christianity which evangelized against the immoral, mortal sinful evil of killing another human being. In 20th century America even abandonment would be preferable to abortion. Wisdom persuades that the moral rational solution is adoption over either abortion or abandonment.

On the subject of infanticide and abortion in China, an interchange of letters took place in the Alpha Omega Alpha Honor Medical Society Magazine (279). It referred to a statement re China in "The Disease of Overpopulation." "Official policy is not responsible for female infanticide. It occurs in rural areas where the farmers desire only male offspring who can help work in the communes (collective farms) but do not wish to lose the financial advantages of maintaining small families. The authorities visit appropriately severe punishment on the perpetrators when discovered" (279).

In response to the above letter, a reply by the original author of "The Disease of Overpopulation" wrote: "China spokesmen decry infanticide and deny forced abortion. However, the official family planning policy is 'one child per couple.' (This) policy has inevitably resulted in forced abortion (of girl babies), female infanticide, and involuntary sterilization. The policy is implemented by a blend of 'birth quotas', front-line cadres to monitor and enforce compliance, and 'grandmothers' to keep track of local menstrual cycles. The consequences are tragic" (280).

All is not quiet on the defensive front for aborting girl babies. An intact fasces-like group is demanding a probe of the sex-selection indication for abortions. "A pro-family lobby in Washington, D.C., concerned that there are growing instances of abortion to choose the sex of a baby, called...for a federal investigation of the practice as a possible violation of the civil rights laws. The evidence suggests that it is "overwhelmingly female fetuses (five to four) who are selected as victims. (This is) a final, fatal form of discrimination against women...In some cases amniocentesis is used to determine the sex of the fetus and on that basis a female fetus will be aborted" (281). When a pregnant woman seeks a chorionic villi* sampling (CVS) and amniocentesis for the specific purpose to ascertain the sex of her unborn child, if it is to be a girl, an abortion inevitably will be the terminal event. The Roe v. Wade decision has now brought the law down to the ridiculous level of *reductio ad absurdum*.

In the beginning of the 1970s when physicians and their patients expressed a favorable opinion in regard to abortion, no one conceived it proper to entertain the thought of utilizing this procedure because the intended parent/parents were disappointed that the future offspring was to be a girl. After Roe v. Wade medical geneticists were surveyed to ascertain the sanctioning of prenatal diagnosis to determine fetal gender with the primary intention of abortion if the unborn had the "effrontery to be the wrong sex" (291). At the time of the first survey only one percent responded in the affirmative. In the first week of January 1989, "*The New York Times* reported a new poll showing that twenty percent of such geneticists approve of the practice" (291).

"This is surely the most frivolous use of abortion yet invented...Apparently many doctors are tailoring their own ethical standards to fit the seeping permission granted under the Roe v. Wade decision...When these operations are not plainly sexist (aimed at reducing the number of females born), they are manifestations of the custom-made-child syndrome...(The) search for the perfect baby now extends to getting rid of a fetus for being the wrong sex. If technology allowed it, presumably some would abort for insufficiently high intelligence or the wrong ultimate height. If we do this, what kind of society do we become? Sex selection is the natural successor to female infanticide as a method of increasing the ratio of males to females. A few feminists are gingerly using the term

* Chorionic villi: The chorion is the outermost envelope of the growing zygote or fertilized ovum which serves as a protective and nutritive covering. The chorionic frondosum is the external surface of the chorion which develops vascular processes (chorionic villi) and later forms the embryonic portion of the placenta.

femicide in a movement that tends to regard abortion as the simple shedding of an unnecessary body part, such as the appendix or a hangnail" (291).

## Medical Research As Excuse

Abortion as a mechanical operative technique is deficiently minus any classical surgical finesse. Even professional abortionists sense the brutality in its performance as medical means of induction are gaining preference over surgical procedures. The advent of the Paris pill will become extremely popular in this regard because of its "hands-off", pseudo-innocent, indirect participation by the physician.

Performing abortions can be looked upon as crude, cabalistic, cannibalism. It is bereft of surgical refinement or manual dexterity worthy of a scientific accolade. The procedure has become so commonplace that anything associated with abortion has not been shocking to the pragmatic, hedonistic populace of this generation. In 1988 controversial publicity in the non-scientific press reported facts, which known to the medical community, was cloistered in sequestration. The notoriety emanated from the utilization of directly aborted infants for biomedical experimentation. What was performed with clandestine surreptition became an overt revelation.

The mental tempo of current, nonprocrustean scientific thinking is not to object to the utilization of human fetal tissue for biomedical research. Practicality in science dictates that available anatomic material for investigative study should not be discarded even if the organs are obtained from an amoral procedure. One can recall the era of the resurrectionists who were grave-robbing anatomists. Medical history teaches that ethical conduct has been ignored frequently in the pursuit of solutions to the unknown mysteries of science.

Any excuse for killing an intrauterine human being cannot be condoned as an acceptable, sanctioned, sacrifice for the benefit of another human person singularly or a group collectively. No matter how altruistic, well-meaning, or honorable the intention, the unborn infant cannot be destroyed intentionally. Any plan to abort a fetus in order to secure human anatomic material for therapeutic research arouses the macabre spectacle of a crucibled witch's brew from cadaveric vice, funereal malice, and lugubrious sin that cries to heaven for vengeance. Past scientific doctrines did not accept human fetuses as a biological harvest to be utilized to bolster pharmacological therapeutics. Such thoughts are not compatible with the noble, established ideals of classical medical history. Epochs of medicine came from dignified, honest endeavors of medical heroes as Hippocrates, Maimonides, Malpighi, Cesalpinus, Harvey, Withering, and countless others less known. None of these medical elders, dedicated as they were to excellence, were tainted by any wafted odiferous indignity that could scorch medicine's untinged, unstained escutcheon.

When a woman aborts her baby to secure human tissue for experimental medical research, humanity is dehumanized. Humanity becomes despised. Opponents of abortion are encouraged by sporadic opposition to experiments utilizing organs from deliberately aborted fetuses. At the National Institutes of Health experiments on fetal tissue were banned. "Researchers had been using fetal organs and tissues to seek cures for illnesses such as Parkinson's disease, diabetes mellitus, and (selected) blood dyscrasias"...fetal tissue was to be implanted into patients with Parkinson's disease when the proposal was blocked by the assistant secretary of health at the Department of Health and Human Services (281).

Objections from multiple sources (religious, political, professional) have curtailed the neophytic, exacerbated enthusiasm for medical experimentation on aborted embryonal organs and hormones extracted from fetal tissues. The evil spectre of abortion is limitless in arousing adversarial exclamations. "The Journal/NBC poll illustrates a vital point in the (abortion) debate: abortion foes tend to feel more intensely about fetal tissue than do prochoice advocates" (283).

The poll found that 75 percent of those people who oppose legal abortion regard the issue as very important to them. By contrast, only 51 percent of those favoring legal abortion said the issue was very important. Further, 55 percent of those who oppose legalized abortion said their concern about the issue has increased over the last year, compared with 44 percent of those who favor legal abortion (283).

One immoral law is sufficient to spawn diverse interpretations of it that generate propagating amorality. The multivariegated excuses for performing an abortion do not negate the immutable, irrifragable biological verity that the intrauterine fetus is a unified living entity whose destruction is murder.

## Infant Deformity As Excuse

Proponents of abortion who advocate the destruction of a deformed baby have no factual data in this regard. Where are their statistics? *De facto*, most aborted babies examined in the pathology laboratory are found to be neither deformed nor disfigured. Moreover, the present state of the medical art can correct many pediatric disturbances that in prior years were considered incurable.

A praiseworthy example is the development of Rh immune globulin. This knowledge has made possible the prevention of erythrobastosis fetalis, also referred to as Rh disease or Rh hemolytic disease of the newborn. Rh immune globulin given promptly (within 72 hours) to an unsensitized Rh negative woman who has just delivered an Rh positive infant or who has had an abortion or an ectopic pregnancy can be expected to block Rh sensitivity in the next pregnancy. Since this prophylaxis is provided by passive immunity, it prevents maternal sensitization only by the currently terminated pregnancy (95).

Science is verifiable truth founded upon experienced trial and error. Personal opinion is emotionalism expressed in terms of individual preference. The latter is not always arrived at through acquired knowledge, rational judgment, or properly documented experimentation. Therefore, let the biological sciences in pediatrics solve the ills of infancy and let personal considerations be the concern of the future mother, who often is the culpable contributor to infant anomalies and mortality.

Clinical gynecological studies have substantiated that women are not without fault as the iatrogenic source of many of their ills. A report on a series of women who presented themselves in an emergency department for chronic pelvic pain were found to have little or no physical finding of organic disease. "This long-standing pelvic pain has been given a series of names, such as pelvic neuralgia, enigmatic pelvic pain, neurodystonia pelvica, and neurological headache — due to its intangible nature and part psychosomatic origin. The etiology of this condition is obscure, but it has been suggested that there are changes in the pelvic blood flow with mood, and pelvic congestion that could be causing the pain. Psychotherapy is appropriate for the management of this type of pelvic pain" (96).

Women who are found to be in this category of pelvic pain patients are attuned to the anatomic pelvic area. Their attitude is genuine. This same concern stirs up false impressions that if they are pregnant the outcome may be a deformed infant. This is not compatible with clinical experience in obstetrics which has found no relationship between psychosomatic pelvic pain and infant deformity or disfigurement.

Many pregnant women persist in exposing unborn children to unnecessary jeopardy. "The prenatal period is the most vulnerable time of a child's life. Although it was once thought the fetus was well protected from external harm, in recent decades hundreds of substances, organisms, and circumstances have been shown to have a deleterious effect on fetal development. Despite widespread publicity about the fetal harm done by such things as drugs, rubella, infection, cigarette smoking, and alcohol, many pregnant women continue to expose their unborn children to needless hazards" (97). At times certain sports, such as scuba diving or the passive exercise of sauna bathing, may harm the fetus.

"About twenty percent of birth defects are caused by environmental factors, such as drugs, viruses, and vitamin deficiences or excesses. Sixty percent more defects result from the interaction of some environmental factor and a genetic predisposition" (97).* The answer to infant deformity or disfigurement is prophylaxis. Correction of, or the elimination of, the etiology of anomalies is to prevent them beforehand. The avoidance of many causes for illnesses is the province of environmental medicine. The obstetrician as the specialist in prenatal care is the one who can reduce deformity as a proffered reason for an abortion.

The disfigurement issue is necessarily contiguous to the proposal that the quality of life is a determinant that persuades some women to seek an abortion. Quality is a disposition of substance. Qualities have their foundation in quantity as color on a surface.

* The remaining twenty percent are due to maternal drugs, smoking, etc.

Visible quality cannot exist without a preexisting quantum. Quality is dependent on quantity, rather than quantity being dependent on quality. Hence, quantity can exist without quality, but quality cannot exist outside a quantity. Opposite qualities may be found in the same subject in different aspects. Contrariwise, quantity is a unit at some fixed point unless it is in the growth process when it increases, or it is being divided, cut up, or made smaller, when it diminishes.

Therefore, it must be concluded that quantity is a measure of substance. Every quantity consists in a certain multiplication of parts. A quantity, however small or microscopic, regular or irregular, round or square, still remains substance, retaining its intrinsic natural characteristics. Thus quality of life does not negate its quantitative presence.

In his final Pastoral Letter, Terence Cardinal Cooke, from his death bed, urged all of us to remember that "the 'gift of life', God's special gift, is no less beautiful when it is accompanied by illness or weakness, hunger or poverty, mental or physical handicaps, loneliness, or old age. Indeed, at these times, human life gains extra splendor as it requires our special care, concern, and reverence" (98).

Impaired quality of life is a poor excuse for abortion. Most abortions performed are because no children are wanted. Very few abortions occur today for any other acknowledged or documented reason. "In New York State, 500,000 consecutive abortions were performed on young adult women (many residing outside New York State) who did not want a child, and for no other reason. It is a dictum worthy of recollection that no one human person has a greater claim to life over another human person. All men/women are created equally to enjoy life" (73).

If a geriatric adult could be shrunken down to the first spark of life in order to commence it again, this may have been the story written. In a diary of an unborn child, the joy of life was soon extinguished. The chronology of this event commences (244).

"October 5—Today my life began. My parents do not know it yet. I am as small as a mustard seed, but it is I already. And I am to be a girl. I shall have blond hair and azure eyes. Just about everything is settled though, even the fact that I shall love flowers.

"October 19 — Some say I am not a real person yet, that only my mother exists. But I am a real person, just as a small crumb of bread is yet truly bread. My mother is. And I am.

"October 23 — My mouth is just beginning to open now. Just think, in a year or so I shall be laughing and later talking. I know that my first word shall be — Mama.

"October 25 — My heart began to beat today all by itself. From now on it shall gently beat for the rest of my life without ever stopping to rest! And after many years it will tire. It will stop, and then I shall die.

"November 2 — I am growing a bit every day. My arms and legs are beginning to take shape. But I have to wait a long time yet before those little legs will raise me to my mother's arms, before those little arms will be able to gather flowers and embrace my father.

"November 12 — Tiny fingers are beginning to form on my hands. Funny how small they are! I shall be able to stroke my mother's hair with them. And I shall take her hair to my mouth and she will probably say, 'Oh, no, no, dear...'

"November 20 — It wasn't until today that the doctor told Mom that I am living here under her heart. Oh, how happy she must be! Are you happy, Mom?

"November 25 — My mom and dad are probably thinking about a name for me. But they don't even know that I am a girl. They are probably saying Andy. But I want to be called Cathy. I am getting so big already.

"December 24 — I wonder if Mom hears the whispering of my heart? Some children come into the world a little sick. And then the delicate hands of the doctor perform miracles to bring them to health. But my heart is strong and healthy. It beats so evenly — tup – tup – tup — You'll have a healthy little daughter, Mom!

"December 28 — Today my mother killed me" (99).

Learned physicians with various specialized competences should never hesitate to make their independent contributions to the developing area of bioethical doctrinal and moral teaching. This is an enterprise worthy of those who defend and praise the virtue of saving human lives. Physicians are in an enviable position to be defenders of the unborn because the law does not pursue these defensive ideals to precise fulfillment.

Lord Chief Justice Coleridge of England wrote an opinion in 1893 which contained these words: "It would not be correct to say that every moral obligation involves a legal duty; but every legal duty is founded upon a moral obligation" (100). Although these words were written in the last century, modern lawgivers have forgotten them. This is not only true in the British Isles, but also American legal decisions have been lukewarm in defining moral conduct. A supreme court decision in New York is pointed in this direction when a definition on this matter was given. It said: "What is generally called the ethics of the profession is but consensus of expert opinion as to the necessity for professional standards" (102).

Average citizens have failed to grasp the Hippocratic heritage of medicine that is dedicated to the preservation of life. Are they not, too often, as insignificant as a leaf in a whirlwind, tossed about by public opinion, weak when they should be strong? There are all sorts of people in this world, some, backed by good training, education, breeding, and correct example grow strong and straight (101). Others, lacking guidance, are easily swayed and know not which pathway to choose when a necessary selection is an imperative necessity. By presenting the written material in this text, perhaps some bioethic guidance will be found when people are confronted with an identified problem demanding resolution. If there is moral stamina in peoples' characters, it is hoped that some of them will arrive at the best decision that leads upward to eternal happiness.

# CHAPTER FIVE

# RELIGION AND ABORTION

*"You are a child of the universe, no less
than the trees and the stars; you have a right to be here."
Engraved on a tablet in old St. Paul's Church,
Baltimore, Maryland, dated 1692.*

The circadian mundane commercialism of American modernity attests to the existence of God. Each homeowner's insurance policy contains a clause stipulating that no reimbursement will be made for property damages resulting from an act of God. The actuality of God as the creator acknowledges the presence of humankind as the created. Religion is the bond between the creator and the created. The word religion is derived from the Latin verb *religare* meaning to tie, to fasten behind, or to bind. Hence, it is a binding between God, the creator, and human beings, the created.

Dictionaries may give more specific, more complicated, or more sophisticated definitions, but the Latin etymology is simple, original, and most appropriate. Among the composed interpretations of the word religion is one that it is a state of life bound by monastic vows. Another is that it is the condition of one who is a member of a religious order — the religious life. It has been defined as an action or conduct indicating a belief in, reverence for, a desire to please, or a divine ruling power. The exercise or practice of rites or observances implying an observance has been called religion. A particular system of faith and worship has been termed a religion (11).

"Recognition on the part of humanity of some higher unseen power as having control of his/her destiny, and as being entitled to obedience, reverence, and worship is religion. The general mental and moral attitude resulting from this belief, with reference to its effect upon the individual or the community with personal or general acceptance of this feeling as a standard of spiritual and/or practical life, is religion. Into the realm of religion dictionaries have listed as a synonym devotion to some principle, strict fidelity or faithfulness, conscientiousness, pious affection, or attachment" (11). As a terse summation, religion is a manifestation of strict adherence to the natural laws of God.

In view of the bond, called religion, that unites God to human beings, all men/women are called upon to obey the natural law. Hence it matters not whether the person is a Roman Catholic, a Protestant, a Jew, a Muslim, a pagan, or an individual who has no religious preference or affiliation. Nonetheless, all people are obliged to become acquainted with and to observe the teachings of the law of nature just as they are obligated to know and observe the civil law in jurisdictions where they live. Thus, the obligations in reference to abortion flow from the natural law.

"If an action is evil in itself and so prohibited by the law of nature (for example lying, stealing, murder), no authority on earth, be it civil or ecclesiastical, can under any conceivable circumstances legitimately grant permission to perform that action. Nor can any authority on earth legitimately forbid an individual to perform an action that is clearly and under the circumstances required by natural law. It follows that a literary work on medical ethics written by a Catholic is not merely a collection of rulings of an arbitrary nature made by his church. It is rather an application of the principles of the natural law. The Catholic looks to his church for guidance in the interpretation of the natural law, for in the role of teacher, the Church has the right to explain and interpret different principles of the natural law and to pass judgment on the applications of these principles. Because of confused notions which have at times arisen with regard to certain prescriptions of the natural law, the Catholic Church has issued clarifying and authoritative pronouncements which serve to protect her subjects from error" (4). Based upon this fundamental concept, it is apparent that the Catholic Church has a right, a duty, and an obligation to speak out against abortion with the instructional objective to repeat, even *ad infinitum*, that: "What is in harmony with man's/woman's rational nature is good. What is opposed to rational nature is evil" (4).

The moral seriousness of the abortion morass has awakened in religious groups other than the Catholic Church the need to have a second look at the ethical side of this controversy. An example in point is the attitude of "Lutherans For Life" who held a convention in La Grange, Illinois in 1984. "The Reverend Doctor Ralph Bohlmann, president of the 2.7 million member Lutheran Church-Missouri Synod, assured the group of his 'personal support of your efforts and actions'. 'Lutherans For Life' draws most of its members from the Lutheran Church-Missouri Synod, but is open to all Lutherans" (103).

"The American Baptist Churches in the U.S.A., a founding member of the Religious Coalition for Abortion Rights, is 'struggling with the painful and difficult issue of abortion'...(finally in June 1988) the Churches' policy-making General Board voted on a statement opposing abortion in some cases and urging member congregations to support alternatives to abortion" (284).

"Protestant denominations — long identified with the pro-choice side of the abortion debate — have begun to revise and reassess their positions on this divisive moral and political issue. The reassessment has come as opponents of abortion within the denominations have begun to organize themselves more effectively, posing the most formidable challenge to the churches' pro-choice views since abortion was legalized in 1973. According to many in these churches, the mainline Protestant activity also is challenging the view that opposition to abortion is purely a matter of Roman Catholic or fundamentalist Protestant doctrine" (104).

After the Roe decision, much dispute distorted the harmony within many church denominations. Various Protestant churchgoers in this nation increased their discussions on abortion out of which came forceful efforts to formulate policy statements thereon. "There is little evidence that the Protestant churches took counsel together in order to seek what for them might amount to an ecumenical consensus...Intensive theological study and ethical dialogue might have produced a useful, if not fully unanimous, formulation. But each denomination chose to go its own way; and the ways were widely divergent" (285).

Among many protestants there was the incipient, volatile fear that abortion was such a bellicose subject that it should be avoided. "The World Council of Churches regarded the question of abortion with such anxiety that discussion of it has been discouraged..The more liberal Protestants permit abortion, but they are flexible or uncertain about hastening the death of elderly persons or condoning suicide. The more conservative Protestants are as firm as Catholics in opposing abortion, but they may sound bloodthirsty in their calls for dispatching major criminals" (285). Hence it is that no one has put on the toga of a Protestant bellwether to be expressive on this medicomoralsocial moraine.

"Jewish tradition does not consider abortion to be murder, but neither does it permit abortion on demand," says a new pamphlet released by the American Jewish Committee. Entitled "Jewish Views on Abortion", it was written by a conservative Rabbi of the Teaneck, New Jersey Jewish Center, chairman of the New York Federation on Jewish Medical Ethics. In the introduction to the study, the director of the committee's Jewish Communal Affairs Department, comments that "it is doubtful whether even most Jews understand the Jewish approach to the subject (abortion). If the matter comes up at all in a Jewish context, people tend to assume unthinkingly that Judaism must support abortion on demand" (105). In 1973, the abortion upheaval had the intimidating force of driving people away from churches. With the advent of 1985, the pronouncement of leaders in Protestantism, Judaism, and Catholicism have the opposite effect of drawing people back to their former congregations, with newer faces being seen in the pews of churches and synagogues. "To some people, the whole notion of an organized church structure is ridiculous. They feel that their relationship with God is their own private business, and the idea that some limited human being would stand up and preach to them or instruct them seems a kind of sacrilege. But by making each person his or her own authority, they are effectively rejecting the value of any religious community or tradition" (106). Currently, this indifferent attitude appears to be changing.

Occasionally there arises out of the smoldering ashes of silence, a non-religious (even an irreligious) author who is compelled by an innate spiritual force to write on a moral issue that is separated conspicuously from his diurnal literary enterprise. Like an unaimed arrow released from the bow of a hidden archer the piercing sound of the feathered, barbed missile passing through space has catapulted an assertive, applauded columnist for *The Village Voice* (published in Greenwich Village, New York City) into national lauded recognition.

"When Nat Hentoff writes against euthanasia, abortion, or infanticide, he cannot be accused of trying to impose religious or right-wing beliefs on anyone...(He) has described himself as one in a tradition of 'stiff-necked Jewish atheists' with a long history of involvement in such causes as civil rights, civil liberties, and labor. "Politically I am on the left. I am a lower case libertarian' with a long track record of supporting civil rights and civil liberties...He describes euthanasia, abortion, and infanticide in the same terms as he sees other issues with which he is concerned: defending the disadvantaged" (286). This confession emblazes the factual reality that even an atheist can be a moralist; that abortion is not a Catholic issue but a universal *cause celebre*.

A return to religion is slow and is often associated with discord. This was manifested in 1984 when lay Catholics were questioning their bishops. "Although criticism by the laity against their bishops is not new, the recent vocal dissent by leading Catholics in public office on the issue of abortion highlights a 'new relationship' emerging between Catholics and the hierarchy of the Church. This is the view of a diverse group of theologians, Church historians, and bishops. In interviews, they said recent conflicts between Catholic politicians and the hierarchy show how both lay Catholics and their bishops have 'matured' — and how they are finding new ways of relating to each other" (107).

"On the one hand, Catholics, increasingly educated, affluent, and rooted in the American mainstream, have come to depend less on the guidance of their bishops. At the same time, many bishops, inspired by the reforms in the Church over the past 20 years, have insisted increasingly that Catholics examine a broad range of social issues in light of Church teachings" (107). "The result has been the recent publications on the public lay hierarchy confrontations over issues ranging from abortion, economics , to nuclear arms which, while significant are not new" (108).

No matter what objections are made or what criticisms are hurled against them, the hierarchy remains adamant on the immorality of abortion. From the Pope down to the least known of his bishops, none have deviated from this doctrinal teaching. Pope John Paul II has spoken openly against abortion during his universal travels to many nations around the world. His antiabortion quotations have been repeated continually on television, other electronic media, and in printed journalism in all modern languages. There is no literate person who is excused from knowing the papal position on abortion.

This antiabortion doctrinal teaching of the Roman Catholic Church has been affirmed, confirmed, and repeated by cardinals, archbishops, and bishops in America. Because of their outspoken efforts to save the unborn, many members of the hierarchy have been publicized in the various news media as individual spokesmen on unified hierarchical Catholic teaching on abortion.

The cardinal who presses the fight against abortion is Joseph Cardinal Bernardin of Chicago. "In a carefully worded column published in the archdiocesan newspaper, the Cardinal said 'A decision to deny protection to human life in the early stages of its development must be judged arbitrary and inadequate.' As chairman of the Bishops' Prolife Committee and the head of the committee that wrote the bishops' pastoral letter condemning nuclear war, Cardinal Bernardin plays a key role in formulating church social policies" (109).

In the forefront and in the fighting lines in the battle against abortion is Cardinal John J. O'Connor. His attacks against the opponents to the right-to-life are universally founded upon abortion as murder of the innocent. He "properly emphasizes that biomedical science identifies the product of fertilization as a distinct and separate human life which develops both before birth and after birth in dependence upon others, including, most importantly, the new human being's mother. Cardinal O'Connor implores physicians to use their great influence to check abortions" (110). "This point warrants repetition: if doctors, in accord with the Hippocratic oath, wanted to eliminate abortions, they could do so almost entirely, because they are the persons who perform the overwhelming number of abortions. Medical schools and medical societies must become target areas for re-education on the dignity of unborn human life" (111, 112).

A cohort of Cardinal O'Connor in the quadrigal chariot of fire racing against abortion is Cardinal Bernard F. Law of Boston. He believes "that achieving a legal ban against abortion could require a long and divisive struggle. But he said it was one the bishops could not back away from, any more than the Protestant abolitionist ministers of New England could have retreated from the issue of slavery in the 1850s. "On March 24, 1984, in my homily of installation, which was prior to the political conventions, prior to the formulation of platforms, prior to any of that, I said I think abortion is a primordial evil, a primordial darkness, and I have been insistent in teaching that and I will be consistent after November" (113). To battle against abortion is a battle for the civil rights of the unborn (114).

Bishop Francis J. Mugavero of the Brooklyn-Queens Diocese has stated publicly that abortion is a national "tragedy" that not only violates divine law but cheapens respect for all life. "Abortion has led our society to accept other evils and, worst of all, it has encouraged acceptance of the falsehood that mankind controls the right over life and death. From this arrogant cynicism our country now has come to accept the deliberate killing of handicapped infants in many of our hospital nurseries" (115). The Bishop was referring to a 1982 incident in Bloomington, Indiana in which a state court allowed parents to withhold medical treatment from a deformed infant. The baby died a few days later. There have been similar instances elsewhere in the nation since that time (116). As in all facets of morality, the Catholic hierarchy is steadfast in its duty not only to proclaim the teachings of Christ, but taking all necessary actions for justice that will benefit the entire Church and its parishioners.

Religion of whatever denomination to be true to its purposeful fulfillment leading to goodness must sustain the moral virtues. "Morality is the relation of a human act to the object, circumstances, and aim which furnish the goodness for that act. Consequently, immorality is the opposite whenever there is an object, a circumstance, or an aim which makes the human act evil by depriving it of its full humanity. Immorality is not limited to selected sins such as those of impurity or drunkenness. These vices have a certain manifest ugliness which makes them sensibly odious; but they cannot claim a monopoly on immorality. There are vices which exceed the sins of the body in immorality, such as infidelity and hatred of God" (117). Immorality is dirt. What is dirt? It is matter out of place.

## Catholicism and Abortion

In decades past, both civil and ecclesiastical authorities had a unanimity of opinion in their moral sentiments on abortion. Criminal abortion was interpreted always as a heinous act. Since 1973, however, there has arisen a disparity between civil law and ecclesiastical canonical pronouncements on the moral culpability of fetal destruction. This discord arises in part from the interpretation of abortion, as has been discussed in the chapter defining abortion.

Vocal and written condemnation of abortion by ecclesiastical authority is the intellectual apostolate of Catholicism in action. "By the intellectual apostolate is meant making Catholic truth appear intellectually respectable and relevant to contemporary people, be they Catholic or of some other faith" (118). The intellectual apostolate has the burden of obligation to defend as well as promulgate Catholic dogma.

The strongest advocate of the intellectual apostolate is Pope John Paul II. "He told Vatican officials that the Catholic Church has a duty to denounce all violations of human rights and to guard against even those who seem to be an accomplice to such violations ... The Church, with respect for the person and for those responsible for the common good, still has the duty to tell the truth, like the prophets who could not accommodate injustices. The Church must not even so much as appear to be an accomplice in situations that harm the fundamental rights of persons. Above all, the Church has the duty to express Christian solidarity with those who suffer injustice" (119).

In uniformity with the papacy, bishops do not promote specific public policies. Episcopal utterances have a purposeful, plenary goal which is the salvation of human souls. The growing activism of bishops in the abortion quagmire is essential to combat the immorality it has engendered. Silence on the part of bishops would approximate dereliction of a pastoral duty. Furthermore, silence would be an assent to it. *Tacit: adsensio* said the Romans. (He who is quiet is saying I agree.) Episcopal outspokenness is justifiable by the ecclesiastical obligation to awaken public opinion to any immoral public policy. This joint effort will bring, one by one, the proabortionists to a confrontation with their own moral fiction.

Within the ranks of the Catholic laity and others in a religious order disagreement may arise that differs from the teaching of the Catholic Church on abortion. Too many Catholics want it both ways. They desire the standards (non-permitted physical pleasures) of the world and the spiritual comfort of the Church. Emotional propulsion may find fault with one of the missions of the Catholic Church, which is to ferret out those human actions that threaten any person's immortal soul, no matter from what source that evil threat may arise. Many American Catholics are at odds with the teachings of the Church on abortion.

"Catholics today are more affluent, better educated, and more willing to question the Church than their parents were. And their independence of conscience is accepted — or at least tolerated — by growing numbers of parish priests and nuns who feel their primary pastoral mission is to meet the everyday needs of the faithful. American bishops, more vocal, perhaps, than ever this year (1989) in promoting the teachings of the Church, are finding it increasingly more difficult to command obedience from either the clergy or the laity" (120). This self-imposed emancipation from Church authority has found itself among the signers of the proabortion ad sponsored by "Catholics for a Free Choice".

"Ninety-seven Catholics sponsored by 'Catholics for a Free Choice', a proabortion lobbying group, took a full page ad in The New York Times on October 7, 1984, in which they asserted that 'there is the mistaken belief in American society' that the teaching of the Pope and the other bishops on abortion 'is the only legitimate Catholic position'. Although most signers were lay academics, the '97' included a few priests, several former priests and a number of males and females from religious orders" (121).

"Many persons who signed the proabortion ad have decided to launch a country-wide campaign for the 'right to dissent' in the Catholic Church. It seems that some of those in religious life who signed the original statement are endorsing this campaign. This decision will surely fix them in the spider's web" (122).

"A variety of ways exists in the Church for scholars and others to test theories and practical solutions that conflict with current authentic and binding Church teaching. Sometimes when persons find out that they cannot win their case on the basis of Catholic theological method, which includes ratification by the Church's teaching office, they resort to contestation, the method of political and social struggle. 'Catholics for Free Choice' must be overjoyed with their surrogate's choice. The big spider now has both the lay and religious signers of the October 7th statement firmly entangled in its web" (122).

"All in the Catholic Church, including laity, priests, and those in religious life, have the right and the duty to follow their upright and informed consciences. When such conscientious judgments, which can be sincerely mistaken, conflict with the commitment priests and religious men/women have made, a clash with Church authority inevitably results. Particularly is this so when such persons choose the method of public contestation to resolve perceived difficulties. Those who exercise Church authority, however, are also obligated to follow their upright and informed consciences. The publicly contesting religious men/women are thus backing Church authority into a corner" (122).

"Since those who accept appointment to Church office or who embrace religious consecration have solemnly pledged fidelity to binding Church teaching, they have no right to reject it. Those who find themselves conclusively opposed to such teaching may invoke processes in Church law to free themselves from their commitment to offices or states of life that presume acceptance of this teaching. In such an event, no one can or should question that they have acted honorably. One must also regret the naivete, if it is that, of those clergy and religious men/women who allowed themselves to be used by 'Catholics for a Free Choice' in a public slap at Church authority. Distressing, further, is the long-standing angry criticism of Church authority engaged in by a few religious signatories to the statement" (121).

"Signers of the public statement dissenting from the Catholic Church's teaching on abortion have labeled the Holy See's action against some of the signers a 'cause for scandal to Catholics everywhere' and an attempt to 'stifle freedom of speech and public discussion in the Church'. In a press conference following a meeting behind closed doors, the group of more than 35 nuns, priests, and lay people strongly criticized the Holy See's directive that the males and females in religious life who signed the statement publicly retract it or face disciplinary procedures under canon law. Failure to do so could result in their dismissal from the religious life" (123).

"The spokesman of the Holy See insisted that the threatened disciplinary action constituted ordinary Church procedure .... The Congregation for Religious and Secular Institutes, recalling the teachings of the Second Vatican Council and canon law norms on abortion, as well as the submission to the magisterium required of people in religious orders, has invited the superiors major of the institutes concerned to ask every single member who signed the declaration to make a public retraction" (123). Obstinate disobedience has attached to it the threat of expulsion from the religious order relative to a provision of the code of canon law.

"In the letter it sent to the superiors, the congregation cited canon 696, paragraph one, of canon law stating that: "the pernicious upholding or spreading of doctrine condemned by the magisterium of the Church especially on an issue of such gravity is a flagrant scandal and is sufficient cause for the dismissal of a religious (secular priest or a person in a Catholic order) guilty of such conduct. The congregation also cited the Vatican II's 'Pastoral Constitution on the Church in the Modern World' which defines abortion as an 'unspeakable crime'. According to canon law, a male and female religious (secular priest or member of a Catholic order) incurs automatic excommunication" (123). As of 1989, this advertisement fiasco has faded into oblivion.

The Monsignor Secretary of the National Council of Catholic Bishops issued a statement joining the United States' Catholic bishops with the Holy See's directive. It concluded: "The Vatican congregation bases its action on the constant teaching of the Church concerning the immorality of abortion, and on provisions of canon law concerning spreading doctrines condemned by the magisterium as cause for dismissal from religious life" (124).

There is need for some corrective guidance on the bioethical, sociomoral disconcerting moods that prevail in American society as the 21st century approaches hastily. Hence, it has been deemed necessary that writings on abortion, AIDS ministry, health, poverty, contraception, and other life-related themes be included in forth-coming Respect Life manuals from the National Conference of Catholic Bishops. October of each year has been designated as the Respect Life Month.

Among those popularizing the October prolife endeavor are men of all religious faiths. A groundswell of opposition to abortion has erupted like a geyser from this unexpected, unanticipated source. The male gender has formed prolife assemblages of outspoken men, many of whom are married. Some have opposed their own wives on this fiery topic of abortion. Husbands are clamoring for their marital rights in any decision pertinent to abortion — even to the utilization of legal clout to enforce their positions.

Men have just begun to fight for the rights of the unborn. * With their *basso profundo* voices, they will outsound the soprano tones of women proabortionists with their contrary exclamations. The year 1989 will be a landmark annual of twentieth century history with the entrance of stalwart men into the fray against abortion. Addition-ally the prediction is that by 1990 the ranks of proabortionists will diminish as the wave of public opinion rises in favor of prolife sentiment stimulated in a large measure by male participation in the antiabortion rally. Legalized abortion in the United States is faltering. Curtailment is on the horizon. Unborn infants will be preserved, protected, and produced to assume their prerogative positions in life as citizens in the world of tomorrow.

Many physicians are misguided by self-assessment or for any other reason when evaluating the immorality of abortion. Within the ranks of the medical profession, there are dissidents who deviate from the nonacceptance of the unethical conduct of legal abortionists and the vice of fetal destruction. Most of the proabortion devotees ignore published bioethical data as they dismiss or deny their conscience. Learned specialists in the pursuit of their obstetrical

* From all categories of social life: husbands, fathers, bachelors, physicians, politicians, policy-makers, etc.

and/or gynecological endeavors have biological proof of intrauterine life, yet they destroy it. These same physicians labor heroically to save one life only to destroy hundreds more with lesser effort.

Proabortion physicians in many instances justify abortion by destructive criticism of the Catholic Church whom they blame for inserting a moral issue into a medical procedure protected under state and national laws. They imply or actually state that religious objection is unwarranted, unscientific, purely theoretical, or unrealistic. Misquotations are made that are tinged with hedonistic pragmatism. Sometimes statements are read that are the epitomization of ridiculosity. When persons do not express their thoughts in oral or written words, their lack of knowledge cannot be exposed. However, when their notions are released by speech or inscription their unfettered ignorance is not emphractic. Effable, self-disclosed obscurantism allows a concealed tatterdemallion mentality, once unfastened, to raise havoc as it escapes igneously into the public domain.

An example of this incredulity was demonstrated by a psychiatrist who wrote in a medical journal that: "It may surprise many Catholics to know that views on abortion within the Church have varied and St. Thomas Aquinas found abortion acceptable in the first few months until the time of 'quickening', after which, in his times, attempts would have meant almost certain death for the woman. Today there is another issue. In our times of sophistication, if not cynicism, the Pope's decisions on abortion, contraception, and celibacy reflect the recognition that when the affectional tie forged by sexual privation is weakened, all hierarchic control is likely to go... I am saying that the subterranean reasons for the Pope's decisions are based on power, while the overt reasons presented are inconsistent ideologic ones. If 'taking a life' is a genuine issue, the Pope has an absolute obligation to command all Catholics to refuse to serve in war, making excommunication the consequence of failure to do so" (22).

The first excerpt attempts to quote St. Thomas Aquinas as favoring abortion in the first trimester of pregnancy. This statement would be acceptable only by a direct quotation from his writings: *Compendium Summae Totius Theologiae*, published in Rome

MDCCLXIII. Having checked the chapters in the above text pertinent to the subject under discussion (Volume 6, Questio LIX to Questio LXIII concerning De Fecundis Nuptus) no verification is found of the alleged statement attributed to St. Thomas Aquinas.

Prior to reading any writing by the "Doctor of the Church from Aquina", an enlightening statement under the editor's preface in the Thomas Aquinas Dictionary should be remembered. "In the preparation of this volume, therefore, I was constantly reminded of Rickaby's admonition: St Thomas is an author particularly liable to misrepresentation by taking his words in one place to the neglect of what he says on the same subject elsewhere. No one is safe in quoting him who has not read much of him" (125).

The mention of the Pope's decisions is persiflage. A continuation of this negation of papal criticism is quoted from a counter-publication in a subsequent issue of the same medical journal. "It indicates that the person expressing opinions about the papacy has little or no understanding of it, and less knowledge of the reigning Pontiff John Paul II. Concerning the present discussion, the opinions of the current Pope are gleaned from the encyclical 'Humanae Vitae' as promulgated by Pope Paul VI" (73).

"In the generality of papal pronouncements there is one constant. The natural law is authentically existential as a constituent of evangelical morality. This evangelical morality presupposes and perfects the natural law even as it goes beyond it. Whenever the Roman Catholic Church, through the papacy, teaches natural law doctrine or a specific application of it to a concrete moral issue, it does so by virtue of the Petrine Commission and not as eminent philosophers or world-renowned metaphysicians. The Roman Catholic Church does give reason for its condemnation of totalitarianism, apartheid, racial discrimination, economic exploitation, nuclear war, abortion, donor-sperm insemination, surrogate motherhood, and artificial contraception. The natural law is so-called not because it is discernible by a natural faculty or human reason, but because it is the law of the nature of man. Nor is it called natural law because it is the law of human reason, but because it is the will of the divine legislator made manifest in the exigencies of human nature as an obligatory norm of moral conduct" (73).

"As to papal excommunication and war, the association with abortion is nebulous in the extreme. However, to digress to this criticism, who is the Pope to excommunicate? The frightened draftee does not have a choice, except to be a conscientious objector. Failure to sign up for the draft or to answer selective service board notice is a federal offense. To excommunicate a soldier is a *reductio ad absurdum,* even as it is a useless emotion. Should the generals be excommunicated? *Cui bono!* They are under orders from the national officials. Those who should be excommunicated are they who start wars and the leaders of world states who propel their nations to war. Excommunication of these men in government (e.g. Russia, Iran, Iraq, Cuba, Libya, North Korea, Vietnam, etc.) would be *a ridiculum.* In the first place, most leaders of nations are not Roman Catholics; therefore, excommunication is *nihil.* Furthermore, the voice of the Pope falls on deaf ears in the world of politics. *De facto*, the Vatican State is never invited (except as a silent observer as in the United Nations) to participate in major world councils on war or peace. Hence, papal excommunication is worthless in this arbitrage world of political chicanery" (73).

Technical knowledge, medicine, law, philosophy, and theology have experts in their ranks. Rarely does the expertise run over into one or more of the other disciplines. Even the most learned among us see only what they know. If they know nothing outside their own region of knowledge, they see nothing. These areas of higher educational specialties, "apart from their methods, engenders attitudes of mind which tend to ignore each other and thus end by opposing one another. The devotees of each branch of learning are concerned exclusively with the matter of their own work, without straying from their chosen path" (2). Trained, specialized, knowledgeable experts in certain fields of educated learning regard in an adversarial manner the pseudo-intellectual intruder who contradicts authority. The interloper may be assertive in the name of some principle, or other social announcement. Audacity is feigned with an assurance of "one untroubled by the least doubt that he/she holds the truth, to meddle with matters about which he/she knows nothing and which he/she has not even taken the trouble to study. Let such intruders stay in their own domain, in their ivory towers. Let them draw up rules for private living, for problems of the personal conscience" (2). Bioethical matters are not to be subjected to the surveillance of those who are not initiated into this newer philosophic aspect of medicosurgical practice. Legalists combined with medical ethicists have their own requirements for interpretive understanding, and let those who seek to conform to such requirements be left in peace (2).

## Catholic Teaching on Abortion

With all the prior commentaries completed, it is appropriate to state the Roman Catholic teaching on abortion in a secular society. This clarification is an urgent necessity because Catholics in high public office have said: "Are we asking government to make criminal what we believe to be sinful because we ourselves can't stop committing the sin? I think our moral and social mission as Catholics must begin with the wisdom contained in the words 'physician, heal thyself'. Unless we Catholics . . . set an example that is clear and compelling, then we will never convince this society to change the civil laws to protect what we preach is precious human life. Despite all the efforts at defining our opposition to the sin of abortion, collectively we Catholics apparently believe — and perhaps act — little different from those who do not share our commitment" (126).

Concurring with these quotations, an auxiliary bishop in New York has given serious reflection to this problem. Referring to the abortion issue, he said, "The major problem the church has is internal. How do we teach? As much as I think we are responsible for advocating public policy issues, our primary responsibility is to teach our own people. We have not done that. We are asking politicians to do what we have not done effectively ourselves" (127).

In an effort to increase the education of people concerning the Catholic standards on abortion, a prestigious Catholic medical research center has made an educational contribution toward the solution of the debate over religion and abortion. "Every member of Congress, every United States Catholic bishop, and the governors of the fifty states have received copies of the lengthy statement on 'Catholic Teaching on Abortion and Secular Society', issued by the Pope John XXIII Medical-Moral Research and Education Center in St. Louis, Missouri" (128).

This publication will fill the void, if one exists, on a so-called need for clarity on the position of the Roman Catholic Church on abortion. For the sake of brevity, facile understanding, and assimilation, the St. Louis pamphlet is presented tersely in a litanized format (129).

1.  Catholic teaching on abortion belongs to a broader teaching about the stewardship of human life. The strong condemnation of direct abortion by the church cannot be separated from the equally strong condemnation of infanticide, euthanasia, and the direct killing of noncombatants in war. Catholic teaching likewise condemns acts of rape and all acts which violate the autonomy of women by causing an unwanted pregnancy.

2.  It also charges society as a whole to assist couples unable from their own resources to provide for their offspring before or after birth. This duty becomes doubly pressing when a woman has been abandoned or rejected by the man who fathered her unborn child.

3.  Catholic teaching does not support either a moral or a legal right to an abortion. It also considers public funding of abortion morally wrong.

4.  In modern times, the Catholic Church presented its official and authoritative teaching against abortion when all the Catholic bishops of the world met in Rome for the Second Vatican Council of 1962-1965. The bishops spoke of abortion as "poisoning human society" in their document on "The Church Today" (130).

5.  The hierarchy taught that whatever is opposed to life itself, such as any type of murder, genocide, abortion, euthanasia, or willful self destruction . . . are infamies indeed. Such acts poison human society. In addition they do greater harm to those who practice them than those who suffer the injury.

6.  The year after the United States Supreme Court decision of 1973, the Sacred Congregation for the Doctrine of the Faith in Rome prepared a long and detailed Declaration on Abortion which Pope Paul VI approved and confirmed on June 28, 1974. This document clearly teaches that the moral wrong of abortion must be seen in its violation of the basic human right to

life. Far from merely violating personal religious beliefs, abortion violates social justice and the public moral order.

7. To be allowed to live is the primordial right of the human person . . . the foundation and condition of all others. It is not within the competence of society or public authority, whatever its form, to give this right to some and take it away from others . . . The right to life does not derive from the favor of human beings but exists prior to any such favor and must be acknowledged as such. Discrimination based on the various stages of human life is no less excusable than discrimination on any other grounds . . . Every human life must be respected from the moment the process of generation begins (130).

8. Even if it is assumed that animation comes at a later point, the life of the fetus is nonetheless incipiently human (as the biological sciences make clear); it prepares the way for and requires the infusion of the soul, which will complete the human nature received from the parents.

9. In the history of the Catholic teaching against abortion, one finds unanimous agreement that abortion from the time of conception is morally wrong. Some church teachers and documents, it is true, entertain the view of delayed animation of a spiritual soul, as Aristotle had taught in the pre-Christian era, but they did not use the time of animation as a moral dividing line between permissible and immoral abortions (131). In a powerful essay, the argument was quieted "that if the philosophical principles of Aristotle and St. Thomas Aquinas are correctly applied to the data of modern embryology, the theory of delayed animation becomes quite implausible" (132).

10. The church does not teach that abortion is wrong only for Catholics. It teaches that abortion is detrimental to society at large. Anyone who accepts this firm Catholic teaching which rejects all direct abortion cannot treat this doctrine as purely a matter of private or religious conviction, even in a secular society. The injustices which the church identifies in abortion affect society at large, and, as the Second Vatican Council declares, 'poison society'. Therefore, every Catholic is obliged in conscience not only to oppose abortion as a personal deci-

sion, but also to oppose its practice in society" (129).

A concluding summation stated succinctly reiterates that the Roman Catholic Church's teaching on abortion is clear and certain. "The teaching is:

"1.That directly intended abortion cannot be a morally right human act;

"2.That abortion is detrimental to society as a whole; and,

"3.That, therefore, abortion must be opposed" (129).

"The three parts of the teaching are inseparable. Anyone who claims to reflect authentic Catholic teaching may not attempt to separate them. Moreover, this teaching is not offered as a 'law' for Catholics only, but as a teaching that has its roots in human nature and which, therefore, applies to all humankind. Catholics in public life are not expected to oppose abortion because they are Catholics, but because abortion is wrong and harmful for society. If they do not accept the church's teaching, they may say so. But if they do accept their church's teaching, logically they must accept it all" (129).

"No society can live in peace with itself, or with the world, without a full awareness of the worth and dignity of every human person, and of the sacredness of all human life. When we accept violence in any form as commonplace, our sensitivities become dulled. When we accept violence, war itself can be taken for granted" (133). Deprivation of basic human rights without reverence for life is a grievous fault.

Sins that cry to heaven for vengeance are those serious transgressions which are of such severe injustice to humanity that God is called upon to avenge them. These sins, according to the orthodox Roman Catholic Church, are: willful murder, sins against nature, oppression of the poor, the widow, the orphan; and depriving laborers of their just wages. Premeditated, consensual abortion falls into this classification of sin.

Directed efforts toward moral good by any one church or all churches of the various denominations collectively cannot change a predetermined, fixed proabortion mindset of certain zealots. This evangelistic ineptitude results from the failure to teach morality at all social levels. It is resurgent proof reaffirming that an ecclesiastical promulgation is ineffectual legislation in a strictly formulated secular government that ostracizes Godliness from statesmanship...This is evidence once again that the voice of God spoken through his church is like the muscular wings of an indefatigable angel beating abyssmally against an eternal void.

CHAPTER SIX

# POLITICS AND ABORTION

*"You shall love your neighbor more than your own life. You shall not slay
the child by abortion. You shall not kill what is generated."*
*The Epistle of Barnabas*
*(circa 138 A.D.) quoted in reference 134*

There does not seem to be any syncretism on abortion between
the moral teachings of the Roman Catholic Church and the judicial/
legislative dicta of civil law as promulgated by people in public
service. The deviation from Catholic dogma by any individual or
groups does not alter the factual truth that their own interpretation
does not prevail against it. This pronouncement has been reaffirmed
by the Cardinal Prefect of the Sacred Congregation for the Doctrine
of the Faith in Rome.

As the highest-ranking theologian at the Holy See, he spoke
about the prevailing materialism of the West, saying, "there is
something diabolical in the way pornography and drugs are ex-
ploited, in the coldness with which humanity is corrupted by taking
advantage of his/her weaknesses. A culture that persuades people
that life's only aims are pleasure and individual interest is infernal.
. . . The Church's morals are lived as if they were a foreign remote
body, which clashes not only with the concrete habits of life, but also
with the basic model of thought. It becomes difficult, if not impossible, to present the authentic Catholic ethic as reasonable; it is too
distant from what is considered normal, and obvious" (135).

"Many moralists in the United States believe they are forced to
choose between dissent with society or dissent with the magisterium. Many choose this last type of dissent, adapting themselves
to compromise with secular ethics which often end up unhinging
men and women from their deepest nature, leading them towards a
new slavery, which initially intended to liberate them"(135).

A personal attitude that attempts to negate the existence of
objective truths of faith is at the core of many theological disquie-

tudes. "In a world in which skepticism has infected even believers, the Church's conviction that there is a truth and that this truth can be defined and expressed in a precise way is considered a shock. It would no longer be the Catholic Church if that deposition was not commonly accepted by everyone. Certainly, unity in faith does not mean uniformity of technical instruments and of the unit type of reflection; but in the end, everything must be referred to a truth which is redeeming and which is unique" (135).

As a precise recapitulation, the Cardinal Prefect has said conformity to Church teaching is a universal obligation imposed upon those who would be or call themselves Catholics. In brief, Catholics must go by the rules of the Roman Catholic Church. To accept contrary views and favor the poet Horace's Lydian advice, "*Carpe diem*", is not allowed even to Americans. No social group, state, or nation is able to establish any functional methodology without guidelines, rules, or rule makers. "We turn to Robert's Rules of Order for meetings. We accept the umpire's call in baseball or basketball and the referee's flag in football, despite the fact that three cameras and instant replays give us livingroom judges a closer look at the game than even the players themselves. We very seldom change the score, even if the umpire is proved to be wrong. It seems logical, then, that we American Catholics have to begin to consider whether we are going to go for individual judgment in disputed cases or accept some kind of referee or umpire" — whether or not all the umpire's calls coincide with our own opinions (136).

"If that seems a simplistic view of the world, I invite you to examine the decisions about Martin Luther and Henry VIII that resulted in severing two great Catholic nations, Germany and England, from the Roman union. That is the only conclusion I can come to about the two most recent missives from Rome which delighted headline writers. 'Deep pain, anger follow Roman letter' was the headline in a Canadian newspaper" (136).

"I thought it another reaction story to the potential expulsion of men and women religious signers of a statement on abortion that appeared as a full page advertisement in a New York newspaper (137). Instead, it told of reaction to the 'secret letter' from the Vatican Congregation for Eastern Churches about the 'suspension' of Ukrainian married priests in North America.

There was deep pain also caused by those letters sent by the Vatican Congregation for Religious to superiors of religious orders who signed the abortion ad" (136). In the matter of the Ukrainian priests, Vatican commentators said that the aim was to "regularize" and assure "liceity" for their ministry. "In the case of the ad signers, their spokespersons say the intent of the ad was to call attention to a variety of views on abortion among Catholics in America. The United States bishop's doctrine committee saw the ad in a different light, as they stated at their November 1984 meeting in Washington" (136).

"The members of the Committee on Pleuralism and Abortion present a personal opinion which directly contradicts the clear and constant teaching of the Catholic Church about abortion, a teaching which they as Catholics are obliged to accept. At the same time, the Committee on Doctrine reaffirms its confidence in the many theologians who explore and present the implications of moral teaching in fidelity to the Roman Catholic tradition" (136). We Americans tend to go by the rules; this tendency should be and is applied to all people who profess to be Catholics.

The one and only Catholic position on abortion is to reaffirm the immorality of it, the statement issued in Washington on September 14, 1984 by the group called the Catholic Committee on Pleuralism and Abortion notwithstanding. This committee, under the auspices of Catholics for a Free Choice, says it is "a mistaken belief in American society that there is only one Catholic opinion on abortion. Catholic teaching comes from the faith of the laity and the work of the professional theologians as well as from pronouncements of the hierarchy. The three groups are 'mutually corrective and mutually supportive'. To hold that only the hierarchy can define Catholic teaching marks 'a fascistic kind of Catholicism' that makes the church like the National Football League in which 'the officials make the rules' and if one does not like them he can only leave the game and play elsewhere (138). This spokesman for the Catholic Committee on Pleuralism and Abortion has said it clearly, "play elsewhere". If so-called Catholics cannot go by the rules, they know what they can do. As in every social group, professional society, or country club, every member must obey the rules, regulations, and by-laws. As President Truman often said: "If you cannot stand the heat, get out of the kitchen".

## Even Under Law Abortion is Immoral

The majority of persons who hold high or low, elected or appointed, political office are lawyers. This includes the executive and legislative branches of government. As such, these educated men/women do know or should know that laws are made to protect human rights, to safeguard humanity, to pursue life, liberty and happiness. Laws are a reflection of the intellectual quantum and the mental health of a nation.

Based upon this fundamental knowledge of the purpose of the law, it is realized that in the abortion problem something is missing. The denial of human rights to the unborn dichotomizes these rights, separating one group from another according to age. Hence, statutory and common law do not fulfill entirely their legal obligations when they do not safeguard the lives of those yet unborn. As a mirror of the intellectual health of the nation, the abortion law is an indicator that all does not go well with American ethical culture.

"The Roman Catholic Church has been plunged into American politics in a way that is unique in modern history. A sudden flurry of activity by the bishops of the Northeast has come at a time of conflict over the political activism of the Protestant right. It has raised questions . . . about why the bishops have acted within a church that in the past has been reluctant to appear too aggressive for fear of stirring a Protestant backlash of the kind that marred their relations for many years" (139). The answer to the query is that most American bishops believe that abortion is "the key issue" in current politics.

"The issue of abortion seems to be at the root of the new clerical activism in the political arena. The unwillingness of some Catholics to accept their church's teachings only makes it more urgent in the minds of the bishops. The Cardinal-Archbishop of Boston said, 'the estimated 1.5 million abortions occurring annually in the United States was a primordial sin, a primordial darkness' that was corrupting society. By describing it as a key issue he did not mean to promote anyone's candidacy but to elevate the issue now and after the November 1984 elections to the high level held by civil rights for blacks in the 1960s. What the Archbishop accentuated was that 'A Catholic believes as a Catholic'. What the bishops were pursuing was not a political strategy to elect someone or to defeat someone" (139). Their aim is to defeat the abortion laws. Politicians must accept this episcopal position, as they are the religious representatives of 55 million Catholics in the United States of America. Failure by politicians to realize this truism will lead to the fact that one by one they will fall victims to their own personal moral imperfection.

In a September 11, 1984 column, the article's title was "The Question Is Law". The writer thereof tried to show that morality and legality are confused in debates on abortion. "Opponents argue that it (abortion) is immoral, but that is not the issue. Many things are immoral, such as lying, adultery, being mean or dishonoring one's parents, but they are not illegal" (140). "Why among immoral acts she mentions, did she stop short of including the obvious example of murder, both immoral and formerly illegal? If abortion is not classified as murder, it is surely the closest thing to it, since it entails the deliberate killing of a developing human being that is alive in the mother's womb. She also neglected to point out that up until recently abortion was illegal, and she seems surprised that the pro-life movement is demanding to make abortion a crime" (141).

The exact point is "that abortion has been in the past considered immoral by the great majority of civilized people, not for religious reasons only, but for the same reasons that murder is immoral or stealing is immoral. They are condemned as being opposed to the well being of the community" (141). "When a society is faced with an attempt to impose views which are repugnant to civilized values, such as the Nazi regime imposed in Germany in the 1930s, it is the obligation of thoughtful people to resist"(42). Voltaire's notorious byword, *"ECRASEZ l'infame* — crush the detestable thing — applied by him with singular venom to the Christian religion, has apparently been adopted by groups of crusaders who are applying it with physical force to abortion clinics and various kinds of munitions or military installations. We have witnessed over the past years several destructive or other terrorist-type attacks upon munitions factories, military personnel, military transports, or installations by persons protesting the nuclear arms race" (143). Now the procedure has been adopted by antagonists to abortion clinics as a protest against the killing of the unborn. Such destructive activity and terrorist tactics cannot be condoned. "Extremists are responsible for the violence and terrorist intimidation mentioned. In neither one nor the other case do they have the support of the citizenry at large. *ECRASEZ l'infame!* Yes, but only by peaceful and lawful means"(143).

The nation's bishops were united in their condemnation of the bombing of abortion facilities. They called these acts dangerous, ill-considered, and deplorable (144). "However, in a statement released on behalf of the National Conference of Catholic Bishops, the Cardinal-Archbishop of Chicago added that the bombings demonstrate that 'violence begets violence' and reflect the violence that goes on inside abortion clinics... Wrong in themselves, they are also symptomatic of the violence unleashed into society by the legalized violence of abortion" (144).

Bad laws that ban human rights are intrinsically, inherently, inchoately evil. Like the Nazi laws against selected human beings, they will disintegrate from within by the decomposition of their very decayed framework upon which they were formulated. Evil laws cannot triumph, but will inevitably crumble to dust. If it were not so, then distributive social justice could not survive. However, to destroy specific evil laws more quickly, a cohort of leaders, crusaders, like the bishops of America, are needed to lead the crusade against abortion.

Some legal methods have been propelled in the direction of diminishing the number of abortions performed through-out this nation. One of the steps taken in this direction was the limitation and/or restriction of federal funds for abortion allotted to Medicaid-eligible women. Medicaid funding was established to treat illnesses, not to interrupt reproduction. Pregnancy is not an illness, it is the fulfillment of one of the ten biological functions of the human organism. As intrauterine infant is not a disease complex but a clinically identifiable process of creativity. It should be the prevenance of true love in all its glorious grandeur. "To measure the impact of this restriction on abortion-related complications, the Center for Disease Control (CDC) initiated a hospital surveillance project in 13 states and the District of Columbia. No increase in abortion-related complications was observed in this surveillance project. An editorial note on this research supports the inference that Medicaid-eligible women are not choosing self-induced or non-physician-induced abortions to any large extent" (145).

A prolife initiative to cut off state funds for most abortions for the State of California was rejected. The antiabortion neophytic effort claimed that the endeavor would not stop all abortions. Moreover, the head of the Catholic Conference postulated the factual reality that a bill of such genre had a minimal chance of approval by the state legislature.

The motivating force to restrict abortion funds in the governmental attempt was cost containment consciousness and not to advance ethical conduct or foment moral responsibility. The "Children's Fund", as it was called, would diminish by $30 million the amount spent each year for approximately 85,000 state-funded abortions. If this financial curtailment became a reality, there would be an abortion retrenchment. The monies salvaged would have been tagged to assist handicapped children and treating premature babies (249). The end result is that living infants in need of medicosurgical treatment will be deprived of remedial care as many more thousands of unborn healthy babies will be destroyed recklessly.

In Congress, a Representative from Michigan has introduced legislation that would require doctors to inform patients that fetuses suffer pain during abortions. The bill would not compel physicians to use anesthesia or restrict access to abortion. "An unborn child experiences organic pain perhaps as early as eight weeks after conception and definitely from thirteen-and-a-half weeks after conception, according to the proposed congressional bill" (22).

"The Catholic Bishops of the United States have endorsed the passage of a constitutional amendment as a necessary step providing legal protection for the unborn because of the Supreme Court decision of 1973. Sincere public officials may disagree with this effort, but the onus falls upon them to find other ways of protecting the unborn. The experience of the past years has not demonstrated that any less difficult program will succeed in overcoming the abortion trauma to our nation" (129).

"Many of our citizens who oppose the suggested amendment take the position that 'I am personally opposed to abortion, but I must not impose my beliefs on others'. Catholic doctrine does not admit this latter exclusion, because abortion is, in fact, a justice issue, and all citizens in a democratic society are obliged to use the democratic process to work for justice for all. The Catholic Church upholds the rights of the unborn, not as sectarian doctrine, but as a right essential for the good of secular society itself" (129).

"However, some legislators are convinced that legislation restricting abortion is too difficult to apply effectively. The Vatican declaration on abortion (1974) considered this claim and found it inconclusive. But whether the law finds abortion difficult to restrict or not, the declaration went on to add a further analysis extremely relevant to the abortion controversy in the United States" (129).

"Whatever the civil law may decree on this matter, it must be taken as absolutely certain that a man/woman may never obey an intrinsically unjust law, such as a law approving abortion on principle. An individual may not take part in any movement to sway public opinion in favor of such a law, nor may he/she vote for that law. He/she cannot take part in applying that law" (146).

"The above statement highlights the most fundamental responsibility of citizens and legislators who are personally convinced that abortion is morally and socially wrong. A personal moral conviction precludes endorsing what is morally wrong in legislation, such as appropriations bills which pay for abortions. To approve public funding is to cooperate directly with the doing of abortion. It is simply illogical to see abortion as a real social evil, while being willing to expend funds for its practice" (129).

What has been written above is a concinnity with the dogma that the faculties and powers of men and women must be used according to the purpose for which they were intended by nature and in the manner evidently prescribed in accordance with nature's biological functions. "If any human act is wrong ethically, one is not only obliged to refrain from it, but he/she is also obliged to refrain from formal cooperation with another in the performance of that act. Evil may never be done that good may result from it. The end does not justify the means" (4).

"Attempts to silence the clergy on matters political or to silence politicians on matters religious are contrary to the spirit of the First Amendment of the United States Constitution. Such efforts to separate religion from politics represent a confused understanding. At the same time, politicians' attempts to conduct affairs of state as if they were an extension of a particular religion" must be avoided (147).

A distinction is to be made "between religion and politics as spheres of belief and action on the one hand, and religion and politics as sources of power and authority on the other hand. When viewed as spheres of belief and action, religion and politics need not be separated. When religion and politics are sources of power and authority, a different picture emerges. Neither may become an arm of the other" (147).

Because politicians have passed laws that involve the moral fiber of social personal decisions, religious tenets were inadvertently (without premeditation) insinuated into the legislative machinery. Statutory law is binding upon all citizens as individuals or as neighbors. Love of neighbor is an intricate part of religious dogma. By serendipity or without design, political involvement has become a newer, modern, pseudo-religion in action.

A medical journal contained a dissertation on abortion in which the author wrote: "Let me say at once that Catholics and Orthodox Jews are entitled to their theological positions but have no right to legislate that view against the best interests of society"(72). By what figment of the imagination does abortion serve the best interests of society? Moreover, by what imaginative authority does this writer categorically and only within her private opinion deprive Roman Catholics and Orthodox Jews of their constitutional rights to freedom of speech? How can any American deprive another American of his/her right to this basic American freedom to speak for or against any public issue?

Since the United States of America is a republic, under this form of government, the majority has a right to rule if the majority legislates. Under a democracy, the majority opinion prevails and the will of the majority becomes the law of the land. In New York State, the Catholic and Jewish population approaches the majority of the people, certainly their combined number is a voice worthy of being heard. To write that this combined religious group speaks against the best interests of society is to propel a fiction (73).

Even as other religious congregations have a right to postulate their opinions on abortion, so too do the Orthodox, Conservative, or Liberal Jews. This was done by the Massachusetts Council of Rabbis, who issued an abortion statement. The president of this council declared the following to be their official statement regarding the question of abortion.

"Because of the recent statement issued by a coalition of various clergy, the Massachusetts Council of Rabbis feels impelled to advise that the Jewish clergymen in the coalition in no way represent the stand of traditional Judaism when they support the call for abortion on demand. It has been stated often that abortion on demand is a direct violation of the right to life and is considered a definite wrongdoing. Only the Almighty can make the decision between life and death of another human being even if it is an embryo. Anyone who would exercise the prerogative to do so as a human being is overstepping his or her bounds. Jewish law is quite clear on this matter. It is, therefore, wrong to state that Judaism allows abortion on demand to take place" (148).

## Single Issue Versus Multiple Issues

There are some religious authorities who assail the single-issue approach to attacking immorality. Others prefer a consistent, compact, totally encompassing advancement to solving or mitigating moral transgressions. An invitation has been made to the Roman Catholic authorities to "reject single-issue politics and adopt a 'consistent ethic' which includes an array of human-life issues" (149). "The policy of abortion on demand needs to be resisted and reversed. But this does not mean the nuclear war question can be ignored or relegated to a subordinate status . . . I am committed to teaching the total moral law against abortion. But I am also committed to the search for what is possible and most effective in the civil area. War and abortion are linked at the level of moral principle . . . I am convinced that the bishops and the Church as a whole must be equally engaged in both issues," said the Cardinal-Archbishop of

Chicago (149).

On the surface, it may appear that these words digress from the primary immorality of abortion. As one bishop stated: "We want to avoid the contest of saying one is more important than the other. We avoid that by taking a seamless-garment approach, repeating a phrase attributed to the Cardinal-Archbishop of Chicago who used the term 'seamless-garment' to emphasize the connection between, and the importance of, an array of social justice issues, including abortion and the arms race" (150).

The difference in thought is founded upon timing. *De facto*, the abortion issue is present *hic et nunc* (here and now). Therefore it should be given immediate primary attention. Let us be practical minded and adhere to the motto, "First things, first". Abortion is *in actu*, nuclear war is *in potentia*. Both are a national worry, each is equally dangerous, but most of our present energy should be directed to eliminating legal abortion if we would have a future population to fight against the proliferation of nuclear arsenals. A diversity of opinion on the precedence of abortion over nuclear weaponry or vice versa does not change the basic immorality of each issue. Rather, it is an attestation to the princely panoply of episcopal intellectual talent that is in America.

Nothing alters the primordial doctrine of the Roman Catholic Church on abortion as it has been decreed formally. It stands as an impregnable fortress against all assailants who would destroy unborn children. This ineradicable teaching is unalterable, cannot accept emendations, revisions, additions, or deletions. When a cause is right and just, it will endure and the diabolic gates of the inferno will not prevail against it. In God is our trust.

## Pornography and Abortion

Licentious art or literature that expresses or suggests obscenity in speaking, writing, theatre, or television is pornography. It has been said that pornography is harmless. A ruling by the United States Supreme Court has rendered a contrary decision. "The sum of experience, including that of the past two decades, affords an ample basis for legislatures to conclude that a sensitive, key relationship of human existence central to family life, community welfare, and the development of human personality, can be debased and distorted by crass commercial exploitation of sex" (151).

Some say, "You cannot legislate morality. On its face this cliche is absurd, because every law legislates morality. Every law sets some standard for its citizens, and every citizen must ultimately make the moral decision to obey or disobey laws. Others imply that they would rather see 'people make love than make violence'. There is no love in pornography. It is totally loveless, debasing women, children, and humanity generally. In addition, violence is inherent in most pornography" (152).

It has been a defense that if you do not like pornographic films and books, you do not have to see them or buy them: but do not interfere with the right of another person to see or to buy them. "The Supreme Court has said that what you do in the privacy of your own home is your own business. However, your privacy right does not extend to the market place. It is against the law for anyone to sell or exhibit obscenity to you" (152). (In this regard, the law is not being enforced.)

Another argument by those who accept pornography is, "Who are you to tell me what I can see or read? You are imposing your morality on me" (158). "Nobody can tell you what to see or to read, but the community can tell you what commercial spectacles and literature cannot be sold or distributed to you — if you choose to live in that community. The local community sets up standards for itself, and has a right to legislate to protect those standards" (152). A community does not have the legal power to restrict or allow the commercial, professional, and personal services you may receive. If any of these are immoral in themselves, the community is not banned from continuing the usage of their executive or legislative powers to eliminate them.

With or without a moral consideration as the initiating moving force, communities have a right under their laws to oppose pornography with an equivalent similar right to negate abortion. Public acceptance is the underlined necessity for the survival of pornography, even as public non-acceptance will be the death knell to the existing abortion laws.

What do pornography and abortion have in common? Very simply answered, they arouse a shared concern for public morality.

This responsibility has found its way into the halls of legislatures, and into the *sanctum sanctorum* of judicial jurisdictions. By their geometric growth, pornography and abortion have made hostile a large portion of the citizen population. The moral animosity to both has enlivened a confrontation on public policy as having a double standard. The protagonists of pornography do not accept it as being against public policy as they divest immorality from it, claiming it is a private matter. At the antipodes are the antagonists to abortion who make opposite claims as they are accused of forcing their personal morality on the general public.

"Most people believe as their forefathers did that moral values are permanent and absolute. Some believe that moral values are situational and circumstantial, meaning that objective moral measurement cannot be defined. The public policy implications of these disparate views are significant. Each view has a different agenda for political and social change in America. People who ascribe to these divergent belief systems are frequently in competition with one another — each attempting to affect public policy" (154).

"But over the last two decades, a double standard has materialized. Those who adhere to a philosophy revolving around situation ethics have repeatedly accused their rivals of attempting to impose their views on everyone else. This accusation is leveled at a time when the former have been busy removing the traditional moral signposts that once anchored the American society. For example, permitting pornography to obtrusively invade the public square is a testament to the triumph of situation ethics. Yet, those who believe in moral relativity have succeeded in, to use their phrase, 'imposing' their views on society" (154). This action they attribute to their adversaries.

"Now that the other side, those who believe in the efficacy of traditional moral values, is on the rebound and is trying to restore the moral signposts that once stood tall in our country, they are being accused of trying to impose their ideas. How disingenuous! In point of fact, in our democracy, public policy is not imposed. Legitimate legislative channels are used to attempt to enact the ideas one advocates. It is not a question of imposing ideas, it is a matter of whose ideas become public policy" (154). Thus laws can be legislated morality.

## Equal Rights Amendment And Abortion

"The hand that rocks the cradle rules the world" was an old adage that children learned in grammar school at the same age that they read the story of "Little Red Riding Hood". This is considered below the dignity of women in these last decades of the twentieth century. "A simplistic view of a woman's role in life is being fought on many fronts, most notably in the Equal Rights Amendment debate. Many women as well as men still feel that the proper and nature-intended place of women in society is that expressed by the 19th century American clergyman, Charles A. Stoddard. 'There can be no higher ambition for a Christian woman than to be a faithful wife and a happy and influential mother. It is the place which God has given woman, and she who fills it well is as honorable and honored as the most illustrious man can be'" (155).

"In primitive cultures, the undisputed major biological role of women in reproduction precluded them from much active participation in hunting or war. In some parts of the world, primitive conditions still exist almost unchanged. In most underdeveloped countries, children are still considered the parents' old age 'social security'. The average woman there is kept busy reproducing" (155). "In the United States and other developed countries, women are being more and more freed from their biological role of reproduction. Ever-decreasing childhood and infant death rate insures that the vast majority of children born will survive to adulthood. Social security is now seen as more of a role for society as a whole rather than one's progeny. The worldwide population explosion has more than adequately guaranteed continuity of the species . . . Many women therefore do not see the need to reproduce and few women desire more than two or three children. These phenomena are among the major reasons for the current 'women's lib' movement" (155).

The ERA momentum conjures up from past memorabilia present reactivation of factual reality that women have current sociojuridical protective rights. Some of these pertain to economic careers. As an example, a pregnant working woman has certain job privileges. With reliance on the statistical fact that women compose 45 percent of the workforce, the physiological event of conception in the employed future mother has been protected.

Prior to 1978, it was not illegal to discriminate against working pregnant women. In that year, Congress amended Title VII of the Civil Rights Act. "Under the amendment, a pregnant woman cannot be refused employment or be fired because of her gravid condition. Neither can she be forced to go on leave at an arbitrary point during the pregnancy nor be penalized if she returns to work after the baby is born" (250).

Employers do not have to pay health insurance benefits for abortions except where the life of the mother would be endangered or where medical complications have resulted from an abortion. On the other hand, employers cannot fire or refuse to hire a woman simply because she has had an abortion. In addition to federal laws, many states have passed legislative measures that bestow upon pregnant workers entitled benefits under temporary-disability-insurance laws or via special sections of fair-employment or labor codes or court decisions (250). As a general statement, the law does not require an employer to provide a specific number of weeks for maternity leave or to treat pregnant workers in a way different from other employees in hiring or promotion practices. In the manner of granting fringe benefits, an employer has to treat pregnant women in the same way that other workers with similar abilities or inabilities are treated (250).

An historical fact is that the Equal Rights Amendment was proposed to Congress back in 1923. Although women were allowed to vote in the Wyoming Territory in 1869, it was not until 1920 that universal suffrage for women was permitted by the 19th Amendment to the Constitution. The proposed 27th Amendment to the Constitution is quoted in part. "Equality of rights under the law shall not be denied or abridged by the United States or by a state on account of sex; the Congress shall have the power to enforce, by appropriate legislation, the provisions of this article. This amendment shall take effect two years after the date of ratification" (155). Passed by Congress in March 1972, the amendment requires passage by 38 of the states for it to become the law of the land.

As a revelation to many women, the ancient Etruscan culture

respected their ladies, elevating them to a dignity equal to that of men. This was accomplished without any dictum, or law reminiscent of an equal rights amendment. Respect for women was via the old-fashioned way; they earned it.

"Most telling of all is the position of women in ancient Etruscan society. Not even the most romantic of these women have claimed that they were early feminists, but their position of freedom and equality was a source of shock and scandal to both the Greeks and the Romans of their day. Lydians and Lycians traced their lineage through both male and female lines — and so did the Etruscans. Women of this civilization had their own names (not merely feminized versions of their fathers' family names, as with the Romans). They could own personal possessions and are seen in tomb paintings partying with the men on reclining couches, and at elaborate dinner parties. They turn up, light, languorous, wearing flowing garments, and elegant gold jewelry. Some are depicted playing at games, dancing, even attending athletic events with their men. Such behavior got them a very bad press at the time, but admiring respect from later generations. Most of the upper-class women had handsome bronze mirrors engraved with Greek mythological figures or Etruscan gods, often inscribed, showing that indeed some Etruscan women were taught to read" (156). In the antiquated *campo santo* in Volterra, Italy, can be seen a carved patrician husband and wife vis-a-vis sharing a sarcophagus cover that reflects the honored role of women in Etruscan society.

Current years have witnessed critical outbursts for equal rights for women that picture them as helpless minions at the mercy of conniving men. This may have been true thirty years ago, but certainly cannot be entertained today. Parenthetically, a study on venereal disease clearly indicates that the so-called weaker sex is far from being weak.

"The increasing rate of venereal disease is due in part to an outgrowth of the women's liberation philosophy that contends women should be as aggressive sexually as men," according to the director of the venereal disease control program of the Nassau County Department of Health (157). "The woman today is the aggressor. She believes she is just as much entitled (to sex) as the male. Years ago it was considered quite a feat to get a girl to submit (to sexual advances). The male was happy as a peacock when he was able to accomplish that act. But today it is the other way around in many, many cases. And this is what we call the sexual revolution. The girls do not want to be considered the sex object, but the subject. They come in here and brag about breaking a man in. This new 'liberation' has compounded the problem of venereal disease because many women are carriers without even knowing it" (158).

Returning to the Equal Rights Amendment, the question has arisen as to whether or not ERA and abortion are separate issues. Many voters who would otherwise support an equal rights amendment fear that it could be used to undermine laws to restrict public funding for abortion. Some experiences prove that these fears are well founded.

Equal Righters have another kernel for thought that is difficult to ingest and probably is indigestible for many. Do-gooders have found an additional cause for advocation. Free elective abortions in prison have their defenders. On May 16, 1988, the United States Supreme Court did not disturb the dictum that pregnant women incarcerated for criminal activity "have a constitutional right to elective, non-therapeutic abortions funded by the government if the inmates cannot afford them" (299). This New Jersey appeal was denied sustaining a decision handed down in November 1987 by the Third United States Circuit Court of Appeals in Philadelphia. "The ruling struck down a Monmouth County (New Jersey) policy that required women prisoners to pay for their own abortions. The decision was binding on all local, state, and federal prisons in New Jersey, Delaware, and Pennsylvania" (299). It was rendered in the matter of "Jane Doe", a 29-year-old inmate at a Monmouth County, New Jersey prison. She requested an abortion at the county expense because she could not cope with pregnancy and her drug abuse.

"Since the 1973 decision legalizing abortion, the United States Supreme Court has ruled that the federal and state governments do not have to pay for even medically necessary abortions sought by women on welfare. However, women in prison were considered to be in a special class because the high court has said the Eighth Amendment to the Constitution, prohibiting cruel and unusual punishment, requires that adequate medical care be provided for prisoners" (299).

From a medical viewpoint, it seems that the courts lack the scientific acumen in some decision-making. To be cognizantly redundant, it is reiterated that pregnancy is not a disease. Gravidity is a normal physiological state that is monitored by the physician so that the pregnancy may reach its normal destination. To intimate that adequate medical care (abortion) for a pregnant prisoner equates with prenatal care (that monitors the progress of the mother and the child) is to postulate an inaccuracy.

"Minutes after the 98th Congress convened for the first time on January 25, 1983, House Speaker Thomas P. O'Neill, Jr. announced to the assembled House that he was designating the proposed equal rights amendment (ERA) as House Joint Resolution No. 1. The Speaker thereby emphasized that ERA was a major legislative priority for that session. The conventional political wisdom was that it would pass easily through the Democrat-controlled House but might run into trouble in the Republican-controlled Senate. It did not work out that way. Instead, when ERA came to the House floor on November 15, 1983, it was defeated" (159).

The *National Catholic Reporter* subsequently published an analysis that began with a simple and accurate summary of what had occurred. "The abortion issue killed the equal rights amendment in a bitterly divided House of Representatives on November 15, 1983. (The operative language of ERA, however brief, is specific.) We believe that this proposal, unless revised, would invalidate restrictions on public funding of abortion, jeopardize the conscience rights of those who choose not to participate or cooperate in abortion and diminish prospects for a reversal of the 1973 Supreme Court decision that legalized abortion on demand. Such judgments are sharply disputed by many ERA proponents, who contend that ERA and abortion are unrelated" (159).

That position was defended at length by Catholics Active For ERA (160). "During the 1983 Congressional session, speakers for pro-ERA organizations have suggested publicly that the purported ERA/abortion connection is a sham issue, raised by enemies of women's rights who are eager to defeat ERA. Following its rejection by the House, a member of Catholics Active for ERA was quoted in the *National Catholic Reporter* as saying that ERA would not affect the abortion law. She said that an amendment to ERA proposed by prolife groups to render ERA neutral with respect to abortion laws was one of several 'dishonest amendments proposed by people who want to kill the ERA'. The Equal Rights Coalition of Utah said: 'This attempt (to link the ERA to abortion) is part of the disreputable propaganda technique known as the big lie'" (159).

"In stark contrast, many ERA proponents believe that abortion and ERA are related issues. Attorneys with the American Civil Liberties Union (A.C.L.U.) and other prochoice groups have attacked laws restricting abortion funding in several states, arguing that such laws violate state equal rights amendments" (159).

The first court in the nation to address the issue accepted the argument on restricting funding for abortion. A decision was rendered by the Commonwealth Court of Pennsylvania, the court immediately below the Supreme Court, which will have a significant effect on prospects for enactment of the Federal ERA (159). Judge John MacPhail held that state laws limiting Medicaid funding of abortion to cases of rape, incest, or life endangerment to the mother were invalid under the state ERA (161).

"In considering the possible impact of ERA on the abortion laws, it is important to keep in mind the prevalence of a proabortion mindset in the Federal Courts. As recently as June 1983, the United States Supreme Court invalidated a law requiring a 24-hour waiting period prior to an elective abortion and other minor forms of abortion regulation. Generally, the lower Federal Courts have been even more hostile to any impediment to abortion. These courts will not take lightly arguments such as those made by the A.C.L.U. The ERA's clearest impact would be in the area of abortion funding. Currently, the Hyde Amendment prohibits Federal Medicaid funding of abortion except when the mother's life is endangered. About 30 states substantially restrict similar funding. An extraordinary level of political consensus is required for any constitutional amendment to become law. It is evident that no such political consensus will exist regarding ERA so long as it is linked with abortion (159).

## The 1984/1988 National Elections

Some public officials become political gypsies whose thought processes and opinions are swayed by an attempt to please the electorate by being all things to all people in order to retain political popularity. This was manifested to the ultimate during the 1984 presidential campaign. One may intimate that so-called Catholic politicians in America are abandoning the Aristotelian philosophy and the Platonic orientation as promulgated by St. Thomas Acquinas and are adopting the pragmatism of Immanuel Kant. "The debate over the appropriate role of religion in politics is befogged by a crucial misunderstanding about the nature of abortion, which is in essence a matter of public and not merely private morality. Several Catholic politicians maintain that they personally oppose most abortions but that they do not want to impose their morality upon others by law. They believe abortion should be legal and that abortions for the poor should be funded publicly. They criticize the Roman Catholic bishops' view that it is 'not logically tenable' to separate 'personal morality and public policy'. Yet, the proper dichotomy is not, as some contend, between law and morality: most laws are grounded in moral concepts. Instead, it is between moral principles that relate to the individual conduct of one's own life, with which the law should not deal, and moral principles that relate to actions that may cause harm to others" (162).

The senior Senator from Massachusetts came close to articulating this point when, on September 10, 1984, he addressed himself to disputed contemporary questions of religion and politics.

"He held that 'religion has no right to harness Government to impose a single view in areas where Government should not intervene at all. Where decisions are inherently individual', the Senator continued, 'or in cases where we are deeply divided about whether they are, people of faith should not invoke the power of the state to decide what everyone can believe or think or read or do.' He cited abortion, prayer, prohibition, and sexual identity as examples (163).

"First, it should be noted that the examples Senator Kennedy gives are quite diverse and need both separate and careful examination. Secondly, those who seek public action on one or other of these issues do not base them on religious tenets but on rational considerations open to the examination of all. These issues are human rights issues.

"That religiously affiliated persons, for example, oppose apartheid in South Africa does not mean that the effort to end apartheid is based exclusively on a religious tenet or that it cannot be considered apart from religious convictions. Thirdly, no one is asking the Government to tell people what they may believe or think or read. Laws can and do, however, prescribe or proscribe certain actions. This is a legitimate function of law.

"Should a person be allowed to keep a slave? To have several spouses? May a person drive while intoxicated? May parents sexually abuse their children? Should the law protect homosexual practices? Should government finance abortions or even approve this killing of the unborn?

"Like the Senator's examples somewhat vaguely expressed, each of these examples, too, would need separate and careful examination. The law has already taken a stance on some. With respect to others, it is true that citizens debate, sometimes very heatedly, positions the law should take. But all these actions are inherently individual actions, which nonetheless affect others. Is the Senator implying that those who choose and effect an abortion do not affect someone, the unborn child, other than those who willingly participate in the act?

"To hold that citizens, whether affiliated religiously or not, must forego seeking enactment of particular laws by the democratic process because society may be divided over the relevant issues is to negate personal integrity and the democratic process itself. Should those who seek 'gay rights' legislation cease doing so because society is in disagreement over this issue? We could never have eliminated slavery or segregation and its ramifications in this country if we adopted Senator Kennedy's view about societal conflict. Those seeking to eliminate apartheid in South Africa or untouchability in India would have to cease their efforts forthwith.

"Religious activism, according to the Senator, is acceptable on the issue of nuclear arms because this, he says, is an inherently public issue', whereas similar efforts to limit the slaying of the unborn are unacceptable because abortion is an inherently private and personal matter. Abortion, rather, is the killing of an innocent and defenseless human being.

"It is entirely evident that the law does command or forbid certain individual actions on the basis of whether they injure the rights of others or are needed to promote the common good. It would not be possible to forbid polygamy or child abuse, or to command needed blood transfusions for children whose parents refuse, unless this was so. Why is the action of killing an unborn child exempted from this category?

"There is, indeed, a difference between private morality and public morality, between the rule of Government and the role of individual rights. With Senator Kennedy we agree that 'not every moral command should be written into law'. But our law should not, for example, approve killing of the innocent unborn child or finance his/her slaughter. This is a gross violation of individual human rights.

"The Senator needs to put his thinking cap back on and write a new speech that accurately identifies and distinguishes the real issues at stake in contemporary arguments over religion and politics. The idea that Government must refrain from protecting the lives of innocent unborn children on pain of imposing a single view on society is absurd. Protecting the inviolable rights of innocent human beings is Government's most basic duty" (163).

Politicians do not appear to grasp the true nature of the human fetus as being an unborn child made to the image and likeness of an adult. "If the fetus is not yet a human person, abortion does not affect others, and religious and other moral leaders should not ask the law to interfere. However, if the fetus is a human person, then an abortion causes harm to someone other than the mother, and abortion is a matter of public morality — one about which laws may properly be advocated by religious leaders. Since the status of the fetus is the very matter most in dispute, it begs the question to rule religious leaders out of the debate on the ground that they are illicitly advocating private morality in the public sphere. In their view, they are not asking the state to impose private morality but to protect the rights of others" (62).

There are persons in high political office and others who "seem to anticipate this point, but they also make a larger claim: that when we are deeply divided about whether an issue is one of public or private morality, the state should intervene. But the notion that division of opinion should end rather than foster debate is an unfortunate one. For decades, we were deeply divided about whether race prejudice was a private matter, and for years the argument against civil rights laws was that Government cannot legislate morality" (162).

In reply to that misbelief, Dr. Martin Luther King, Jr. "used to point out that the law cannot make one love one's neighbors but it can — and should — keep one from lynching them.

He did not hesitate to invoke the Bible in support of his position. As Dr. King well knew, the mere existence of disagreement cannot justify politicians, religious leaders, or anyone else in tolerating injustice — still less in assisting it" (162).

In a letter to the editor of a Catholic newspaper, a reader wrote: "The changing of the political system (or a politician) will not bring one single person closer to God" (164). This statement is false. An example to contradict the letter writer is the change of heart of our president on the abortion laws. When as Governor of California he was proabortion, now he is a prolifer. Not only is he a guardian of the right to life, his actions justify his position.

A second letter to the editor of the same newspaper praises the President thusly:

"In the first place, saying can be a form of doing. The very fact that the President spoke about the provoking issue of fetal pain during abortion before the National Religious Broadcasters in January 1984 focused national attention on the humanity and suffering of the unborn. Second, he applied the Hyde Amendment to the Indian Health Service by regulation to stop federal funding of abortions of Native American children. Third, he supported the Office of Personnel Management's denial of abortion coverage under Federal employees' health plans. Fourth, he held a widely attended Conference on Alternatives to Abortion on May 3, 1984 at the White House to draw attention to model organizations which help unwed mothers. And so on.

"Last, and perhaps most moving of all, was the appearance of the

President's scholarly article, "Abortion and the Conscience of the Nation", in the Spring 1983 Human Life Review. The article has grown in prominence and is now available in book form with additional essays by the U.S. Surgeon General and the English writer Malcolm Muggeridge. The President's renowned skill as a communicator should not be undervalued here. During a silent holocaust, our constant testimony on behalf of the least of our brothers may be the factor that will gain us a national consensus to end this national tragedy" (165).

As a continuum of the President's stand in prolife disputes, in July 1984, his restrictions on foreign aid for abortion programs led to disagreements. "As representatives from 149 countries gathered in Mexico City for the United Nations International Conference on Population, the Reagan Administration formally announced its intention to impose tighter restrictions on United States aid to population control programs abroad. While the United States would continue its support for voluntary family planning, it would no longer contribute to private organizations that perform or actively promote abortions" (166).

## Dichotomy In Politics

When, in 1984, the Governor of New York spoke at Notre Dame University, in which he discussed religion and politics, there was a wide variety of reactions to his opinion (126). Some disagreed with his views, others praised him. One commentator called it "an American Catholic classic" (168). Several statements made by the Governor were challenged. Among these was the Governor's warning that "abortions would divide America because a majority of the public, including Catholics, wants them kept legal" (168).

On October 3, 1984, the Governor of New York addressed a public forum at St. Francis College, Brooklyn Heights, New York as a continuation of his theme. The title was: "Religion and Politics - A Personal Reflection". He took "the occasion to clarify some points" he had made earlier at Notre Dame University regarding religion and politics . . . He asserted that in a pleuralistic democratic society it is consensus which gives certain ideas or values the force of law. Mere popularity, however, does not guarantee that the view held is a correct or good one, and consensus alone need not go unchallenged.

To challenge the current consensus on abortion, the Governor declared that: 'Those of us who believe abortion to be wrong and wish to convince the rest of the public must first demonstrate the validity of our position'. This technique is better than merely loudly demanding that others accept it. He went further by stating that abortion is not merely a Catholic or even a religious matter. It is a human one. Even a radically secular world must struggle with the question of when life begins, under what circumstances it can be ended, when it must be protected, and by what authority" (168). The Governor on that occasion did not repeat his often quoted dictum: "I am personally opposed to abortion, but I will not impose my personal views on others" (175). As evaluated in 1989, all governmental executives should know that practical experience, biblical to modern history, particularized cogitation declare that when left to multitudinous, variable human consciences, moral norms are not decided by consensus.

Citing the Cardinal-Archbishop of Chicago, and the National Conference of Catholic Bishops, the Governor concurred that those who demonstrate a concern for fetal life should also be concerned with "the whole spectrum of life issues" (168). To examine these multiple social problems, the Governor announced the formation of a non-partisan "Task Force on Life and the Law" which will strive to answer the question: "What can a society that professes a profound respect for life do to realize its ideals?" (168).

The proposal to establish a task force under the State Health Commission to study medicolegal situations within the perimeter of current professional ethical standards is laudable. However, it does not alter the hubris attached to abortion. Thus, the Governor's plan for a state task force "on end-of-life and beginning-of-life issues has drawn Catholic response ranging from cautiously optimistic to warmly positive" (169).

The associate publisher of the *Brooklyn Tablet* applauded the Governor's recommendation with the following words: "It is only through this kind of study, analysis, and dialogue that people can arrive at a consensus for a change of legislation" (170).

"A more cautious assessment of the Governor's proposal came from the Pope John XXIII Medical-Moral Research and Education

Center in St. Louis. 'I do not think we ought to condemn such an idea, but it is fraught with a number of questions. There is no doubt that these issues need to be taken up publicly. But I would not laud a panel just for its broad representation of opinion. It would depend on what they concluded'" (170).

The formation of a state task force to discuss (prayerfully to solve) multiple medicolegal ethical problems does not and cannot dilute the concentrated immorality of abortions. It remains still the quantitatively ponderous, public, primordial moral impropriety practiced in the United States during this century. Millions of human beings have been destroyed via the horrendous, infamous act of abortion. Death from all the other moral subjects to be discussed by the state task force, when taken collectively, are infinitesimal by comparison. Any digressive, political tactic, however altruistic, is an ineffectual void in an attempt to detract from, mitigate the gravity of, or sidetrack the heinous moral offensiveness of slaughtering innocent human beings before their birth.

The disputations on abortion became so prominently publicized in the 1984/1988 presidential campaigns that many people on both sides of the controversy believe that it will not evaporate. "Members of the 'right-to-life' movement have been comparing the issue to slavery in the last century and to racial discrimination in the South prior to the enactment of Federal civil rights laws in the 1960s. Their opponents compare it to the drive earlier in this century that led to the addition of the Prohibition Amendment to the Constitution, which after a period of strife had to be repealed. Whatever the comparisons, they contain forebodings of social division" (171).

"In the past, most seekers and holders of public office have tried to avoid the abortion debate as a difficult and sensitive one that could be politically damaging no matter what position they took. In the years since the Supreme Court overturned state laws against abortion in the landmark decision of Roe v. Wade, the issue was only a marginal concern in presidential campaigns. In 1984/1988 it was at the center of the controversy over religion in politics. The question was argued at length in the presidential and vice-presidential debates" (171).

The 1984/1988 Democratic nominees stated that abortion is a

private matter and they do not want the Federal government intruding in the private lives of citizens (171). The 1984 vice-presidential candidate of the Democrats said "that as a 'devout Catholic' she has fully accepted her church's position on the issues for herself, but as a public official could not impose it on others" (171).

She also stated: "I do not believe in abortion. I am opposed to abortion as a Catholic. I also feel very, very strongly about the separation of church and state" (172). Her attitudinal utterances have strengthened the antiabortion crusade that has defeated candidates at various levels of government (171). From episcopal hustings and the hierarchy's podium, the abortion dispute has been elevated above other social concerns. "The morality of abortion is now a truly national issue" (171).

President Ronald Reagan's overwhelming re-election victory and the plurality election of President George Bush sharply raise the question, "Whatever happened to the Democratic Party?" Critical observation suggests some answers (13). Among these are:

"First, many analysts point out that the Democratic Party has become fiercely protective of particular interests, like feminists' rights, public school teachers, homosexuals, and organized labor. Consequently, it has failed to be assertive about national interests; and,

"Secondly, some analysts observe that the Democratic Party harbors contempt for such traditional values as family, matters Christian, and moral values" (173).

"Catering to the demands of feminist interest groups, the Democratic Party has become the Proabortion Party. It not only gives full approval to the killing of unborn children, but demands that unrestricted killing be funded by American taxpayers. Catering to the demands of the National Education Association and the AFL-CIO, the Democratic Party penalizes Christian and Jewish parents who want their children to receive an education with religious and moral values by denying them education tax funds. Supporting abortion-on-demand and denying parents' rights in the education of their children are attacks on the family — the most important and most fundamental institution in our American society" (173). "Democrats have grown uncomfortable lately in the presence of traditional values like flag (patriotism) and family, while the Republicans have cornered the exclusive franchise to the issue of flag and family" (174).

## Justification Of Political Position

Catholic politicians cannot attempt to justify their positions against Catholic dogma and remain Catholics. Without an adherence to Catholic teachings, they remain politicians, but cannot be called Catholics. You are either with the Catholic Church or you are against it. The justification of a moral position or social stand by a Catholic is only in accordance with the teachings of the Roman Catholic Church. In the drama of justification, a united purpose leading to goodness, morality, and virtue is the roadway to divine grace for Catholic politicians.

Thus, it is not logically tenable for politicians to draw a dichotomy between the personal morality and public policy. "This position would be as unacceptable as would be the approach of a candidate or office-holder who pointed to his or her personal commitments as qualification for public office, without proposing to take proper steps to translate these into policies and practical programs. With regard to many issues, of course, there is room for sincere disagreement by Catholics and others who share their moral convictions over how moral principles should be applied to the current facts in the public policy debate. But with regard to the immorality of the direct taking of innocent human life (e.g., by abortion or by direct attacks on noncombatants in war), these views are not simply policy statements of a particular Catholic organization as the United States Catholic Conference. They are a direct affirmation of the constant moral teaching of the Roman Catholic Church, enunciated repeatedly over the centuries, as in our day, by the highest teaching authority of the Roman Catholic Church" (176).

The pronounced Catholic teaching on abortion may be attacked hubristically in private or politely from the public lectern. No persiflage or pseudoscientific discourse will alter this teaching of the Catholic Church. No one is prepared "to say that a moral issue or decision ought to remain private, rather it should be the beginning and not the end of moral discourse" (177).

"No church or religious group should insist that its morality be translated into civil law, if the issue is one of private morality. But abortion touches the public order as an issue of human rights and demands restrictive action by the state ... Politicians who personally oppose abortion but refuse to press for a legal ban are morally inconsistent" (109).

"The protection of human rights, including the right to life of the unborn child, is such an issue (touches the public order). In this matter, there is no dichotomy in reality and there should be none in the practice either of individuals or society, between the public and private stance of persons and their public responsibilities or between private and public morality" (9).

Addressing a direct question to nominal Catholic politicians, did you forget the words of Christ who said: "Go forth and teach all nations what I have taught you". Have they forgotten that the Catholic Church is one, holy, universal and apostolic, or do they eliminate the word apostolic? Has their fading memory forgotten the great missionaries of the past, or have they erased from church history the Society For The Propagation Of The Faith? It appears that some politicians are one-sided Catholics or have an incomplete knowledge of the Catholic faith and/or Catholic teachings.

Pope John Paul II in Rome at the general audience on January 9, 1985, continued his reflections on the role of catechesis in the Church. On that occasion, he said: "We have recalled how catechesis is a work of the Church that spreads the Good News throughout the world and seeks to deepen its sacramental life through a better knowledge of the mystery of Christ. Through catechesis, as through the overall work of evangelization, the Church is aware of responding to man's most essential problems, those which each one has already asked or will ask sooner or later in the course of his life. Where does man come from? Why does he exist? What are his relationships to God and with the invisible world? How must he behave in order to achieve his life's goal? Why is he subject to suffering and death, and what is his hope?" (178).

Now that the tumult and shouting of the 1984/1988 presidential election campaigns have subsided, it is fitting to evaluate in general the Catholic politician. Past experience has demonstrated clearly that the majority of Catholics elected to public office have an abundance of political rhetoric and a paucity of Catholic deeds.  It seems that election to public office achieves a quantitative acceptable increment in personal aggrandizement, often at the expense of moral depreciation.

It is strange to relate that some Roman Catholics in public office forget their religious heritage.  In the face of probable voter opposition, the Catholic politician embarks upon a policy of retrenchment or strategic withdrawal from those beliefs and teachings that should be accepted by devout Roman Catholic persons.  Contrariwise, a black politician elected to public office does not oppose anti-discrimination laws.  Similarly, a Jewish politician does not and is not expected to be negativistic toward Israel.  Catholic men and women are the only social group who feel that complete political acceptance is denied to them unless they suppress their professed religious convictions.

Unfortunate as it may be, Catholic political fortunes in the United States of America rise and fall with the abortion issue.  The liberal abortion movement is the solitary, most perilous evil confronting American society.  It is a question to which the answer must be defined as to yes or no.  The person responding to the question is readily susceptible to measurement as to his or her position on this subject.  Thus, the abortion question is the astrolabe.  Via the Catholic politician's position, he/she is observed and tested as to the caliber of his/her Catholic adherence to the most poignant moral issue of this century.

The written record proves the startling fact that almost all the Catholic politicians who have risen to national governmental prominence are notoriously conspicuous by their support of legalized abortion.  An excuse is given for this attitude under the benevolent guise of political expediency.  Politicians repeat to the point of echolalia, "I am a devout Catholic.  Personally I am opposed to abortion, but I do not want to impose my morality on others."

This diandrous statement produces an ethical dichotomy.  Devotion to Roman Catholic doctrines does not allow an intellectual weakness in moral stamina or a crumbling ethical stability that leads to spiritual bankruptcy.  A political mentality that fears to hazard criticism, if support is given to the unborn child, seems to be attuned to opposing governmental financial aid to parochial schools as being indigenous to the concept of separation of church and state.

Paralleling the rise of Catholic politicians in the national arena, is a simultaneous fall in their personal religious strength. In the decades prior to 1960, as long as Catholic politicians believed there was no hope to elevate themselves to the presidency, they acted according to their religious conviction serving the interest of their constituencies. With the election of President Kennedy, Catholicism in the Catholic politician became submerged.

National political ambition dampened religious ardor. A self-imposed quietus on Roman Catholic tenets led credence to the voter's interpretation that some Catholic politicians do not take their religion as seriously as their political endeavors. Proof of this dictum, called neutral Catholicism, resides in their political acceptance of the abortion laws plus their avoidance of any positive interface discussion on tax aid to parochial schools. With the passage of time, other political controversies will be forthcoming that will test the Catholicity of people in high political office. Based upon past performance it will be sad to realize that many so-called Catholics in political life will be found wanting in their support of the written words, dogma, and rubric spirit of Roman Catholicism in America (179).

In 1984, "a major political party adopted as part of its platform a promise to nominate to the Federal bench (Supreme Court of the United States) only those individuals opposed to abortion. These developments threaten to create the impression that the Federal judiciary is a third and powerful political branch of government" (180). This quotation is from a former judge of the United States Court of Appeals for the Second Circuit, where he served from 1973 to 1980.

This same judge wrote: "At her 1981 confirmation hearings, Justice Sandra O'Connor handled the senatorial inquisition masterfully. Numerous senators attempted to extract her views in general and on the Supreme Court's benchmark decision in Roe v. Wade in particular. That decision, authored by Justice Blackmun, prohibited state interference, under certain circumstances with a woman's decision to have an abortion" (180).

Justice O'Connor "steadfastly refused to respond to the litany of abortion-related inquiries, believing them to be beyond the scope of permissive questioning at a confirmation hearing. Not only was the constitutional integrity of the Supreme Court preserved, but Justice O'Connor was confirmed by a vote of 99 to zero" (180).

Under the covenants of a political platform, a foundation can be fabricated that influences appointments to the highest court in our land. "The tempest that today swirls about the abortion issue might make it impossible for a Supreme Court nominee to repeat Justice O'Connor's feat. And it is feared that pronouncements on controversial issues made by a nominee at a Senate Judiciary Committee hearing would profoundly impair the public's respect for the Supreme Court as an impartial interpreter of the Constitution of the United States" (180). This same senatorial pattern was pursued by the Judiciary Committee hearings of Judge Antonin Scalia, Judge Robert Bork, and Judge Anthony Kennedy.

## Voting On Election Day

At times, it is difficult for human private virtue to overcome the compromising barrier erected by political expediency between personal ambition and the intransigency of irreconcilable dogmatic morality. Citizens can arrive at their own judgment on the character or reputation of people in public office or who seek it. By the power of their vote, they are heard when they select those whose philosophical outlook is compatible with their own. Therefore no one who has the franchise to vote should refrain from exercising this prerogative.

"The hallmark of a democratic nation is its ability to engage the voice of its people in a broad range of public decisions . It is necessary on the occasion of every election year to emphasize the importance of responsible voter political participation. In 1976 and in 1979, statements were issued calling for a 'committed informed citizenry to revitalize our political life'. We now reiterate that call and ask all citizens to ensure that our elections become the vital and popular forum they can and must be if our vote is to address democratically the crucial issues that face us in the years ahead" (181). Thus reads a statement of the United States Catholic Conference Administrative Board on Political Responsibility.

"The American voter's concern should be for a just, peaceful, and humane society, both in our country and throughout the world. Each citizen's personal participation in the democratic political process by speaking out for justice and by intelligent voting is the key to this goal . . . Voting for candidates who share our principles, our values and goals is the only way to realize them. Wishing will not make it so" (182). Active encouragement like President Bush's wish for a "kinder and gentler nation" is praiseworthy.

"All candidates, happily, support arms control (curb) and bilateral disarmament, though they differ on the important questions of the means most effective at present to achieve these goals. On abortion, unfortunately, some candidates differ not only on strategies to protect unborn human beings, but on whether or not some such human beings deserve any protection at all. When we vote, we ought to consider what effect can the candidate, if elected, have on implementing and achieving the principles, values, and goals judged best for our country?" (182).

Holy scripture teaches: "Their words are bold but their deeds are few . . . All their good works are performed for effect.... They love places of honor at banquets, marks of respect in public places. 'Listen to what they say but do not imitate them... They will tie together heavy burdens for other men to carry while scarcely lifting a finger themselves'. The fact that these words appear in the Gospel reading just before Election Day seems to be purely coincidental, but the coincidence is instructive. Clearly, public figures were subject to the same temptations in those days as our leaders are today" (183).

Modern politicians may or may not fit into the classification as described in holy writ. To insure that bad politicians do not succeed in public office, citizens must act by voting. Every single vote is valuable. "An important and consistent message of the Christophers' Movement is that one person can, and does, make a difference. Each of us has basic human dignity as a child of God; each of us makes a difference in family life and in society. As a free people, as citizens of the United States, we have in the electoral process a basic right, and an important moral and civic responsibility. Here, too, each of us makes a difference" (184).

"As citizens we are called to become informed, active, and

responsible participants in the political process. The Roman Catholic Church's part in the political order includes the following:

"1.    Education regarding the teachings of the Church and the responsibilities of the faithful;

"2.    Analysis of issues for their social and moral dimensions;

"3.    Measuring public policy against Gospel values;

"4.    Participating with other concerned parties in debate over public policy; and,

"5.    Speaking out with courage, skill, and concern on public issues involving human rights, social justice, and the life of the Church in society" (181).

On Election Day "we choose those who will serve us in the highest elected offices in our land, as well as members of Congress, the judiciary, representatives in our state legislature, and officials in local government. The candidates for these positions of public responsibility, trust, and service have something to say about their hopes for the positions which they seek, and of what they aspire to bring to public office. Voters are encouraged to be conversant with the issues, be they of national or local significance. Be informed about the candidates, and their positions on these issues, so that you may intelligently, and responsibly participate in the electoral process so important to us and to our form of government. You can make a difference — your vote makes a difference! Be sure to exercise this privilege and fulfill this important responsibility on Election Day" (184).

## Abortion Laws Invade Europe

The political expediency of legalized abortion has been manifested by its acceptance elsewhere. Successful passage of abortion laws in America and in other countries encouraged similar actions in Europe and continues to permeate occidental nations. The pervasiveness and spread of abortion like a conflagration is due in part to the claimed safety of American medicosurgical methods of inducing abortion and evacuating the uterus.

The practice of American medicine and surgery is the best in the world. As factual proof is the testimony that when American physicians work overseas, the medical care, and medical education rises rapidly. As applied to abortion, this same professional performance is repeated. The United States has the dubious distinction of being an early pioneer in elective abortion. But the technical excellence that liberates parents from infant responsibility is not indigenous to American medical superiority.

The abortion rates in several Eastern European nations are much higher than the rate in the United States. "There was one abortion for every three live births in the United States in 1975, compared to 8.5 abortions for every ten live births in Bulgaria. Abortion laws are being liberalized in several parts of the world except Hungary. Tighter laws in Hungary cut the abortion rate from more than eight per ten live births in 1970 to four per ten live births in 1977. Hong Kong and India reportedly have the lowest abortion rate, with only one abortion for every 1,000 women of childbearing age. The report from the United States Census Bureau noted that women under twenty had the highest abortion rate among developed nations in 1977. This high rate in the United States was 30.8 percent. Japan and Tunisia had the lowest rates, with 2 percent of women under twenty reporting abortions" (185).

The performance of an abortion under certain specific circumstances has become legal in Spain. As a concerted group, the Catholic Spanish bishops have warned their flocks that anyone cooperating "physically or morally" in the abortion process will be excommunicated. Beginning August 3, 1985, Spanish women can have legal abortions in cases of rape, malformed fetus, or danger to the life of the mother. Prior to that date, all abortions had been illegal in Spain, which historically and traditionally has a 99 percent Catholic population (251).

Formally educated physicians have been aware that directly induced abortion is not solely a disdainful procedure but an act infused with a variety of moral veils and social ostracisms. The Hippocratic oath included specific prohibitions that condemned feticide. These unquestionable words are: "I will not give to a woman a pessary to produce abortion..." (300).

Nonetheless physicians have faced demands by disaffected women for relief from unwanted pregnancies reciting personal excuses not medical reasons. During the 19th century in England (also in the United States of America) women decreased their fertility dramatically. One of the principal means was induced abortion. Medical authorities tended to oppose this practice for their own different reasons (288).

One of the advanced objections to abortion was an ardent patriotism that included pro-nationalism among physicians. They disfavored a diminishing middle-class population. As good bourgeoisie their hostility fulminated against the so-called wise women and the irregular, devious practitioners who helped women intent upon restoring their menses (288).

"In her book, *Abortion In England,* Barbara Brooks provides a history of the debates about induced abortion from the 19th century passage of criminal statutes specifically prohibiting the practice through the clarification and liberalization of the law in the 1960s. This monograph fits well with other (non-medical) works on fertility control and public policy in human reproduction" (289).

Brooks argues that the debate over abortion was controlled by lambastic professional elites who were more concerned with declining birth rates plus apparent threats to stabile family life than with the reproductive civil rights (of privacy) of individual women. "She believes that induced abortion, when performed by competent practitioners, was a relatively safe procedure by the early 20th century...She criticized social leaders for failing to understand that induced abortion was a traditional method of fertility control which was essential to the well-being of millions of women especially those in the working classes" (289).

"The movement to reform the law was led by middle-class feminists who sought to use official concern over maternal mortality as justification for legalizing the practice of abortion. The author is critical of liberal reformers for 'medicolegalizing' abortion (as she) stresses the loss of autonomy experienced by many women as traditional self-help practices were displaced by surgery" (289).

The above statement seems to contradict the maternal morbidity concern for legalizing abortion..."Self-help," what does it mean? If it means self-induced abortion, this is a source of infection that increases maternal morbidity and tempts mortality. "The weight of the literature on population control supports (the author's) contention that widely held social values were major factors in the evolution of medical attitudes toward abortion" in the United Kingdom (289). Maternal health, welfare, or well-being seem to be a myth in this specious discussion.

The major adversary to the rising tide of abortion is Catholic truth. It is the motivating force that can free the world from legalized abortion that chokes life before its first inhalation of oxygen. "Christian truth can bear the greatest fruits in life. No truth has the capacity to free us from sin the way Catholic truth frees" (186). This means a commitment to Christ's teachings and the upholding of the dogma of his Church. "To believe in Christ is to look for ways of living out that belief. We do not wish to confine our belief to the sanctuary and thus prevent it from influencing our entire lives. We also do not wish to neglect it and think that all that matters is the good actions that we perform. The Christian life is a tension. While we have committed ourselves to Christ, how that commitment affects our daily lives keeps changing because our lives keep changing. Christian living is not easy. But upon comparison, it does make other styles of living seem relatively superficial and unattractive" (186).

CHAPTER SEVEN

# SEPARATION OF CHURCH
# FROM STATE

*"One nation under God with liberty and justice for all."*
*Pledge of Allegiance to United States*

Emotional upheavals initiated by disputes on the separation of religion from the state are secondary only to those sensitive arousals induced by the debates on abortion. The simple display of a cross or Star of David on public property instigates a lawsuit — often with churlishness. The sorrow is that oftentimes the crescent animosity grows surreptitiously to only a hairbreadth away from truculence.

"If there is a difference between what is ethically good and what is ethically evil, there must be a reason for the difference and the reason ought to be discoverable. The writers of our Declaration of Independence believed that certain facts concerning mankind, his rights, his duties, and his destiny could be known with certainty. They said: 'We hold these truths to be self-evident: That all men are created equal; that they are endowed by their Creator with certain unalienable rights; that among these are life, liberty, and the pursuit of happiness'. If such facts were discoverable by reason in 1776, they are discoverable today. Therefore, men and women by the exercise of their reason can know what is right and why it is right" (4).

Our colonial founders escaped from European oppression under the guise that they did not conform to state religion. It was the loss of religious freedom that they did not want in their new found homes. Although that was their purpose, our forefathers and their families were neither agnostics nor atheists.

Apropos of the theme on the separation of church and state, to understand it without prejudice or bias we should surrogate ourselves in the place of the colonists. What was their intention in the constitutional recording of the separation of church from the state? With the historical back-ground as was known in their century and the years before it, the governmental concept was that the reigning monarch had the divine right of kings. Some royal heads of state believed they had godly powers, even to the performance of miracles. The astute Dr. Samuel Johnson had scrofula, which he thought would be cured if he could be touched by the King of England. Monarchs did not discourage this credo. Rather, they encouraged it as the head of the nation's state religion. Thus, the royal personage had a dual authority — one temporal and the other spiritual.

The new world was pervaded by the Puritans with their ideas on religion and government being persuasive. In two areas, their force and influence on colonization was manifested. These were Virginia and New England. History records that the attempt to found a settlement on the Kennebec River in 1607 failed. Later, Captain John Smith was sent to explore this land after his return to Virginia from England. In 1614, he mapped the coast from Cape Cod to Nova Scotia. He gave the region the name "New England", but no settlers came to inhabit the territory.

In the meantime on the British Isles, the policy of James I was sowing the seeds which later ripened under his son. "His conceptions of the powers and responsibilities of a king embraced secular and religious questions alike. There were growing up in England little congregations which refused to be bound by the usages and doctrines of the established Church of England. Under Queen Elizabeth, they had been treated with severity which was much increased under James I. The ministers were driven from their churches, and both ministers and leading church-goers were imprisoned. As a result, many made their way to Holland, where alone in Europe religious tolerance existed" (187).

Life in Holland was unsatisfactory in many ways, and the leaders determined to seek a home in Virginia. A grant of land was obtained from the London Company, and capital was secured from some London merchants. Both the company and the merchants extracted severe financial demands from the emigrants. "It was a hard bargain, but the would-be colonists had no choice, for they were poor and friendless. Leaving Delfthaven in 1620 in the 'Speedwell', they joined some friends who had embarked on the 'Mayflower' at Southhampton" (187).

Both ships had for their destination the colony of Virginia. However, the "Speedwell" had to return to port. The little Mayflower, with 100 passengers, was blown off its course, finally drop-ping anchor at the northern end of Cape Cod. "After exploring the coast for a month, they landed at a spot which had been called Plymouth on Captain John Smith's map" (187). The date was November 20, 1620.

"The Pilgrim Fathers were Separatists who had definitely left the established Anglican church. There was in England a large Puritan party, which, claiming the right to remain in the church, demanded that it be further 'purified' from errors. This party was strong, wealthy, and influential. During the bitter contest with Charles I, some of the leaders determined to emigrate to America where they might worship in the simple form which their individual conscience demanded" (187).

To the colony in the new world came settlers and supplies in rapid sessions. At least 20,000 new arrivals were counted within fifteen years. "After that time, the struggle with Charles I, and the subsequent triumph of the Commonwealth, the Puritans remained in England" (187). Hence, the chief growth of the colony was from within itself. The increment was so rapid that it was able to send settlers to other colonies.

Although those who left the original colony to go elsewhere claimed membership in the established Church of England, within a short time they became as thorough Separatists as the original Plymouth settlers. "In 1631, it was provided that none but members of a church in the colony should be freemen, i.e., members of the company and voters. This shut out not only non-church members, but those who accepted doctrines or theories of church government other than the rigid Puritan view. As a result, the number of voters was small, for not all could satisfy the examiners of their orthodoxy. Usually, an 'inhabitant', as distinguished from a 'freeman', was not molested if he or she was quiet. If disorderly or if he/she attempted to make converts to other theories, he/she was punished or banished. No mercy was shown to a confessed heretic" (187). The rigid rules of the clergy and those who thought like them in Massachusetts was one of the reasons for founding other colonies.

Out of this puritanical turmoil, internecine discord, animosity toward religion, and personal frustration came the determined desire to separate church activities from government on the part of early Americans. Their anticlerical feelings are readily understandable as an expressed rebellion against Puritanism.

It is difficult to attach present day interpretations on colonial intentions. With much doubt can it be implied that the authors of the United States Constitution intended that a school prayer, a display of religious symbol, or the carrying of a child in a public school bus to a parochial school is a violation of our Constitution. More realistically, on this subject the Constitution refers to government authority not to impose a state religion, or to unify state power with the dicta of a specific religion. Separation of church from state means that there is to be no state religion and government is not to impose any one religion upon its citizens as the law of the land. It does not mean the denial of God or His Commandments.

To reiterate, the Constitution does not contain the words "separation of church and state." It does stipulate that there shall not be a state religion and that no law shall be enacted to prevent the freedom of religious worship. The phrase "separation of church and state" was interpolated in subsequent decisions by jurists years after the ratification of the Constitution in 1789.

"It was John Adams who believed that our law was rooted in a common moral religious tradition, one that stretched back to the times when Moses went up on Mount Sinai. All of our founding fathers agreed that our liberties were God-given and should be exercised responsibly. They believed there was a distinction between liberty and license" (154).

Many precedents exist in which the name God has been mentioned by our American ancestors who are listed among the great patriots of our nation. This traditional acknowledgement of God is compatible with the words of John Adams. Commencing with the first president, history records many references to God in their utterances.

George Washington, in his First Inaugural Address, said: "No people can be bound to acknowledge and adore the Invisible Hand which conducts the affairs of men than those of the United States." In his Farewell Address, his words were pertinent to the twentieth century. "Of all the dispositions and habits which lead to political prosperity, religion, and morality are indispensable supports — reason and experience both forbid us to expect that national morality can prevail in exclusion of religious principle" (188).

Abraham Lincoln, whose belief in God was never questioned, extended the hand of unity to the South with these words: "With malice toward none, with charity for all, with firmness in the right as God gives us to see the right, let us strive on to finish the work we are in to bind up the nation's wounds" (188).

In the same American virtuous spirit, Dwight David Eisenhower said: "Without God there could be no American form of government nor an American way of life ... Thus the founding fathers saw it; and thus, with God's help it will continue to be ... Each day we must ask that Almighty God will set and keep his protecting hand over us so that we may pass on to those who come after us the heritage of a free people, secure in their God-given rights and in full control of a government dedicated to the preservation of those rights" (188).

At the Constitutional Convention where the idea of a separation of church and state was originated, as well as adopted, God was mentioned. A man known for his worldliness did not ignore divine providence. Benjamin Franklin said: "The longer I live, the more convincing proofs I see of this truth that God governs in the affairs of men" (187).

The founding fathers of the American Republic were very cognizant of the need for a separation of church from the state. They were opposed adamantly to a national church which was the accepted *via vitae* in those countries (especially England) from whence most colonists had emigrated. Early settlers in the Colonies had witnessed personally, were indoctrinated by their peers, parents/elders, or read of the persecutions attributed to religious sects. Anglicanism's growth was marked by confiscation of real property, imprisonment, torture, and death.

Early Americans did not intend to have their new homeland contaminated or tarnished by such recurrences of that past history. This does not imply that there was a unanimity of opinion on this matter. There was much rankling in early America with an overabundance of aggressive grievance in action among multiple disputants. Calvinism flourished in the colonies. If a census had been taken at that time most of the settlers would have listed themselves as Calvinists.

In New England Calvinism was first, Unitarianism was the second most popular religious group. Virginians like Jefferson, his followers, his friends, and political colleagues were Episcopalians who despised Calvinism. American Baptists in later years increased their numbers along the southern coastline of the Atlantic Ocean. They had an especial appeal to the poor, the hungry, the down-hearted, the depressed, and the disadvantaged.

The colonial religious machinations have a subtle continuum into 1989 perplexing modern Americans as it did their colonial ancestors. When reference was made to the United States as a "Christian Nation" many Americans were affronted. Supreme Court decisions were cited to the effect that this is a Christian nation. In the opposite corner reference was made that our government is prohibited "From making adherence to a religion relevant in any way to a person's standing in the political community" and prohibited as well "from conveying or attempting to convey a message that religion or a particular religious belief is favored or preferred" (292, 293). The rhetorical question raised is: "How can a state be committed to protection of the unfettered conscientious rights of Christians and non-Christians while at the same time giving 'recognition' to the divine origin and truth of one favored religion?" (293).

Knowingly or not the colonists had to grapple with the amalgamation of justice with the social order that was under the umbrage of prejudice and ever-threatening violence. The educated men in the colonies knew history and read literature on political philosophy. Among the philosophers whose political views were persuasive was John Locke (1632-1714). His concepts influenced the colonists in their political thinking. As the first great British empiricist he denied the existence of innate ideas, categories, and moral principles. Hence in his opinion the union of church and state was an obnoxious combination. His thoughts were not atheistic. Locke was a political, economic, and religious thinker of note. He was a "latitudinarian," a broad churchman in theology, and a liberal in politics.* His arguments were against the divine right of kings, the

---

* Latitudinarianism: (1) A party in the Church of England (middle of the 17th century) aiming to reconcile contending parties by seeking a broad basis in common doctrines. (2) A term applied to a liberal opinion which allows diversity in unity.

authority of the Bible, the state church, and maintained that political sovereignty rests upon the consent of the governed, and ecclesiastical authority upon the consent of reason. He was an ardent defender of the freedom of thought and speech. Locke's themes are visibly woven into the pattern of the United States Constitutional Amendments.

This is noted especially in the directives of the First Amendment concerning no state religion, and no impediment to the freedom of religion. By inference there was to be no established religion in the individual future states. The tendency to have a state (as opposed to a national) religion was not abhorred in many newly-formed commonwealths. Thus the firm stand against a state or national religion was fortified in positive statements in writing or in spoken words.

The framers of the Constitution had a unified thought on the "no religion" influence on government. This sentimental sensitivity was inculcated into their thought processes by personal experience or other sources. The strong influence of European philosophers and political sages of that era was very persuasive. Western sociopolitical intellectuals of the 17th and 18th centuries struggled with identical, critical civil issues that burdened with perplexity the early colonists.

Roman Catholicism blossomed in Maryland as a minority religion in the thirteen colonies. Catholics were neither specifically despised nor hated. They were accepted as freely as other religious groups but were tolerated often without equanimity. Notwithstanding this adverse propensity, Lord Baltimore opened the gates of his colony to all religions. A Jewish community was prominent in colonial Maryland. One of the oldest synagogues in America is extant in Baltimore.

If by serendipity or otherwise, a definite religion was to be a national religion in colonial times, most likely it would have been Calvinism. The majority of the colonists were of that denomination, which was a factor in magnetizing others into their ranks. Geographically the division was simple. Episcopalians were in the South and Calvinists were in the North. With each succeeding generation New England Calvinism faded. Unitarianism was preserved in Massachusetts eventually amalgamating with the Universalists.

Episcopalian influence in Virginia continued but gradually diminished in vitality. A newer type of non-apostolic, non-denominational religious politician appears in the person of Abraham Lincoln. In his early life he was a free thinker. Later in his maturer years his utterances sounded Calvinistic. A masterpiece of American Christian doctrine is preserved in Lincoln's Second Inaugural Address. His words on that day enlivened the concept of a Christian nation that makes every patriot a Christian and every Christian a patriot.

The influence of religion over the 200 years of American history has been present but not advertised. A centrality of religious thinking in government policy is necessary for the maintenance of democracy in public institutions. In America all religions may not mingle with each other as they are not fungible. Nevertheless the many imported national foreign customs that identify the various ethnic groups do intermingle. Under one diadem they all conform to the laws of one great affectionate heritage of "fatherland" which is the United States of America.

Early Colonial America was preserved as a nation by Protestant Evangelism. Non-sectarian education protected, preserved, promoted, and prompted morality in early nascent America. Protestantism instilled ethical propriety into pre-revolutionary and post-revolutionary colonialism.

The power of religion was demonstrable as a sectionlist force prior to the Civil War. Protestant sects separated from each other above and below the Mason-Dixon Line into the northern and southern sections of the same denominational churches. This schizophrenic partition was not hidden as visible reciprocal attempts were made to heal the breach. The emotional disengagement and the disclosed disingenuity that prevailed only deepened the dissension between the North and the South.

By 1850 Roman Catholicism, an intruder by the volume standards of colonial religions, became the largest religious denomination in America. Papists replaced Deists in 1847. A 1989 estimation is that the number of Roman Catholics in the United States of

America is 55 million. The voice of Catholicism is not drowned by the boisterous turmoil that brings the subject of abortion into a sharp bioethical focus. This potent force persists even though the proabortionists raise their objections to the invasion of their rights to privacy which sustains their constitutional permission to abortion.

Although the Constitution does not explicitly mention any right to privacy, the Supreme Court has held that some guarantee of personal privacy does exist within the penumbra of the Bill of Rights (294). The High Court has fortified the right to privacy in the Roe v. Wade majority opinion (295). It is based on the Fourteenth Amendment's concept of personal liberty and restrictions upon state actions. Specifically the United States Supreme Court has recognized this privacy right as it relates to marriage, procreation, contraception, family relationships, childrearing (including education), and abortion (296).

In the quest for proselytes in the fight against abortion, the apostolate of Roman Catholicism welcomes the friendship of other religions. Collegiality among divergent churches stabilizes a democracy without insinuating their doctrinal beliefs into civic ventures. Religious diversity is a social reality in the United States of America. It will endure timelessly as it preserves the aquiline motto *E Pluribus Unum*.

Modern American citizens have deviated from the deified beliefs of our renowned ancestors. During the last several years an anti-religion fervor has been observed. It has been termed neopaganism. Although this assumption or mental attitude of neopaganism is morally disturbing to the observer, there is an uncertainty as to what can be done about it.

"By neopaganism is meant the view of life that leaves no room for God or the supernatural. It is a thoroughly one-dimensional view of existence. A description of neopaganism does not infer a real hostility to religion. Neopagans are not angry at God or anti-religious or eager to wipe out Christian faith or other religious denominations. In one sense, each of these attitudes would be a step in the right direction. At least they would indicate that God, religion, and faith were being taken seriously. In the vision described as neopaganism, no strong feelings toward any supernatural realities are entertained. To neopagans, God, religion, and faith are remote ideas that have no important role in life. They are not real to the neopagans" (189).

Neopaganism reflects the two prominently propelling forces in current American and European society which are secularism and commercialism in its diffuse, unrestricted meaning. "Secularism or atheistic humanism provides a detailed vision of human existence in which there is no place for God, life beyond the grave, or any supernatural realities. The secularist sees the purpose of human existence totally in worldly terms. Although human beings are explainable through the process of evolution and, therefore, completely material, nevertheless, we should love one another. For the secular humanist the goal of personal existence is to enrich human personality as much as possible. Commercial consumerism tells us that our value is to be understood entirely in terms of buying and selling. Thus, we are things and our value is determined in the marketplace. Neopaganism leads to personal fulfillment derived from the possession of things" (189). As a secular proposition it fails in the realization that buying and selling are among the neopaganistic activities belonging to mundane civitan commerce. As morally neutral endeavors they have neither ethical beginnings nor endings, unless *evil conduct* unbalances the status quo. With such misconduct goodness evanescences which causes that which is visible to become valueless. When a person has nothing of intrinsic, spiritual value to sell, that individual is ethically bankrupt and socially expendable.

This neopagan phenomenon may be a contributing factor to the ardent vocal antagonism to moral proprieties which are being obliterated under the veneer of a purported violation of the constitutional separation of church and state. This credo of separation has found advocates in high places. The head of a prestigious religious group has expressed his opinion thusly. There is a "need for the separation of church and state and warned that each can corrupt the other. He also warned against what he described as a tendency to mingle patriotic and religious fervor. . . Religion and politics have distinct functions that must be kept separate" (190).

With equal solemnity and with the dignity of a similar episcopal position, the Cardinal-Archbishop of Manila said: "Separation of church and state is like a railroad track. Both government and church serve the same people on different rails. If the rails are too close, you will have a derailment. The same is true if they are too far apart. Separation should not be isolation . . . When there is union of church and state and abuses are committed, the abuses are relegated to the church" (191).

Religion, churches, and their spokespeople readily accept the contexts of American law that enunciates a state's right to define the quality of their lives. Objections arise from religious groups when legislated immorality finds its defense under the aegis of the law. "Local communities can regulate land development through zoning ordinances as well as the size and style of houses. The rights and freedoms of homeowners, landowners, and builders are circumscribed by law in the name of assuring local standards. A community that has the right to outlaw a plastic factory or a two-family dwelling should have the right to regulate what is against public morals — such as pornography" (154).

Separation of church and state does not mean that church influence for the common good of a nation's citizens should be silenced. "The Constitution of the United States prohibits the promulgation of laws that abridge free speech. But the First Amendment was never intended to be a license for public practitioners of pornography (or other public indecencies). Does anyone seriously believe that the framers of our Constitution would have condoned pornography, immorality, or abortion?" (154).

Opponents to anti-pornography or antiabortion legislation argue that such laws compromise freedom, personal choice, invasion of privacy, denial of free choice, and so on *ad infinitum*. Do they mean to imply, suggest, or actually say that legislating against immorality mitigates total freedom?

"Total freedom means total power to exercise one's will.. Civil liberty is the antithesis of total freedom . . . Civil liberty imposes mutual restraints in order to further mutual liberties. These restraints are imposed on the individual and upon all institutions — church, state, school, family, labor — and everything else. The concept of civil liberty implies a measured degree of state-imposed restraints in order to further freedom" (154). This quotation does not intimate that goodness is to be restrained in preference to evil. Humanity from its origin favors goodness even as human valor is an uncommon virtue in the combat against evil.

Many who separate church from the state in their bid to deny morality as a government concern often argue that issues such as pornography (or abortion) cannot be defined in the terms of those who oppose their persuasions. "It is regrettable that such people condemn themselves to a life of perpetual uncertainty. The yard-stick used to make moral judgments allowing society to define pornography (or abortion) is not based on arbitrary whim. Rather, it is founded on the accumulated traditional wisdom that has been given to us by the revealed moral truths of our Judeo-Christian heritage. It is not a matter of 'imposing' one's value on others" (154).

If state or national legislators, or other government officials need a definition of terms that are associated with morality, the separation of church and state does not allow or imply that there is one definition applicable when uttered by a church with a second dissimilar definition to be applied to the same term when used in government. For example, "to define pornography, we apply the standards of our civilization, of our Western heritage, of our Judeo-Christian culture" (154). This tradition provides us with the moral strength to recognize pornography as merchandized filth, a lascivi-ous business, and not as a constitutional right.

"In a democracy, all values must be debated freely in the public square. Those values that emanate from revealed religious truths have just as much right to compete and prevail as those values that have a secular origin" (154).

"America's history is rife with countless scenes of civil episodes of religious discrimination, persecution, prejudices, and bigotry. Thus, our government has been used as an instrument of retribution for private resentments. Although many people might say such injustices could not occur in a religiously free and protected society, courts and juries have closed their eyes and ears to blatant instances of discrimination and persecution. From the days of the American Revolution, when anti-Catholic sentiment was so prevalent that 'Rhode Island was probably the only colony in which a Catholic could practice his religion freely' (later Maryland). Today, people and groups have used government channels to vent their wrath on particular religious expressions of which they do not approve" (192).

An example of intolerance was described in early New York. Although the English were tolerant of Catholics (who were few in number) in the early years of their rule of New York, a policy of intolerance and persecution was introduced after the overthrow of James II, the Catholic king, in 1683. The English "Penal Laws" against Catholics were enforced more strictly in the colonies than in England.

"In 1700 (August 9), the Royal Governor of New York, Richard Coote, Earl of Bellomont, and his assembly enacted a law which excluded Catholics from the rights of citizenship and banned priests from the colony under pain of perpetual imprisonment and death, should they escape imprisonment and be recaptured. This law remained on the books until repealed in 1784" (193).

Separation philosophy has not prevented governmental intrusion into the religion of its citizens. Officials of the state can be driven by hatred or religious intolerance or motivated by greed to vaunt their vengeance upon persons of different religious convictions. Other (non-governmental) individuals or groups of people (overtly or covertly) have discovered that government can be used effectively (usually through the courts) as a weapon of destruction or as a device to invade or destroy traditions or symbols of religions not their own.

An example illustrating this tendency was an adverse reaction to a Federal publication. "Distribution by the United States Education Department of a speech that described the United States as a 'Christian Nation' has been denounced by the executive director of the American Jewish Congress. The director said he found it 'particularly shocking' that the Acting Secretary of Education saw nothing wrong with the federal distribution of the speech. 'This is but the latest in a series of administration actions that betray a lack of knowledge of American history and an appalling insensitivity to the pleuralist character of American democracy' the American Jewish Congress leader said" (194).

Another incident is recorded at about the same time. "Government erection of religious symbols for a war memorial in a public park is unconstitutional, according to a court brief filed by two national Jewish organizations. The American Jewish Congress and the Synagogue Council of America filed the brief in the U.S. Court of Appeals for the Fifth Circuit in opposition to the display of three Latin crosses and a Star of David on public property in Houston's Bear Park. The American Jewish Congress and the Synagogue Council of America said that by placing the Religious symbols on public property, Harris County succeeded in 'the creation of a chapel', which is unconstitutional for government" (194).

Another expression of thought on this separate accentuation was made by the president of a chapter of the American Jewish Committee. He stated that: "The vitality of our religious institutions rests on the fact that they are voluntary in nature and disentangled from government. The experiences of both Catholic and Jewish minorities in Nassau County, New York attest to the wisdom of safe-guarding a public policy of separation of church and state. The place for religious symbols is the church, the synagogue, and private property" (195).

The policy of separation of church and state cannot and does not now deprive any religious group from persuading public opinion in their direction on ethical conduct or moral problems. The Catholic Church through its prelates speaks out against evil in any and all its forms. Certain moral issues of national prominence have placed the Catholic Church at the intersection of public opinion and public policy.

"The recent statements by the bishops on abortion, nuclear war, and the letter on the economy are examples of how the Catholic Church is to work at that intersection. The relationship of the Catholic Church to public opinion locates its distinctive role theo-logically and constitutionally in a democracy. Public opinion does not dictate policy choices, but public opinion does set an atmosphere and framework within which decisions are made by elected and appointed officials. Public opinion establishes some clear demands and it draws defined lines, beyond which democratically elected leaders move only with great difficulty. The Catholic Church has access to a major section of the American public and therefore it is mandated to teach and exemplify a comprehensive moral vision" (196).

The physical presence and the spiritual strength of the Catholic bishops in the fifty states testify to the fact that Catholics belong in America and are here to stay. They are like St. Paul who stood erect before the Roman commander and declared "I am a Roman citizen and I demand to be treated as such." Citizenship entitles one to be accepted as a full-fledged member of a civic society with all the rights and privileges guaranteed by the fundamental law of the specific nation.

As any other citizen of this country, a lay Catholic and the Catholic clergy are entitled "to enjoy freedom of speech and religion, to be treated equally under the law, to be respected in the newsprint and electronic media, to bring moral principles into public debate on political issues". Unthinking political partisanship is conducive to a "self-destructive inferiority mindset common to many Catholics. This fixed state of mind is: As a Catholic, I really do not deserve to enjoy freedom of speech and religion, to be treated equally, etc. This mindset renders the American Catholic citizen psychologically incapable of saying in imitation of St. Paul: 'I am an American citizen and I demand to be treated as such'. Many Catholics willingly and without protest accept the suppression of their rights and liberties to which they are entitled as full-fledged citizens" (197).

The timidity of some American Catholics has made them cowl in the presence of proabortion groups, advocates of pornography, and similar situations. They are fearful to speak out the Catholic principles they know are just. To be silent cannot fulfill what "Vatican II and Pope John Paul II have urged bishops and priests to do in order to bring Gospel values into the political arena. In America, this entails the exercise of their First Amendment rights to freedom of speech and religion" (197).

On the opposite side of Catholic critics, an observation by a non-Catholic cannot be overlooked. A distinguished law professor said that "he becomes appalled at what he sees as the aftermath of the Supreme Court's landmark 1973 abortion decision. But what concerns me the most right now is another dimension. This is claims from civil liberties organizations and parts of the proabortion movement anytime a Catholic speaks against abortion; that banning abortions would be a violation of the separation of church and state. It is a fallacious argument, a calumny, to make that kind of argument that the position of people who are prolife, therefore antiabortion, can only be justified on the grounds of the theology of one religion. Hence, if they succeed in getting prolife legislation passed, that is a violation of the separation of church and state. The debate is over issues of morality, ethics, and true values. Of course, these questions are not irrelevant in religion, but they are not identical to or confined to any particular religion" (198).

When going into the voting booth, religion is not left outside the drawn curtain. "Should one's ethical or moral convictions about fundamental human rights and dignity influence the decisions one makes as a voter, the policies one adopts as a candidate for public office, or the course one pursues as a public official pledged not only to uphold the existing law, but to seek its greater perfection in safeguarding and enhancing these same human rights?" The answer is yes. The affirmative reply persists, even in the face of a criticism. "Some commentators seek to formulate their principle in another way — a way that presents the Catholic hierarchy as urging Catholics 'to work toward transforming the Church's doctrinal positions into public policy and law as attempting to impose their hierarchal beliefs on others through the political process'"(199).

If this was the intention of the Roman Catholic Church, the Pope would not demand priests and nuns who held political positions either to give them up or leave the religious life. This papal advisory was applied to the United States and other countries. "Over a period of several years, the bishops of Nicaragua, backed by the Holy See, have asked and now have directed under pain of suspension, four priests holding high government office to leave their posts. The reasons for this action can be stated simply. Canon law, both the former, in effect 1918-1983, and the new Code of Canon Law for the Latin Church that became effective in November 1983, prohibits priests and, also, Religious (male or female) from holding state offices that involve the exercise of civil power. Permission can be granted, however, in extraordinary and exceptional circumstances for such service" (200).

"In our national life today, there is considerable concern for the appropriate relationships between government's public policy and the involvement of religious institutions in those issues. Questions arise as churches give witness to the moral dimension of public issues. In a pleuralistic society, it is sometimes obscured that in the mutual care for justice and basic human rights, both church and state, though separate, draw from common sources. Such phrases as 'unalienable rights' are not the exclusive language of religion. They are also the words of our nation's founding fathers, affirming the basic dignity of man and his/her 'right to life, liberty, and the pursuit of happiness' — upon which rest the foundations of a just civil government. It is a proper role of religion, in common with civil government, to reflect upon these transcendent, fundamental, and unalienable human rights, and to witness them to the community-at-large. They are presented not merely as lofty ideals, but as the real and necessary fabric of present personal and social life, to be translated appropriately into the fabric of public policy by the whole citizenry through its free and democratic process" (129).

CHAPTER EIGHT

# COMPLICATIONS OF ABORTION

*"Wrong is wrong, even if everyone is doing it, and right is right,*
*even if no one is doing it.*
St. Augustine of Hippo (354-430)*

The performance of an abortion, even upon an apparently healthy woman, is not always an innocuous procedure. An abortion complication, as defined by the Center For Disease Control, includes any illness related to either an induced or a spontaneous abortion that causes a woman to go to the acute care facility at a particular hospital (145).

The most common immediate complications following an abortion are bleeding and/or endometritis. A delayed, distant, or future complication can be the loss of cervical competency. This means that nature's berm has been impaired or destroyed. Specifically, it indicates that the uterine cervix no longer has the anatomicophysiological functional capability of retaining the closure capacity which maintains a subsequent pregnancy within the uterine corpus (body). Thus, spontaneous evacuation of the conceptus can occur in these women who have undergone an abortion. Hence, it is not an uncommon acknowledgement in a lady patient's history to find recorded that an intended pregnancy was not retained following an abortion procedure.

"In August 1977, federal funds for abortion available to Medicaid-eligible women were restricted. To measure the impact of this restriction on abortion-related complications, the Center For Disease Control (CDC) initiated a hospital surveillance project in thirteen states and the District of Columbia. No increase in abortion-related complications was observed in this surveillance project" (145).

As a statistical evaluation to determine the merits of federal funding for abortion, the hospital surveillance project selected non-related areas for study. "Data on women coming to obstetric, acute-care facilities were collected from 24 institutions located in the District of Columbia and thirteen states scattered across the country from October 10, 1977 through June 10, 1978. Ten institutions were located in states where, because of the absence of public funds, legal abortions might be less available. Fourteen institutions were in states that were continuing to use state funds to finance Medicaid abortions. Out of the 3,157 abortion complications reported through this hospital surveillance project, seven occurred after admitted illegally induced procedures. In three other instances in which complications occurred, the women did not name the source of the abortion. For analytical purposes, it was assumed that these women also underwent an illegal or self-induced abortion" (145).

Interpreting the relationship between federal funding for abortion and the occurrence of complications, the conclusions reached were as follows. "None of these ten complications occurred in women reported to be a Medicaid recipient. No abortion deaths related to either illegal or legal abortions were detected through the hospital surveillance. There was also no significant difference between institutions in funded and non-funded states in the proportion of Medicaid women with abortion complications over the eight months" study period (145).

A nationwide mortality observation on this theme of funded abortions resulted in obtaining some information data. "Although no abortion-related deaths were detected through the hospital surveillance project, three abortion-related deaths of Medicaid recipients living in non-funded states have been documented since August 4, 1977, through CDC's epidemiologic surveillance of abortion mortality. One was directly related to the absence of public funds for abortion. It was in regard to a 27-year-old woman who died in a hospital on the Texas-Mexico border on October 3, 1977, from septic complications of abortion" (201, 202, 145).

"In two other instances, the abortion-related deaths appeared to be associated indirectly to the absence of public funding. In one case, the Medicaid-eligible woman delayed her procedure, in part due to medical reasons, in order to locate a facility which would perform a combined abortion and concurrent sterilization procedure with public funds. In the second case, a Medicaid-eligible woman was informed by two free-standing abortion clinics that she was too far advanced in pregnancy to allow the suction curettage procedure that she was planning to finance with private funds. After learning this, and because procedures  performed late in pregnancy are more expensive, she attempted to induce an abortion herself, which eventually produced complications requiring a hysterectomy. She died from a pulmonary embolism ten days after the hysterectomy"(145).

Abortion methods and sequelae were studied at the London Hospital, England. The authors stated: "Induced abortion is a safe procedure when done in the first trimester of pregnancy by a competent practitioner. It has a mortality rate of less than 1/100,000 operations." In the next sentence, it is stated: "The United Kingdom has lagged behind the United States where in almost two million abortions analyzed between 1972-1974 the mortality rate was 3.4/100,000 operations. In 1,475,458 abortions performed in England and Wales between 1963 and 1979 there were 96 deaths, a mortality rate of 6.5/100,000 operations" (203). Although the comparative mortality rate as compared to the operations performed is assessed rather lightly, death before its time is not an insignificant consideration.

Complications seen in a free-standing clinic from elective abortion have been documented by authors from the Department of Obstetrics and Gynecology at the Washington University School of Medicine and Reproductive Health Services, St. Louis, Missouri. "Experience is reported with the elective first trimester abortion 16,400 pregnancies during a thirty-one month period by a free-standing clinic. Incidence of complications was 1.54 percent. The most common of these were incomplete evacuation, excessive postabortal bleeding, and uterine perforation. In patients with unquestioned perforations of the uterus, the use of  laparoscopy has been very valuable. It is used in ascertaining the exact nature of the perforation, in avoiding unnecessary laparotomy, and in giving intra-abdominal visual guidance to concomitant suction evacuation in cases of an incomplete procedure. Aspects of the other complications have been discussed. In general, the findings support the view that even in the first trimester, the earlier in pregnancy that suction abortion is performed, the less likely it is to result in major complications" (204). Even in a modern free-standing clinic with its ultrascientific equipment, abortions are performed with complications, even though the rate is low.

From the Departments of Obstetrics and Gynecology of Emory University in Atlanta, Georgia, were published the results of a study on legal abortion and placenta previa. The anatomic organ on the wall of the uterus to which the embryo is attached by means of the umbilical cord and through which it receives its nourishment is called the placenta. When a placenta is superimposed upon or implants itself about the internal os of the uterus, the term describing this misplacement is placenta previa. This condition can produce serious hemorrhage during labor.

For this reason, any discussion on placenta previa may be the source of knowledge that can save a human life. "Legal abortion has been postulated to be a risk factor for placenta previa in subsequent pregnancies. To examine this hypothesis, two investigators analyzed the deliveries of 28,665 women. Sixty-eight of these had had placenta previa. These obstetrical histories were compared to those of 68 controls randomly selected from the same group of deliveries. The crude risk ratio for women with a history of one or more legal abortions was 1.4. Standardizing the crude risk ratio for the effects of age and gravidity reduced the risk ratio to 1.1. In the population studied, legal abortion does not appear to have a significant association with placenta previa in subsequent pregnancies" (205).

This placenta previa conclusion must be reviewed with some understanding of statistic gathering in this special circumstance. "Ascertainment bias can be an important limitation of any case-control study in which exposure information must be obtained from existing records. In pregnancy cohort studies, the later in pregnancy a history of previous abortion is determined, the more likely is an adverse outcome to affect selective recall. Under-reporting of previous abortions is another potential problem in studies of this type" (206).

"Critics have challenged previous comparisons of mortality from legal abortion and childbirth for contrasting population groups with different clinical characteristics. They allege that most women dying from abortion were young, white, and healthy, while those dying from childbirth had serious underlying conditions. To address this question, three researchers calculated standardized abortion and childbirth mortality rates between 1972 and 1978" (207).

Among their enlightened discoveries was that: "More than one in three women who died from legal abortion between 1972 and 1978 had preexisting medical conditions serious enough to qualify them for therapeutic abortions. Chronic heart disease and morbid obesity were the two predominant, preexisting conditions. However, hypertension, chronic respiratory tract disease, and chronic renal disease each occurred in at least three of the abortion deaths. The death-to-case rate from legal abortion for women with one or more preexisting conditions was 39 times higher than that for healthy women" (207).

"Some life-threatening complications of legal abortion may require hysterectomy as treatment. Although the frequency of such hysterectomies may reflect the incidence of serious morbidity from legal abortion, there is little information available on the frequency of hysterectomy as treatment of complications from legal abortion. The largest case-series files from single institutions have reported hysterectomy rates ranging from 0.3 to 14.0 per 10,000 abortions (209). These rates were affected by gestational age and abortion method. However, up to 1984, there have been no multicenter investigations examining hysterectomies resulting from complications of abortion. The study undertaken on hysterectomy is a collaborative study conducted in the United States from 1970 to 1978" (108).

In this collaborative study, the objective was to determine the use of hysterectomy for the treatment of abortion complications as well as for the specific complications for which the hysterectomy was performed. Abortion complications leading to hysterectomy were divided into two groups according to the method employed to perform the abortion. These are termed curettage abortion and instillation abortion. The complications from curettage abortion were listed as:

1.  uterine perforation;
2.  hemorrhage;
3.  cervical trauma;

4.  ectopic pregnancy; and,
5.  infection.

Instillation of saline complications for abortion were:

1.  hemorrhage;
2.  uterine rupture or perforation;
3.  ectopic pregnancy;
4.  infection;
5.  cervical trauma; and,
6.  failed attempted abortion (208).

"Complications of legal abortion severe enough to require sacrificing a woman's fertility in order to preserve her health appear to be rare in the United States" (208). However, when it is performed there is a finality about it. No matter the indication, the irrevocable ending is that hysterectomy renders a woman sterile forever.

## Psychological Trauma of Abortion

Sixteen years have passed without any harmonious equipoise noticeable in discourses on abortion. The subject has appended to it an emotional tremor that can erupt at any time like a smoldering volcano. One aspect of the abortion controversy that produces adverse opinions with ascerbic denials is that of postabortion complications. Medical records contain scientific facts that in addition to the physical distresses many psychological/psychosomatic symptoms have occurred in women who have had one or more abortions. Contradicting other equiparance opinions clinical evaluation of some postabortion patients does indicate that there are psychological symptoms if the patients will admit their existence.

The proabortionists have taken unto themselves an immobile emotional niche to which they adhere tenaciously. With this programmed Pavlovian emotionalism mutual accord is facilitated to fortify the tenuous external appearance of calm that masquerades the internal moral dissipation. Oversimplified as it may appear, this monotone mindset is conducive to stagnation of reason which contributes to replicated allergy to truth, personal sacrificial giving, and distributive justice.

A preconceived, purposeful study aimed at determining postabortion complications brings to light that some women who thought or believed that legalized abortion would solve their maternal problems are disillusioned. The law has not become a confessional with the power to absolve sin from a troubled soul. There are some women who have been plunged into deep despair with a postabortion period (or residual lifetime) of regretful guilt deriving from one irreversible deed done under pressure, panic, persuasion, or perturbation.

"Recalling the years when abortion was a crime, a grandmother tells of the horrors of going underground in Washington, D.C. to end a pregnancy" (293). As the City of the District of Columbia was in consternation over the abortion demonstrations during the April 24, 1989 week, a group of local women "traveled to Baltimore to advocate the right to abortion, and to share accounts of their illegal abortions during the years before Roe v. Wade" (297).

"A 59-year-old grandmother was one of 13 women who stood up before one hundred-plus spectators at the Aurellino Theatre at John Hopkins University to relate her personal experience. In 1966, the grandmother was a 36-year-old mother of a daughter, 15, and a son, 12. After fifteen years as a housewife, she was about to embark on a retail career to help build a college fund for her children...She did not realize she was pregnant for nearly two months. Her physician finally informed her of the positive signs of gravidity. She exclaimed, 'I did not want a baby again.' When she told her doctor, he refused to help. In 1966 abortion was illegal" (293).

In order to obtain her druthers the chatelaine grandmother and her husband made arrangements to have an abortion operation in a Puerto Rican hospital where abortion was legal. Due to an aviation strike she could not get to Puerto Rico. She was recommended by a friend to a well-known local D.C. abortionist. The preoperative arrangements included cash payment in advance. As to the actual D-and-C performance she was given no anesthesia, no one was present (no witnesses), and she had to walk out of the office immediately afterward unassisted" (297).

"I never regretted my own abortion." She disputes the assertion that abortion is murder. Her other recorded words are, "To me an undeveloped fetus is not a person. Every time a woman has a miscarriage, are you supposed to have a funeral? Who do they (anti-abortionists) think they are preventing from having abortions?

People who cannot afford to have children" (297). This story is that of a woman whose sorrow has not passed but lingers on after more than two decades of mental torture.

The clinical presence of major/minor psychological or psychosomatic trauma following abortion differs from the Surgeon General's opinion as expressed in his television statement in the Spring of 1989. On that occasion he failed to mention the occurrence of mental complications following abortion. Rising to the surface from innermost anxieties are the admissions by aborted women that the lingering evil of their past decisions has haunted them. These troubled "mothers" are seeking help along their own *via dolorosa* as they attempt a salutary comeback to spiritual and emotional wholesomeness.

Church assemblages have established programs called Project Rachel which is a postabortion reconciliation program (298). Lady psychotherapists participate as counselors who have been "drawn to Project Rachel because they had encountered a number of people in their practices who were suffering because they had an abortion" (298). As an asset to the amelioration of the postabortion mental trauma, "a specially developed Bible study workbook, 'Women in Ramah', provided a format (for this novel project). (The reference is to the place, Ramah, where the Old Testament figure, Rachel, is said to have mourned her dead children.) Postabortion counseling programs number over sixty throughout the fifty states" (298). This advice effort is helping to alleviate the self-diminishment stymieing aborted women years after the actual event.

When any discussion, written or spoken, is held on the studied question of postabortion complications the psychosomatic disturbances cannot be removed from this evaluation. Mental remorse can be more intolerable than a physical postabortion morbidity. "Women participating in Project Rachel admit they do not have to be told that abortion is a sin. They know it is a sin. It is this very recognition of mortal sin that causes the guilt which, in turn, produces the mental symptoms. Even with counseling, the difficult problem which cannot be elucidated in many women is that some among them believe this (abortion) is an unforgivable sin, that God could never forgive them" (298).

A participating priest who supervises one of the Rachel programs "was contacted by an 80-year-old woman who had suffered for sixty years with the pain of having undergone an abortion when she was twenty. A summarized, explanatory diagnosis on this woman's medical protocol by a lady psychotherapist stated "that as the denial encouraged by the societal approval of abortion 'breaks' (months, years, or decades after the act), people are more aware of specific pain (mental anguish). They may suffer nightmares, or be unable to tolerate the presence of small children. They may have a sense of feeling numb or of overreacting. The psychotherapist recalls women telling her, 'All of a sudden it was a tidal wave.' For healing to take place, the truth of what happened must be confronted, and that can be a deeply painful process" (298). This illustrative mental history exemplifies the clinical picture of a long festering postabortion complication that curtails any selected one of life's favorite, ecstatic pleasures.

The focus on the relatively low rate of maternal mortality in abortion reflects an incomplete, limited, streamlined subset of the ill-health residuals of abortion on pregnant women. "Numerous studies by independent medical sources have concluded that abortion frequently results in significant, negative, and often permanent physical, psychological, social, and familial effects. The studies of abortion's effects often reach conflicting conclusions, and many suffer from methodological limitations. However, these studies demonstrate that mortality rates alone do not reflect the scope of the negative health impact of abortion cognizable by the state. The Supreme Court need not find these studies conclusive to recognize the significant disagreement that exists over the validity of the scientific premise of Roe v. Wade" (302).

Deductive inaccuracy, indisquisition, statistical insufficiency, reporting inadequacies, and other fallacious defects disallow a plenary evaluation of postabortion complications. The surgeon general "laments the difficulty inherent in documenting the adverse physical (and mental) effects of abortion for two reasons: (1) approximately half of the total abortions are done in free-standing abortion clinics where records are not kept, and (2) fifty percent of the women who have an abortion deny having one when questioned (by a physician, social worker, professional medical assistant, nurse, etc.)" (302,303).

Adverse psychological complications of directly induced abortions have been studied by different investigators. Among the most common clinical symptom complexes discerned are litanized herewith:

1. Grief reactions;
2. Guilt, anxiety, depression;
3. Psychoses;
4. Shame, sorrow, lower self-esteem;
5. Distrust/hostility toward self, spouse, family, and others;
6. Postoperative stress due to an inability to forget abortion (304, 305).

"As repeat abortions show higher levels of medical sequelae, repeat aborters demonstrated significantly higher emotional stress scores in interpersonal relationships than other women. A study of 71 women with multiple abortions showed that they had more often considered suicide and scored higher on borderline personality pathology and depression than the comparison sample (control group). Forty percent of the women reported anniversary reactions and half of the women aborting sought psychotherapy months or even years after the procedure" (307).

It has been said that "abortion is medically easy, but medicolegally risky for the doctor" (210). Thus, there is a counter- complication of abortion that falls upon the abortion-performing physician. An erroneous impression may have arisen that abortion entails a low liability risk to the physician.

"To ward off a malpractice claim, a physician who does an abortion must take exceptional care in keeping records and obtaining an informed consent. Although legislators have not been able to outlaw abortion again, they have surrounded it with as many restrictions as the courts will allow" (210). The doctor who performs an abortion is the object for judicial and/or legislative scrutiny. A physician who agrees to do an abortion is particularly susceptible to having his work closely observed and any mistake seized upon as professional negligence.

Recent malpractice cases reflect the extent of this liability susceptibility. "One lawsuit was brought by a woman who suffered a staphylococcus infection after an abortion because an operating room nurse had failed to scrub her hands properly. Although it was clear that the surgeon maintaining the sterile field did not have absolute control over the hospital employee, the plaintiff counted on a jury that would be hostile to the doctor. She lost that gamble when the jury rendered a verdict in favor of the defendant" (210).

Another plaintiff claimed that she sustained a uterine prolapse and chronic vaginitis as consequences of her abortion. "In examining her, the doctor had calculated that the pregnancy was too far along to be interrupted. But the woman had been so eager for the abortion that she had deliberately misled the physician about the date of her last menstrual period. The fact that the doctor made a note of the date she gave him cleared him of ignoring the deadline" (210). These case studies are suggestive of the reality that the final scene has not been written in the drama on medical hazards and legal complications attached to abortion procedures.

Another legal, non-medical complication of abortion is the possibility of the birth of the baby. Late-term abortions generally involve the injection of a salt solution (hypertonic saline) into the womb that usually kills the fetus. In Pennsylvania, the law formerly required doctors to use other methods when the fetus might be viable.

The United States Supreme Court struck down a Pennsylvania law requiring doctors to use the abortion method most likely to save the life of a viable fetus. The original Pennsylvania Abortion Control Act was held "to be unconstitutionally vague in its definition of 'viability', thereby subjecting abortionists to possible criminal charges for abortions performed in the latter stages of pregnancy" (211).

The general secretary of the National Conference of Catholic Bishops, in response to the majority opinion as expressed by the Supreme Court, commented that by this ruling the Supreme Court "has once again made it clear that it is pursuing an advocacy role with respect to abortion. The Supreme Court has abandoned its constitutionally defined role and has acted solely as a maker of social policy — policy which the people rightly reject. The decision demonstrates an insensitivity and hardening of the heart on the abortion issue that I had not previously wished to think possible. The decision serves only those who are determined that every abortion will result in a dead fetus, even in those cases in which present medical techniques would have spared that innccent human life" (212). The Pennsylvania law struck down the rule that required doctors to try to save the life of the fetus when the physician's "experience, judgment, or professional competence tell him/her that it is viable, or when he/she has sufficient reason to believe that the fetus may be viable" (213).

The State of Missouri concerned itself with abortion complications when that state imposed a number of controversial restrictions and conditions on the medical procedure to produce abortion. The Missouri Attorney General argued that a saline amniocentesis after twelve weeks gestation would result in harm to the woman's health. The state's contention did not prevail.

Victory was for the plaintiff in this case, not the state, when it was decided that the law impermissibly restricted the doctor's right to practice medicine. The plaintiff also contended that the law would require efforts to save fetuses during an abortion procedure. The lower court ruling pointed out that there may be constitutional problems with a requirement that reasonable measures be taken to safeguard the life of an aborted fetus. The lower court found the statute too broad in not referring to particular stages of pregnancy (214).

As a parenthetical advisory, attention is drawn to the scientific fact that sexual indiscriminate promiscuity accelerates, with unrestrained proliferation, venereal diseases. It must be recalled to fading memories that the gender freedom and sexual revolution of the 1960s have fulminated the rise in sexually transmitted diseases. The older venereal diseases of gonorrhea, syphilis, and lymphopathia venerea are still with us. Equally dangerous and contagious are the newer diseases called AIDS (Autoimmune Deficiency Syndrome), herpes genitalis, and chlamydia. Among the complications of some of these diseases when they are untreated and reach the chronic pathologic stage are infertility (as from gonorrheal salpingitis) or death (as from AIDS).

"Chlamydia trachomatis is a bacterium that was once thought to be a large virus. This organism is the most common cause of sexually transmitted disease in the United States. In adults, it causes urethritis, epididymitis, pelvic inflammatory disease, endometritis, and may cause an unusual form of hepatitis (perihepatitis). The urethritis and epididymitis are usually self-limited disorders. As a result of careless personal hygiene, conjunctivitis often occurs by manual transfer of the organism from the genital tract to the eyelids. The conjunctivitis usually subsides spontaneously without sequelae. A neonate can acquire C. trachomatis infection during passage through an infected birth canal. Either conjunctivitis or pneumonia (or both) may result. A third of the cases of neonatal conjunctivitis and a third of the cases of neonatal pneumonitis are due to C. trachomatis infection. Clinical signs of infection usually begin 2 to 14 weeks after birth. The infections usually resolve spontaneously but the pneumonia may be severe. Antibiotic therapy is indicated as soon as the diagnosis is made" (245, 246, 247).

Medical researchers universally seek newer medications or technical procedures that may diminish mortality or morbidity. Abortion is not excepted from these medicosurgical programs. In 1986, much public sentiment was aroused by the research project on RU486, known as the abortion "pill". This is a hormone that makes the endometrium (inner lining of the uterus) inhospitable to pregnancy. It is an antiprogesterone [progesterone is a hormone from the ovum (egg) after ovulation]. RU486 administered with prostaglandin experimentally induces uterine contractions (cramps) which evacuate the uterine contents. As a complication, fever and bleeding from the uterus have occurred. This new research hormone is not the "morning after pill", which is an estrogen taken for three consecutive days that changes the endometrium, by blocking progesterone, from a propregnancy to an anti-pregnancy physiological state.

The usage of the RU486 has other indications than inducing an abortion, it should not be condemned as a future medication until its effectiveness in other areas has been evaluated. When administered solely or exclusively as an abortifacient, in the form of a medication, it does not become a mask to camouflage the intent for which it is taken. The moral onus of abortion is not mitigated by the manner in which it is accomplished. An abortion performed surgically in public, as in a hospital, or in the privacy of a person's bathroom/bedroom does not alter in any manner the immorality of the act. Unethical conduct performed *in pais* or *in camera* does not change the intrinsic, purposeful nature of that specific action.

Therefore, hormonal induced abortion is equated with an abortion accomplished through any other means. The method employed does not diminish the gravity of the intention nor is it an argument for paucity of the grievous matter that is inchoate to abortion. An evil end is not mitigated by a less formidable procedure to accomplish the intended result. Every human person dies spiritually when he/she fails to stand up for that which is right in the physical order of life, no matter in what disguise the evil may appear.

This chapter on the complications associated with abortion procedures has not been written with the determined intention of instigating fear in anyone. A realization of the existence of complications may be a deterrent to a woman who opts for an abortion. Inherent risks of abortion cannot be eliminated even in the best of medical hands using the optimal scientific equipment.

The motivating force behind this chapter is not only to assist the would-be abortee to reconsider accepting abortion as a solution to personal difficulties, but what is spiritually important the universal moral obligation to fulfill divine teachings to help our sisters who are God's children. Hopefully, these modest efforts against abortion may be acceptable in some way toward securing personal spiritual salvation.

One should not be unmindful of the words in the gospel so beautifully written by Matthew (25:31-46). "Come, you that are blessed of My Father! Come and possess the kingdom which has been prepared for you ever since the creation of the world. I was hungry and you fed me, thirsty and you gave me to drink. I was a stranger and you received me in your homes; naked and you clothed me. I was sick and you took care of me. I was in prison and you visited me." I wanted an abortion and you persuaded me against it. *Deo gratias!*

CHAPTER NINE

# ALTERNATIVES TO ABORTION

*"When one door closes, another opens.*
*But we so often look so long and so regretfully upon the closed door*
*that we do not see the one which has been opened for us."*
*Alexander Graham Bell (1847-1922)*

Before a woman arrives at a decision to destroy her unborn baby via an abortion, she must be warned that the final decision is her own. No matter the circumstances of her pregnancy occurrence, to kill the unwanted child is her responsibility and she must bear the burden of whatever ill effects pertain to it, be they physical, psychological, or spiritual. Blame cannot be placed upon anyone else. Therefore, it is well to remember the words spoken by the prophet: "I, the Lord, search the minds and test the hearts of men. I treat each one according to the way he lives, according to what he does" (Jeremiah 17:5-10).

As weighty testimony against the preferential selection of abortion that destroys the innocent child, two facts are worthy of repetition. The first is that no baby is unwanted. There is always someone who will adopt a baby. Secondly, the preservation of life is a moral responsibility to all believers in God, as well as a civic duty to everyone.

Within their hearts, most women who have had an abortion know they have done something wrong. The poignancy of the sin may be tampered with, but the core of the act remains an evil memory. Proof positive of the psychological trauma to postabortion women is verified when a medical history is taken by a physician. Women hide this aspect of their past medical curriculum. It can be elicited if the inquirer persists in the questioning. Extracting this history from the subconscious mind is not with the willful cooperation of the patient. No matter how it is hidden, there is a little voice within us that always speaks out against evil. It never sleeps. Even the hard-hearted cannot silence the voice of human conscience.

Any effort, written or spoken, that stems the rising tide of abortion is not a dissipation of time. It may annoy proabortionists, but that is their subjective reaction. A defeatist acceptance to the right-to-life is not a universal attitude. Let it or let it not be said that many people are stubbornly obtuse. For there are many who look but do not see, who hear but do not listen. Yet, there are others who see wrong and try to correct it.

Alternatives to abortion would not be necessary if the primary function of genital function was recognized, accepted, and adhered to, according to the normal physiologic dictates that physical love is for human procreation. To be against promiscuity is to be accused of moral electioneering, speaking a homily, lecturing on ethics, being cloaked with the vestments of pontification. All these slings and arrows of adversity do not change the basic requirements of human behavior that are consonant with human dignity, propriety, civil conduct, and deportment

Men in the prime of their youthful reproductive period should not perform like jack-rabbits. Likewise, women should not act as *filles-de-joies* in the social community. It is sad to relate that the scarlet woman is not a new character in history. Long before the sexual revolution, there have been women with a messalina complex. One of the greatest of saintly women who fought against this rampant physical immorality lived in the fourteenth century.

In Sweden, there dwelled a remarkable woman called Birgitta (1303-1373). She was the mother of eight children and was not afraid to take a stand on the burning issues of the day. In fact, one could call her a real women's liberationist. She espoused woman's equality to man. She was adamant in her fight against abortion, a practice popular among certain of the Swedish nobility. "She also said that some women behave like harlots. When they feel the life of a child in their wombs, they take herbs or pursue other means to cause the miscarriage only to perpetuate their amusement and unchastity" (215).

If persons of both genders embraced in seeking the supreme ecstasy of true human love, the physical act of love would cease to be seduction and be confined within the sacred bonds of matrimony. The marriage vows sanctify the deep rooted reality that the physical

act is an expression of spiritual love and is not an animal performance to gratify a transient emotional stimulus.

Under marital circumstances, there would be very few unwanted children to be aborted. The connubial, celestially ordained
love would be transmitted to the child as a reflection of the combined
love between a man and a woman. A loved baby will not be destroyed,
for it is the triumphant physical presence that is the visible continuous product of love in action.

Reality does cover over this ideal wish. Youth is bereft of many
sentiments shared by previous generations. The young of America
do not appear to share the optimism of their parents. To them "the
future is nebulous, distant, and even frightening. Consequently, the
youths of today want the rewards of the future now, believing that
time is short and that there are many riches to be had" (216).

Lack of faith in themselves, in their parents, and in God is the
common denominator. This faithlessness has evolved into the
"stockpile mentality" wherein there is an overabundance of "preoccupation with the accumulation of possessions", including multiple
acquisitions of persons of the opposite gender (216). "Many young
people have become intoxicated with the embroidery of life, the
frivolous little extras that are not essential for existence. They have
a hunger for the desserts of life and seem to want to be surrounded
by them" (216).

When this philosophy of life is applied to premarital, pleasurable
genital activity, pregnancies increase, babies are unwanted, and
abortions flourish. Unfortunately, at times this youthful impatient
loss of provident guidance is carried over into marriage. This leads
to a faltering flame of love that must be saved. Efforts to rekindle the
fire of marital love have been exerted. Helping troubled married
couples to rediscover their love is the aim of a new program in many
dioceses.

"*Retrouvaille* means rediscovery. Its name is French because it
was founded by Catholics in French-speaking Canada. The goal of
the program is ambitious: to help couples (whose marriages are
seriously troubled — even couples who have begun to live apart, have
been legally separated or even divorced) in the process of rediscover-
ing the love they once had for each other. The program consists of a

week during which a group of couples spend time with a team of presenting couples and a priest. The presenting couples are those who have come through serious marriage difficulties" (217).

The hopeful expectation of this encounter group is to assuage the grief between husband and wife. By so doing, the hurt between them will vanish and hopefully love will return burning brightly as exemplified in Juliet's quotation about her Romeo.*

Returning specifically to the alternatives to abortion, consideration is given to a report from the Center For Disease Control. According to one of their publications, a pregnant Medicaid-eligible woman in a state which does not fund abortions has several alternatives. "She may:

"1. Carry her pregnancy to term;

"2. Seek and qualify for a Medicaid-funded legally induced procedure;

"3. Use private funds for a legally induced procedure;

"4. Seek a less expensive abortion from an unlicensed practitioner; and/or,

"5. Attempt to abort herself" (145).

"A hospital study project was designed primarily to examine whether there would be an increase in self-induced or non-physician induced abortions, since these options have the greatest potential for causing an increase in morbidity and mortality" (219). For example, in 1972, before abortion became widely available in the United States, illegal abortion was responsible for 39 deaths. Five years later, in 1976, three fatalities resulted from illegal abortions (220). However, no increase was noted, supporting the inference that Medicaid-eligible women are not choosing self-induced or non-physician-induced abortions to any large extent. What conclusion can be drawn from that statement from the Center For Disease Control?

"The CDC has initiated an active surveillance system for the reporting of sporadic cases of illegal abortion complications when they occur — whether or not they are related to public funding. CDC

* *"When he shall die, Take him and cut him out in little stars, And he will make the face of heaven so fine, That all the world will be in love with night"* (218).

does not have data to explain the later mean gestational age after legally induced abortions in Medicaid-eligible women observed in non-funded states. For each week of delay after the sixth week of gestation, the risk of complications after legally induced abortions increases approximately 20 percent. The risk of death increases approximately 50 percent" (145, 221, 222).

Of the statistical studies (with or without any decrease in postabortion morbidity or mortality) on the five alternatives presented by the Center For Disease Control, the first proposal is advocated as the primary alternative to abortion. The Archbishop of New York is an outstanding spokesman for this preferential alternative.

"Properly emphasizing that biomedical science identifies the product of fertilization as a distinct and separate human life which develops both before birth and after birth in dependence upon others, including, most importantly, the new human being's mother, the Cardinal-Archbishop implored physicians to use their great influence to check abortions. His point warrants repetition: 'If doctors, in accord with the Hippocratic oath, wanted to eliminate abortions, they could do so almost entirely, because they are the persons who perform the overwhelming number of abortions. Medical schools and medical societies must, then, become target areas for re-education on the dignity of unborn human life" (223).

"When there is question of a young unmarried woman who is now with child, the physician is in a position to help her make arrangements so that the fact of her pregnancy will remain secret. The physician will usually know of some out-of-town home or hospital to which the unmarried mother may retire until after the birth of the baby. The doctor can acquaint the woman with this possibility, advise her concerning the time when she should go away, and suggest reasons for leaving that she can give to her family, employer, and friends. In such cases, it would ordinarily be preferable for the young mother herself not to undertake the rearing of the baby, but to provide, through the hospital authorities, for a good home for the infant" (4).

"The attitude of the priest or the professional theologian towards members of the medical profession, whether doctors or nurses, contrary to what they may imagine to be the case, is one of very deep sympathy. It expresses itself as helpfully as possibly by endeavoring to discover a *modus vivendi*, whilst preserving intact the moral teaching of the Church, in cases where their professional reputation or even their employment in hospitals is at stake. In the last resort, some material loss may have to be faced rather than offend against the law of God in so grave a matter. The issue between causing and not causing direct abortion is, at all events, a matter which has wider interests than purely medical ones. We find it hard to believe, though we are open to persuasion, that the professional reputation of a doctor would gravely suffer in the long run if he/she pleaded these wider interests, religious, legal, social, moral, or whatever they may be, in justification of refusal directly to cause an abortion" (224).

Compassionate and compelling, the Archbishop of New York has accepted the challenging gauntlet of abortion alternatives. He has pledged his church's help to all women considering an abortion. "The Archdiocese will do everything to assist pregnant women who choose to allow their unborn children to live and be born. He does not hesitate to say that he, like any other priest, would do everything to help women who had abortions to recover from the physical, psychological, and spiritual trauma it has caused" (110).

More specifically, the archdiocesan outreach antiabortion program stresses that no woman need ever feel she has no choice but to have an abortion. The Archbishop is on record as saying: "I can assure every single or married woman facing an unplanned pregnancy that the Archdiocese of New York will give you free, confidential care of the highest quality. It makes no difference whether you are Jewish, Protestant, Catholic, Muslim, Orthodox, of any other religion, or of no religion at all, or single or married ... A wide variety of services ranging from prenatal care and housing through adoption services for those who desire them and financial aid and support services for women who choose to rear their children. Simply and straightforwardly, the Archdiocese of New York is prepared to do everything in its power to help you and your unborn baby, whoever you are" (225).

If, by selecting an alternative to abortion, one human life is saved, in contrast to the 4,000 abortions performed daily, it will be an occasion to rejoice. Contrariwise, if an alternative is not chosen, melancholy will prevail, as was expressed in the words of John Donne (1573-1631), the parochial poet, who wrote: "Any man's death diminishes me, because I am involved in Mankind; and therefore never send to know for whom the bell tolls. It tolls for thee" (226).

Many are cognizant of and fully conversant with the other alternatives to abortion. However, it seems that one of the most widely publicized alternatives is ineffectual. Reference is made to the Family Planning Clinics and the Planned Parenthood groups. It is estimated that more than 50 million dollars are spent annually to educate people to their various offerings. Yet, the number of abortions continues to rise. These pre-need planning activities consist in rendering services in family planning that accentuate birth control. "The methods of contraception provided to patients include natural family planning (rhythm), oral contraceptives, intra-uterine devices (IUDs), and other mechanical contrivances. There is specialized counseling about each method and education on the method of choice. In addition, voluntary sterilizations are provided to both men and women" (227).

On the sterilization alternative, certain observations cannot be set aside without comment. Prior to doing so, the quotation from the president of a sterilization association has been made available. "According to the most recent studies (in 1977-78), almost 75 percent of American couples use one of the three most effective methods of birth control: the pill, the IUD and voluntary sterilization. Voluntary sterilization rivals the pill in prevalence of use in the U.S.A. Of the over one million voluntary sterilizations, about 60,000 were done by Medicaid funding, according to the General Accounting Office. The rest were funded privately"(228).

Up to 1969, there were some guidelines adhered to before a gynecologist would sterilize a woman. A numerical figure was necessary based upon age. Thus, a woman's age times the number of children she had must equal 120 before she could qualify for voluntary sterilization. This rule is no longer applicable.

"Sterilization has not followed an identical course in public policy and perception to other methods of contraception. Because it is a surgical method, it has been confined to the province of the physician and the hospital rather than to the clinic and counsellor. * * * The Association for Voluntary Sterilization is working with the Planned Parenthood Federation of America to support a program to increase access to outpatient sterilization" (228).

Many patients are not fully informed on the biological nature of sterilization. The availability of government funds for involuntary sterilization has led to deception for financial gain in performing surgery that is unnecessary to preserve life. There is abuse in federally funded sterilization programs. Under the by-line of "current opinion", a learned medicolegalist discussed involuntary sterilization (229).

One aspect of his presentation was ludicrous to a fault. It concerned a report from "a Cherokee physician who revealed that an Indian woman who had been sterilized by means of a hysterectomy after childbirth, asked for a uterine transplant. The request revealed that this patient never understood the permanence and irreversibility of hysterectomy as a contraceptive device. Although the patient did sign a consent form, she was uninformed" (229).

Obtaining an informed consent is not only a moral, but a legal imperative. In part, this urgent consent need arises from the due process clause of the 14th amendment of the constitution (229). In 1923, the Supreme Court stated that "freedom from bodily restraint and the right of an individual to marry and establish a home and bring up children is consistent with the due process clause of the 14th amendment. In a subsequent decision, the Supreme Court recognized the right of procreation as an independent constitutional right and as a basic civil right (231).

Later decisions by the Supreme Court have warned against any governmental interference with "the basic human right to procreate". Any interference with this right is a violation of the 14th amendment (232). In 1941, Mr. Justice Douglas invoked the 13th amendment to prevent the states from curtailing the right of free movement of the poor because this "would introduce a caste system utterly incompatible with the spirit of our system of government. It would permit those who are stigmatized by the state as indigent, paupers or vagabonds to be relegated to an inferior class of citizenship" (233).

"By the same line of reasoning, a lifetime of childlessness is a form of involuntary servitude if it is not desired. Does not voluntary sterilization (the result of a procedure performed with an informed consent) place the victim in a state of permanent inferiority? Is it not a 'stigma' or 'badge' of inferiority? If it is, then voluntary sterilization is violative of the 13th amendment" (229).

"Dr. Constance Uri, a Cherokee physician, condemned the U.S. Government as being guilty of genocide. If, indeed, sterilization is performed on Indian women for socioeconomic or birth control purposes, or as an anti-poverty device, then involuntary sterilization is genocide" (229). The Supreme Court expressed it well when the majority opinion was: "The power to sterilize, if exercised, may have several far-reaching and devastating effects. In evil or reckless hands, it can cause races or types which are inimical to a dominant group to wither and to disappear" (231).

To failing memories, it must be recalled that the United States participated in the Nuremburg trials. "There it was learned that a legislatively represented majority determined that there were others who were less fit to procreate. These eugenic theories were popular in Nazi Germany. Such ideas are opposed to our belief that each human being and each social class is capable of full development, if given equal opportunity" (229).

## Morality, Contraception, and Rhythm

Average citizens are not prepared to give up worldly pleasures or mundane possessions. Less willing are they prone to sacrifice sensual gratification. Many are like children who want what they want when they want it. Human desires have popularized contraception, even as it has enriched the coffers of those who manufacture and distribute anti-fertility pharmaceuticals or mechanical birth control devices.

Since 1975, the contraceptive enterprise has become a billion dollar industry in New York and other states (with the discovery of AIDS in the early 1980's it has doubled). In 1975, the Federal Court for the Southern District of New York found unconstitutional provisions of a New York statute which:

1. Prohibits the sale or distribution of contraceptives to persons under sixteen;

2. Prohibits the advertisement or display of contraceptive products; and,

3. Prohibits the sale or distribution of contraceptives by anyone other than a licensed pharmacist (234).

As an alternative to abortion, contraception seems to be a reversal in logic. Abortion is a result of the failure of contraceptives to prevent pregnancy. Abortion is an ignominious back-up to contraception. As a reasonable alternative to abortion, contraception resurrects the logical fallacy of *"post hoc, ergo propter hoc"* (after this, therefore on account of this) in which it is argued that a consequent is caused by an antecedent simply because of the temporal relationship (10). Factually, the advocates of more "effective and widespread contraception" have erred in their enthusiasm.

"*Newsday* told its readers on August 20, 1982, that the best way to prevent 1.5 million abortions annually in the U.S. is for government to take a more active part in promoting contraception. The editorialist latched on to findings published elsewhere to the effect that oral contraceptives, though possibly harmful to women over 35 who smoke, have demonstrated positive effects in preventing a multiplicity of female disorders . . . But the editorialist makes no mention of the evidence identifying the contraceptive pill as achieving its primary effect by preventing nidation, that is, blocking the fertilized ovum's attachment to the uterine wall and thereby effectively aborting the newly conceived human life shortly after fertilization" (235).

The same proponent of accelerated contraception education left "unmentioned the actual increase in abortions following the ever-increasing use of contraceptives in this country. A 550 percent rise in abortions among unmarried teenagers has taken place since the federal government began providing free birth control services to them in 1970. Statistics on all abortions in Nassau-Suffolk Counties for 1981 show a 30 percent jump from the previous year, or six abortions for every ten live births" (236).

A reviewing editor of the above article wrote that: "*Newsday's* stance seems to take fornication and promiscuity for granted because so many abortions are performed on unmarried, often young, even teenage women. We do not find in the editorial any mention of chastity, any advertence to the need, cited by Pope Paul VI, to create 'an atmosphere favorable to education in chastity, that is, to the triumph of a healthy liberty over license by means of respect for the moral order' (236). Thus, the recommendation for a more active U.S. government participation in promoting 'more effective and widespread contraception' to prevent abortion lacks realism and attention to fundamental ethical values" (235).

Those who defend the unborn's right to live do not condone the artificial alternatives to abortion listed as the three most effective means of preventing conception. The only method of contraception acceptable is prudential restraint, which is the practice of rhythm. The brief history of the practice of rhythm or periodic continence has been marked by controversy and confusion. From the viewpoint of moral law, there is a great difference between rhythm and the use of contraceptives. "The practice of rhythm has been subjected to some highly questionable past publicity. On the one hand, it has been proclaimed as the answer to modern family problems as the 'natural' or 'Catholic' form of birth control, and the way to happiness in marriage. On the other hand, it has been roundly condemned as an abuse of a noble faculty, a symbol of modern secularism, and an escape into selfishness. Avoiding these two extremes, a more moderate group has expressed their uneasiness about the practice by calling it 'evil sounding', or an 'unhappy compromise'. However, it would seem the better part of prudence to avoid these emotion-laden terms. Rhythm must be evaluated in the clear light of reason and faith — as is done in other areas of human activity" (237).

It is not within this province to discuss the assumptions and physiological facts upon which the practice of rhythm or periodic continence is based. The present concern is to answer the question as to the ethicity of the practice. "When is a couple morally justified in making use of this practice? The question has several aspects which had best be treated separately" (237).

"In the first place, the practice of rhythm represents a means to achieve an end. The couple deliberately restricts marital relations to a definite period in the menstrual cycle in order to avoid or promote pregnancy. Hence, in judging the morality of the practice, one must consider first whether or not it is a morally permissible means considered in itself; and secondly, whether or not its use is morally legitimate under the circumstances" (237).

As to the first point, "the practice of rhythm, considered in itself, does not constitute a deviation from the right order or the moral law. It does not interfere with the normal, physiological process of reproduction freely set in motion by the act of intercourse. As is well known, it is the positive and direct interference with the natural physiological process of reproduction which constitutes the essential evil in the use of contraceptives" (237).

When rhythm is adopted as a marital plan for physical bliss, "the couple engage in normal marital relations and respect the natural physiological respite of the reproductive process which they have initiated. Profiting by their knowledge of the period of fertility and sterility, which the functioning of the female reproductive system establishes in the menstrual cycle, they restrict marital relations to those periods which are considered favorable either for the avoidance or promotion of pregnancy. Hence, considered as a means, the practice of rhythm must be considered morally indifferent. It is the purpose or reason on account of which it is used that makes it morally good or evil" (237).

Out of this adiaphorous status flows the second consideration which asks the question: under what conditions is the practice of rhythm morally permissible? "Inasmuch as rhythm, for whatever purpose it may be used, involves the restriction of marital relations to limited periods in the menstrual cycle, two conditions required for its licit use are evident. First, both partners must freely agree to the practice. The marriage contract confers the mutual right to marital relations and the consequent mutual obligation to grant the reasonable request for the use of that right. Neither one nor the other party may restrict the partner's use of this right without the partner's consent. Second, both partners must be capable of bearing the tension and restraint which the practice of rhythm may involve. If the restriction of marital relations to limited periods places either partner in the proximate occasion of sinning against chastity, or if the accompanying tension seriously threatens the growth of mutual love and harmony between husband and wife, the use of rhythm is illicit" (237).

The fulfillment of these two stipulations is required whenever there is licit restriction or limitation of marital relations for any reason whatsover (237). St. Paul summarizes the Roman Catholic position on this point in his first letter to the Christian couples of Corinth. "The husband must give his wife her due, and so too the wife her husband. The wife has no right over her own body; that right belongs to her husband. So, the husband has no right over his own body; that right belongs to his wife. Of this right do not deprive each other except perhaps temporarily by mutual consent, that you may be free for prayer; then resume your common life, lest in case of lack of self-control, Satan tempt you" (238).

In the final analysis, of all human actions in life, humanity proposes, but God disposes. A moral palingenesis is needed for unbelievers to accept abortion as murder. Until then, we are the surrogate voices of the unborn crying from their mother's wombs, hoping to exit into the full radiance of the external world.

# CHAPTER TEN

# EPILOGUE

*"Neither dost thou fear God, seeing thou art under the same condemnation? And we indeed justly, for we receive the due reward for our deeds, but this man hath done no evil."*
Luke 23, 40-41 (239)

The devastating contabescent diseases from the famine in Ethiopia, the Sudan, and elsewhere invoked the financial altruism in charitable Americans. Their generosity accumulated millions of dollars to help the starving children of these arid lands. Most of these victims of drought and malnutrition will not survive. Nevertheless, they have not been abandoned.

Contrarily, this same benevolent nature, proneness to charity, and American compassion turns away from the unborn — most of whom are healthy. Their only need is an opportunity to live. *"O! tempora, O! mores"*, to quote Cicero; how many unheralded Shakespeares, Verdis, DaVincis, Steinmetzes, Einsteins, Lincolns, George Washington Carvers, or Mother Theresas have been destroyed? How illogically have Americans defined their moral duties separating starving children to be saved from unborn children to be killed? Who has divided charity into unreasonable categories?

Charity is love. As such, its presence is not selective. It embraces all human beings. When it is needed, its awareness is superbly publicized by the electronic media and printed journalism. This attention brings forth a commendable, tangible, popular response. Thus, the needs of the unfortunate are met generously by the caring people of our nation.

In the abortion dilemma, to many groups, this same benignity is not demonstrated. Perhaps it is because some people refuse to accept the veracity that abortion is murder. That to kill is contrary to God's law. To them the words of the early Christians have been forgotten.

Did not Peter the Rock say: "Whoever disobeys even the least important of the Commandments and teaches others to do the same, will be least in the Kingdom of Heaven" (240)?

The premise advanced in this book is that abortion is murder of the unborn child. Oral and written opposition to this exordium has not changed this belief one iota. Scientific, medicolegal, philosophic, socioeconomic, and theologic research on the subject of abortion has strengthened this stated position. The flimsy excuses offered in favor of abortion are not acceptable.

The detraction that the inexactness of the ensoulement time eliminates the moral responsibility that human life exists, leaving the fertilized ovum in the nonspecific category of a mass of protoplasm, is not tenable. From embryonic reasoning, the time of animation has been postulated. It is founded, additionally, on physiologic motility which allows a moral immunity for medical means to be employed in the protective treatment of the victims of rape or incest.

To those who have expressed the opinion that the Roman Catholic Church does not have a uniform teaching on abortion, the answer is contained in this textbook. Between these covers is found written substantiation, dogmatically recorded, of the printed Roman Catholic doctrine on abortion. It is documented and expressed by the Pope John XXIII Medical-Moral Research and Education Center in St. Louis, Missouri (129).

Included in this doctrinal guideline is the abolition of the alleged Catholic politician's dichotomy of personal opposition to abortion without the right to impose individual moral beliefs on others. Religion and politics, separation of church from the state, have been chapters for discussion because they are inextricably entwined with the abortion disputation. Under both these chapter titles, the right of Catholic bishops to speak out on abortion is defended as their moral duty as well as an American civic responsibility as incorporated in the Constitution of the United States which guarantees freedom of speech to all its citizens.

The physical medicosurgical complications of postabortion procedures founded upon purposeful studies at certain major hospitals are brought into scientific focus. The assembled research data verifies that the medicosurgical procedure of abortion performed with the most modern techniques under sterile surroundings, and with the latest instruments, is not free from the physical hazards of morbidity and mortality. The psychiatric residuals of abortion have not been classified didactically, but they do occur.

Alternatives to abortion are suggested as offerings to the pregnant woman. Some of these proposals existed long before the legalization of abortion by the Supreme Court in 1973, or the state laws that preceded that decision commencing in 1970. The American Medical Association had a program for unwed mothers almost since its inception as a national medical organization more than 100 years ago.

Church groups of the various denominations had similar facilities to care for unwed mothers which managed adoption procedures for the child and granted financial aid for postnatal care to the natural mother. The chain of tactful, discreet services were prescribed with dignity and in a gentle fashion. Under this methodology, there was no war waged against unborn infants, rather they were protected from birth until they were placed into the arms of loving, caring foster parents. "The day may soon arrive when a woman who wants to terminate a pregnancy would do so by going through delivery and having the newborn infant taken to a neonatal care facility for immediate adoption" (45). In this way, the human soul within the small body will remain in its proper worldly habitat.

If this does not eventuate, then the diary entry of a Russian Censor in 1866 would prevail. "How coarsely these naturalist fellows treat the human soul, considering it part and parcel of the human flesh. They stare at it coldly through their microscopes, plunge their scalpels into it, and are disinterested in anything the microscopes or the scalpel cannot divulge. Naturally, they believe only their own senses. But is everything that is knowable available to them alone? Why does materialism have a greater right to our trust in what concerns the most vital part of man than does idealism? Both of them are ignorant in this sphere. But at least our spiritual interests are harmonious with idealism, without which man would be no more than a beast, a scoundrel, and the most pathetic creature" (241).

An additional purpose has been to assist in the clarification of those nebulous areas that camouflage the fundamental immorality of abortion. We do not sit in judgment, for we are mindful of the gospel. "Do not judge others, and God will not judge you. Give to others and God will give to you. Indeed, you will receive a full measure, a generous helping poured into your hands — all that you can hold" (242).

Like the prophets in old biblical history who spoke in terms of hope, we do not despair that the abortion tragedy will lessen and eventually fade into nothingness. May all unborn children be a St. John the Baptist. He is without equal among the prophets, not only because he heard the voice of Christ and baptized him, but also among the saints of the Old and New Testaments he alone was sanctified *in utero*. John was blessed in a special way before he was born. The incident is recorded by St. Luke: "When Elizabeth (mother of St. John) heard Mary's greeting, the baby leapt in her womb" (243). May all the unborn babies in our time leap from their mothers' wombs out into nature's atmosphere.

By their conjugal act, two adult human beings of different genders produce another human person whom they start on the voyage of life. To obstruct or destroy it is an interruption to that natural pathway necessary for the betterment of all human life. Abortion is the estoppel to future intellectual grandeur and glorious, spiritual, joyous enlightenment. Abortion interrupts the entrance of another human being into the universe through the threshold of life. It negates to another the right to partake in the living experience that may lead to masterful accomplishments which enrich all phases of human existence. Every human being is entitled to embark on life's voyage.

Consideration is given here to a conceptual essay on "human subjects injured in biomedical research". It targeted on a disputation that provoked the controversy of deontological versus utilitarian thought (252). Deontology was defined as "pertaining to the theory of moral obligation". The utilitarian interpretation of the subject material had for its proposition the belief that sees "social justice as the greatest good for the greatest number of people" (252). As an explanatory remark, it was specified that: "This view, however, is not equivalent to Rawl's theory of distributive justice which is concerned with a just distribution of burdens and benefits among members of society" (253).

The microscopic scrutiny of factual knowledge on the subject of abortion does not allow any acceptance that under the canopy of deontology or utilitarianism a moral obligation is a theory. The insinuation of distributive justice (as expressed under utilitarianism) into any segment of the abortion intricacy is not applicable. As in any medical discussion of maximum gravity, it is scientifically dangerous to speculate whenever the ken of the discussant or the available honest facts do not bolster authoritatively the expressed opinion or contemplated conclusion to be postulated.

To discuss the debated abortion issue from every conceivable aspect demands a knowledge of embryology, physiology, an understanding of the law (unborn fetuses have rights under the law), a profound, ubiquitous concept of philosophy including its subdivisions, a proper definition of the theological terms employed, precise quotations from scholastic philosophers and/or theologians, plus a genuine search for the ultimate criterion of things in the light of pure reason. Failure to pursue this roadway to truth is to employ pedantic sophistry. Hence, any medical, legal, social, or philosophic dictum not founded on truth degenerates to a canard (73).

The intrinsic moral nature of humanity is such that there exists a spontaneous respect for all forms of living creations. Hence, it is common to see signs: Do Not Walk On The Grass, Seeded Lawn, or Keep Off The Flower Bed. Thus, vegetative life is protected even in its incipiency. Protectors of animal life express their concern under banners such as: The American Society For Prevention of Cruelty To Animals, and The Anti-Vivisection Society. Other groups protest research experimentation that injures or destroys animal life with or without the tranquility of euthanasia. If there is noticeable resentment against the destruction of vegetable or animal life, how much greater attentive concern must be given to the protection of human life? Is not humankind the steward of all creation?

# GLOSSARY

This commentary is not to be construed as a partial dictionary or as an exercise in palillogy. Rather it is an essential, supplementary, partial elucidation of the historical abortion ruling by the United States Supreme Court Justices on July 3, 1989. The fragmented, splintered opinions need some clarification in order to preserve the seminal ingredient of the judgments rendered.

The glossary is warranted because of the complex detail of the many statements and dissents in the 86-page document that often necessitates microscopic disentanglement. In the main majority statements the minuscule imbalance between conservative judges versus liberal judges is manifested by the narrow 5-4 vote on most occasions. This slight margin of victory results from the deciding vote cast by the most recent judicial appointee Mr. Justice Anthony Kennedy who is a conservative *in pectore*.

The quintessence of the eristic, voluminous decision is outlined sequentially.

1. The court voted 5-4 to reinstate key provisions of the Missouri abortion regulation law;

2. Majority vote was cast by Justices Rehnquist, White, O'Connor, Scalia, Kennedy;

3. Dissenters were Justices Blackmun, Brennan, Marshall, Stevens;

4. By 6-3 the court reaffirmed the Missouri statutes that bar the use of tax money for "encouraging or counseling" women to have abortions;

5. Additionally that section of the Missouri law was upheld that prohibits abortions by public employees or in public facilities (hospitals or in hospitals built on ground owned by government) plus requiring tests on fetuses 20 weeks or older to determine their survivability outside the mother's body;

6. Justice O'Connor, who is acclaimed as a key voter in the majority conservative group by some interpretive authorities, supported the Missouri law indicating that it could be done without altering the Roe v. Wade dictum of January 22, 1973;

7. By allowing the Roe decision to survive, women retain their constitutional privacy right to abortion, concurrently it endan-

gers the Roe framework by the state's power to regulate the performance of abortions;

8. The Supreme Court in the Roe matter gave women an absolute right to choose an abortion during the first three months of pregnancy, states can restrict abortions during the second three months (trimester) only for reasons "reasonably related to maternal health'";

9. After the fetus becomes viable (able to live outside the mother), usually 23-24 weeks, states can restrict or prohibit abortions except when the mother's health/life is threatened;

10. Justice Rehnquist stated that "trimesters and viability" are not found in the text of the constitution, thus, "the result has been a web of legal rules that have become increasingly intricate, resembling a code of regulations rather than a body of constitutional doctrine." Hence "we do not see why the state's interest in protecting potential human life should come into existence only at the point of viability"; and,

11. The Missouri law preserved by the Supreme Court was passed in 1986 but was not implemented because a United States District Court and the 8th United States Circuit Court of Appeals declared it unconstitutional. The provisions of the law as reinstated on July 3, 1989, now are enforceable, i.e., it is a violation of the law for public employees to perform or assist in performing an abortion, taxpayer money cannot be dispersed to encourage/counsel women to have an abortion, public facilities cannot be used to perform an abortion, specific indications are prescribed by Missouri law for fetal testing as to age, weight, plus lung maturity (309).

The 213th anniversary of Independence Day does not equate with a peace treaty between the abortion factions. Fragor with discord has not diminished. Foreheard rumor strongly suggests that the July Supreme Court ruling giving to states autonomy to restrict abortions within its borders will infiltrate the 1990 elections. Predictions are rampant that each side of the abortion travail will spawn vociferous bombardments of state legislatures.

No longer can elected members of state assemblies, senates, or House of Burgesses become uninvolved by stating abortion is in the realm of the courts. With this latest Supreme Court decision state legislators have no alternative but to assume responsibility for the abortion contestation. People in state political arenas cannot take a leave of absence from their obligations in this tristful division in America.

It is predicted that further attrition of the Roe v. Wade decision will be witnessed during the autumn/winter session of the High Court after it listens to the pleadings in three abortion cases. Arguments were ordered in two instances concerning parental notice requirements for non-emancipated minors who seek an abortion. The Supreme Court has consented to listen to these two adversarial petitions requiring parental notification for minors that have originated in Ohio and Minnesota. The third dispute to be heard involves the licensing of abortion clinics (310).

From both the pro- and con-abortion camps, the bright fires of the distressed campers are visible. In cahoots with their colleagues they are planning connived strategies to bolster their cause. The seething hatred must be constrained because hatred breeds violence and violence bursts into uncontrollable destruction.

After the July 3rd, 1989 Supreme Court majority dicta President Bush said: "The court appears to have begun to restore to the people the ability to protect the unborn...I have confidence that the American people will continue to express their deeply held convictions on this subject within the bounds of civility and our legal institutions" (309). Forecasters envision a future America that allows abortion to remain legal, but it may become impossible to obtain one.

Amalgamating contentious contraception with baneful abortion is an unfounded concept of wild, imaginary fancy. It is a legally insinuated version of the mixed-species, monstrous Chimeras of grotesque Greek mythology. The *fons et origo* (source and origin) of which is an obscured figment of the imagination. To interpose contraception in the abortion disputation is a revealed bifurcated disunity indicating the exigency of the embarrassed predicament in which the abortion forces find themselves. In attempting to aid their cause by confusing the opposition, the abortion devotees have epiphanized the pressing debilitated state of their efforts to preserve the *status quo*.

For comparative mindful diffusion the strict interpreters of the constitution and the procrustean adherents to the laws sustained by the Supreme Court of the United States must separate contraception from abortion even as they vehemently proclaim the separation of church and state. Attentive legal thinking seems to be in a vacuum of erroneous inconsistency. When discussing the separation of church from the state, the judiciary adamantly upholds this division. However, when contraception is introduced into the abortion fracas, this commingling is not frowned upon. *Insuper* the lawgivers, the eager-heedful observers, who can only stand and wait, seem to be in the limbo assigned to non-participating, no-choice outcasts.

The haste in terminating the mid-term session stimulated the Supreme Court to rouse out in July 1989, an opinion, with dissents, concurring data plus photographs (appended to the pleadings as properly introduced court exhibits) a no-sense decision on the separation of church from the state. It centered on the well-known targeted Pittsburgh legal action on the depiction of the creche and the menorah during the Christmas holidays.

By a 6 to 3 vote, the wisdom of justice manifested itself when the Supreme Court ruled that displaying the menorah was permissible. The creche was judged to be illegal by the narrow margin of 5 to 4. Mr. Justice Blackmun, writing in favor of the 18-foot-high Hanukah menorah indicated that its presence on the steps of the City Hall did not violate the First Amendment. This constitutional amendment forbids the establishment of religion which was not violated because the menorah was next to a Christmas tree. Although both are religious symbols the presence of more than one item eliminates the endorsement of any one specific religion. Contrariwise in the same City of Pittsburgh, the solitary creche had no companion ally to militate against its religious significance. As a solo performer it was interpreted as an endorsement of Christianity. Therefore such displays are not permitted under the First Amendment.

*O! tempora, O! mores*, what has humanity done that we despise each other? Normally established, acceptable religions of whatever denomination are not injurious to America. Displays during the Christmas weeks are festive delights that bring joy to elative communities large and small. Hospitality increasingly flourishes, friendliness flows, and the air is filled with cheerfulness radiant by the religious symbols brilliant with the multicolored lights of Christmas-tide. These filamented bulbs should be neither dimmed nor extinguished because duskiness and darkness bring gloomy sadness. Americans flourish under the glow of religious tolerance which is an integral part of the crural heritage intended for us by our colonial ancestors.

A new invalidation of personal rights called no-choice has been manifested by self-aggrandizing pseudo-philosophers and hedonistic legalists. This propensity is obvious in the decisions rendered on separation of church from the state, the flag-burning opinion, and the past, present, and probably in future abortion dicta. Under the no-choice doctrine the unconceived ovum has no-choice as to whether or not it is to receive a spermatozoon. A zygote has no-choice as to its survival or demise. The fetus has no-choice as to the determination of its own viability. Prior to 1973 an American infant was protectively cuddled in its mother's womb. Now babies may be destroyed capriciously at someone else's whim. Advocates of prochoice for women simultaneously are no-choice advocates for the unborn.

# REFERENCES

1. Peyton, Rev. Patrick. A Special Time For Prayer. Family Rosary Crusade, Executive Park Drive, Albany, N.Y. 12203, 1984.

2. Flood, Dom Peter. New Problems In Medical Ethics. Translated from the French "Cahiers Laennec" by Malachy Gerard Carroll. Published by the Newman Press, Westminster, Maryland, 1954.

3. Marcel, Gabriel. Psychological and Moral Incidences. In New Problems In Medical Ethics quoted in reference 2.

4. Healy, Edwin F. (S.J.) Medical Ethics. Loyola University Press, Chicago, Ill., 1956.

5. Pregnancy in Anatomical Illustrations. Presented by Carnation Company. Published by the Medical Department of the Carnation Company, Los Angeles, California, 90036, 1969.

6. Dorland's Illustrated Medical Dictionary, 25th Edition. W. B. Saunders Co., Philadelphia, Penna., 1974.

7. McElin, T.W. Ectopic Pregnancy. Chapter 18 in Obstetrics And Gynecology, 3rd Edition, by David N. Danforth. Published by Harper and Row, Hagerstown, Md., 1977.

8. Pegalis, S.E. and Wachsman, H.F. American Law of Medical Malpractice, Volume One. The Lawyers Co-Operative Publishing Co., Rochester, N.Y., 1980.

9. Bernardin, Joseph Cardinal. The Chicago Catholic, Sept. 28, 1984. Quoted by Religious News Service in The Long Island Catholic, p. 11, October 25, 1984.

10. The Dictionary of Philosophy. Edited by Dagbert D. Runes. Published by the Philosophical Library, New York, N.Y. (no date).

11. The Shorter Oxford English Dictionary. Revised and Edited by C.T. Onions. Oxford University Press, Ely House, London W.I., England, 1977.

12. Feldman, Walter S. Frozen Embryos. To Be or Not To Be, That is One of the Questions. Legal Aspects of Medical Practice, Vol. 12, No. 10, Oct. 1984. Publication of the American College of Legal Medicine, Chicago, Illinois.

13. Auci, D.L. Tolerance and Dialogue Needed. Letter to the Editor. Long Island Catholic, October 4, 1984.

14. Rugh, Roberts, Shettles and Landrum. From Conception To Birth: The Drama Of Life's Beginning. Harper and Row, New York, N.Y., 1971.

15. No author. The Faith of Scientists. Robins Reader, Fall- Winter Issue, 1984. Published by A.H. Robins Co., Fairview, New Jersey.

16. Eckstein, Walter. Rights defined. In The Dictionary of Philosophy. Reference 10.

17. Black's Law Dictionary by Henry Campbell Black. Fourth Edition by The Publisher's Editorial Staff. West Publishing Co., St. Paul, Minnesota, 1951.

18. Holland's Elements of Jurisprudence. Quoted in Black's Law Dictionary. Reference 17.

19. Austin's Province of Jurisprudence, Paragraph 264. Quoted in Black's Law Dictionary. Reference 17.

20. Sweet's Law Dictionary. Quoted in Black's Law Dictionary. Reference 17.

21. Ficarra, B.J. (M.D.) Newer Ethical Problems In Medicine And Surgery. The Newman Press, Westminster, Maryland, 1951.

22. No author. Some Doctors Endorse Reagan Fetal Pain Remark. Long Island Catholic, Thursday, March 22, 1984.

23. Ficarra, B.J. (M.D.) Surgical And Allied Malpractice. Charles C. Thomas, Publisher, Springfield, Illinois, 1968.

24. Verkennes v. Cornien, 38 N.W.2d 838 (D. Minn. 1949).

25. Raney v. Horn, 72 So.2d 434 (D. Miss. 1954).

26. Holder, A.R. Prenatal Injuries. JAMA, Vol. 214, No. 11, pp. 2105, 2106, December 14, 1970.

27. Bonbrest v. Katz, 65 F.Supp. 138 (D.C. D.C. 1946).

28. Prosser, W.L. Handbook Of The Law Of Torts, Third Edition. West Publishing Co., St. Paul, Minnesota, 1964.

29. Stetson v. Easterling, 161 S.E.2d 531 (D. N.C. 1968).

30. Williams v. Marion Rapid Transit Co., 87 N.E.2d 334 (D. Ohio 1949).

31. Woods v. Lancet, 102 N.E.2d 691 (D.N.Y. 1951).

32. Amann v. Faidy, 114 N.E.2d 412 (D.Ill. 1953).

33. Norman v. Murphy, 268 P.2d 117 (D.Ca. 1954).

34. Endresz v. Friedberg, 248 N.E.2d 901 (D.N.Y. 1969).

35. Arnold, L.C. Prenatal Injuries: A Treatment and Prognosis of the Law. DePaul Law Review, Vol. XVIII, Nos. 2 and 3, Summer, 1969.

36. Rodriguez v. Patti, 415, 496, 114 N.E.2d 721 (D.Ill. 1953).

37. Mitchell v. Couch, 285 S.W.2d 901 (Ky. Ct. App. 1955).

38. No author. Unborn Child Found Entitled to Benefit. American Medical News, p. 22, March 2, 1984.

39. Presley v. Newport Hospital, 365 A2d 748 (Sup. Ct. R.I. 1976).

40. Delgado v. Yandell, 468 S.W2d 475 (Tex. Civ. App. 1971).

41. Mone v. Greyhound Lines, Inc., 331 N.E.2d 916 (July 16, 1975).

42. State v. Magnell, 51 A. 606.

43. Wells v. New England Mutual Life Ins. Co., 191 Penna. 207, 43 A. 126, 53 L.R.A. 327.

44. Peoole v. Luckett, 23 Cal. Cal. App. 2d 539, 73 P.2d 658, 659.

45. Dujardin, R. Technological Advances Cause New Conflicts Between Medicine and Ethics. Long Island Catholic, November 29, 1984.

46. Connell, Very Reverend Francis J. Preface in Newer Ethical Problems In Medicine And Surgery by B.J. Ficarra, M.D. Reference 21.

47. No author. Murder Charges Filed After Failed Abortion. The New York Times, October 5, 1984.

48. Editorial. Dr. Melnick's Lethal Act. The Long Island Catholic, Thursday, February 7, 1985.

49. No author. Unborns Rate in D.C. The Washington Times, October 22, 1984.

50. The Bible. Genesis 4, 3-16.

51. The Day of the Lord: 33rd Sunday in Ordinary Time, November 18, 1984. Published by J.S. Paluck Company, Inc., P. 0. Box 2703, Schiller Park, Illinois. With Ecclesiastical Approbation.

52. Madigan, W.A. Letter to the Editor from Carmack, N.Y. Long Island Catholic, November 1, 1984.

53. Planned Parenthood v. Danforth (No. 74-1151) Mo (Appealed from the Sup. Ct. of Missouri to the U Supreme Court

54. Barid v. Belotti, 3 Massachusetts Lawyers Weekly 462.

55. Roe v. Wade, 225 U.S. 215-216 (1973).

56. Holman, E.J. United States Supreme Court and Abortion. Parts I, II, III. JAMA, Vol. 225, No. 2, 3, 4, July 9, 16, 23, 1973.

57. Ficarra, B.J. (M.D.) A Psychosomatic Approach to Surgery. Froben Press, Inc., New York, N.Y. 1951.

58. Sheen, Most Reverend Fulton J. Peace of Soul. Whittlesey House, McGraw-Hill Book Co., New York, N.Y., 1949.

59. Bourke, V.J. Ethics. Chapter 11, "Justice and the Persons of Others." The Macmillan Co., New York, N.Y. 1951.

60. Scremin, Luigi. Il vizio solitario. Istituto di Propaganda Libraria, Milan, Italy, 1949.

61. McFadden, C.J. (O.S.A.) Medical Ethics. Chapter 2, "The Foundations of Morality." F.A. Davis Co., Philadelphia, Penna., 1951.

62. O'Donnell, T.J. (S.J.) Modern Medical and Surgical Means for the Preservation of Life. Linacre Quarterly, Vol. 18, No. 2, pp. 22-31, February 1951.

63. Farrell, P. (O.P.) In The Groove. Published by the National Headquarters of the Holy Name Society, New York, N.Y., 1949.

64. Cassidy, Ferrer, O.P. The Knowledge Of Evil. Published by the National Headquarters of the Holy Name Society, New York, N.Y., 1951.

65. Jacobson v. Massachusetts, 197 U.S. 11, 25 S.Ct. 358, 49 L.Ed. 643 (1905).

66. McIntosh v. Milano, 168 N.J. Sup. Ct. 466, 403 A.2d 500 (1979).

67. People v. Privitera, 23 Cal.3d 697, 591 P.2d 919 (1979), 153 Cal. Rptr. 431.

68. Tarasoff v. Regents Univ. of California, 17 Ca1.3d 425, 131 Cal. Rptr.

69. Areen, J., King, P. and Goldberg, S. Law, Science, and Medicine. The Foundation Press, Inc., Mineola, New York, 1984.

70. Advertisements in New York Times Sponsored by Planned Parenthood of New York City, Inc., 380 Second Avenue, New York, New York, 1984.

71. Trunk, K.M. Letter to the Editor, Long Island Catholic, Thursday, November 1, 1984.

72. Abortion Unalienable Right. New York State Journal of Medicine, Vol. 72, No. 16, pp. 1772, 1774, July 1, 1972.

73. Ficarra, B.J. (M.D.) Letter to the Editor. "The Abortion Issue". New York State Journal of Medicine, Vol. 72, No. 19, pp. 2460, 2462, October 1, 1972.

74. Castiglioni, Arturo. A History of Medicine. Alfred A. Knopf, publisher, New York, New York, 1941.

75. Arey, L. B. Developmental Anatomy. W. B. Saunders Co., Philadelphia, Penna., 1935.

76. No author: First Embryo Transfer Baby Born. American Medical News, Feb. 7, 1984. 77. O'Beirne v. Superior Court of Santa Clara County, Cal. (Dec. 7, 1967).

78. Huxley, Aldous. The Many Faces of Love. Quoted in Robins Reader. Reference 15.

79. McTigue, J.A. O.P. Equipment For Crises. Published by National Headquarters of the Holy Name Society, New York, New York 1949.

80. The Chicago Tribune. Quoted in Robins Reader. Reference 15.

81. Fishbein, Morris. Abortion Reform. Editorial in Medical World News, June 2, 1972.

82. Rosenfeld, D.L., Garcia, C. and Shippen, W., Jr. Injuries Incurred During Rape. Medical Aspects of Human Sexuality, Pages 77, 78, March 1976.

83. Breen, J.L. and Cooke, C.W. Treating the Rape Victim. Medical World News, pp. 50-58, March 8, 1976.

84. Sternback, G.L. Treatment of Rape Victims. Emergency Medical Services Magazine, pp. 8-15, January/February 1976.

85. Medical News report on sexual behavior in an abnormal situation, JAMA Vol. 245, No. 3, pp. 215, 216, January 16, 1981.

86. Webster, W. Uniform Crime Reports for the United States. U.S. Dept. Justice, Washington, D.C., pp. 14, 15, 1978.

87. Schelble, D.T. An 18 Month Evaluation of the Akron General Medical Center Assault/Rape Protocol, Annals of Emerg. Med., Vol. 11, No. 1, pp. 9/27, 17/35, January 1978.

88. Guzzardi, L.J. Emergency Care of Rape Victims. Annals of Emerg. Med. Vol. 9, No. 12, p. 76/649, December 1980.

89. Metzger, D.A. Evidence Collection Vital in Rape Cases: Forensic Expert. Discussion at U. of Michigan Med. Center. Reported in Emergency Dept News, p. 15, October 1980.

90. Cryer, L. and Mattox, K.L. Rape Evidence Kit: Simplified Procedure for the Emergency Dept. Jour.,Am. College Emerg. Physicians, Vol. 5, No. 11, pp. 890, 893, November 1976.

91. Milne, D. R. Ethinyl Appears Contraceptive for Rape Cases. Report from the National Institute for Child Health and Human Development, Bethesda, Maryland. Reported in Emergency Dept. News, Vol. 3, No. 1, pp. 1-15, January 1981.

92. Special Report on Rape. The Long Island Catholic, p. 4, Thursday, Jan. 7, 1982.

93. Erlich, R.F. Author's Reply on Emergency Care of Rape Victims. Annals Emerg. Medicine, Vol. 9, No. 12, p. 76/649, December 1980.

94. Ficarra, B.J. (M.D.) Medicolegal Handbook. Marcel Dekker Inc. publisher, New York, New York, 1983.

95. Ingraham, H.S., Health Commissioner's Directive, Dept. of Health, State of New York, Albany, N.Y., Sept. 5, 1973.

96. Gillibrand, Pharic. Psychotherapy May be Answer to Pelvic Ills. Report from Southhampton University, England. Quoted in Emergency Department News, Vol. 4, No. 3, Page 4, March 1982.

97. Brody, Jane E. Personal Health. The New York Times, Wednesday, January 6, 1982.

98. Executive Directors' Letter. Quoted in The Catholic Charities of the Archdiocese of New York Annual Report for 1983.

99. Scanlan, Patrick (Editor). Diary of an Unborn Child. The Brooklyn Tablet, exact date unknown (newspaper clipping).

100. Regina v. Iustan, I.Q.B. at 453, Great Britain, 1893. Quoted by Kim Rimirez in a book review in the Journal of Legal Medicine, Vol. 5, No. 2, pp. 332-342, June 1984.

101. Ficarra, B.J. (M.D.) Leaf In The Wind. Exposition Press, New York, N.Y., 1962.

102. Cherry v. Board of Regents of University of State of New York, 289 N.Y. 148, 44 N.E.2d 405, 412.

103. "Lutherans For Life." Long Island Catholic, Thursday, November 22, 1984.

104.    No author. Protestants Begin to Reassess Positions on Abortion. Long Island Catholic, Thursday, October 25, 1984.

105.    Religious News Service (New York). AJC Issues Pamphlet on Jewish Views on Abortion, Long Island Catholic, Thursday, October 25, 1984.

106.    Marrin, W.C. (Rev.). The Word of God, Long Island Catholic, Thursday, August 23, 1984.

107.    Religious News Service (Washington), Catholics v. Bishops: Signs of Maturity, Diversity. Long Island Catholic, Thursday, November 29, 1984.

108.    Ellis, John Tracy (Msgr.). Quoted in reference number 107.

109.    Briggs, K.A. Cardinal Presses Fight on Abortion. New York Times, September 28, 1984.

110.    Editorial. Compassionate and Compelling. Re Archbishop John J. O'Connor. Long Island Catholic, Thursday, October 18, 1984.

111.    Klein, Joe. Abortion and the Archbishop. New York Magazine, October 1, 1984.

112.    Goldman, Ari L. New York's Controversial Archbishop. The New York Times Magazine, Sunday, October 14, 1984.

113.    Herbers, John. Archbishop Explains Abortion Stand. The New York Times, Sunday, September 23, 1984.

114.    Falwell, Jerry (Rev.). Speech on behalf of the Moral Majority. Harvard Law Forum, Cambridge, Mass., September 20, 1984.

115.    Excerpts under photograph of Bishop Francis J. Mugravero. Long Island Catholic, Thursday, October 11, 1984.

116.    Goldman, A.L. Bishop Links Abortion to the Killing of Infants. The New York Times, October 5, 1984.

117.    Lehner, C.M. (O.P.). Morality vs. Immorality. Published by the National Headquarters of the Holy Name Society, New York, N.Y., 1949.

118.    Lander, R.E. (Rev.). Marvelous Gift by a Scholar. Long Island Catholic, Thursday, December 13, 1984.

119.    Pope John Paul II's speech before members of the Vatican Justitia et Pax (Justice and Peace) Commission, November 30, 1984. Reported in Long Island Catholic, Thursday, December 6, 1984.

120.    Sciolino, Elaine. American Catholics: A Time for Challenge. The New York Times Magazine, Sunday, November 4, 1984.

121.    Editorial. Judging the Issue. Long Island Catholic, Thursday, January 3, 1985.

122.    Editorial. Spider's Web. Long Island Catholic, Thursday, January 24, 1985.

123.    No author. Signers of Abortion Statement Criticize Vatican Action. Long Island Catholic, Thursday, January 3, 1985, p. 9.

124. Hoye, Daniel F. (Msgr.). Statement as General Secretary of the National Council of Catholic Bishops. Quoted in reference number 123.

125. Stockhammer, M. (Editor). Thomas Aquinas Dictionary (Ethics I, p. 131). Published by the Philosophical Library, 15 E. 40 Street, New York, New York, 1965.

126. Cuomo, Mario (Governor). Speech on religion and politics. Delivered at Notre Dame University, September 1984.

127. Blum, Virgil C. (S.J.). Do Catholics Teach About Abortion? Long Island Catholic, Thursday, October 18, 1984, p. 7.

128. No author. Catholic Research Center Distributes Abortion Statement. Long Island Catholic, Thursday, November 29, 1984.

129. Catholic Teaching on Abortion and Secular Society. Published by the Pope John XXIII Medical-Moral Research and Education Center, St. Louis, Missouri, 1984.

130. Liebard, Odile M. Declaration on Abortion. In Official Catholic Teachings: Love and Sexuality. Consortium Books, McGrath Publishing Co., Wilmington, North Carolina, pp. 413-414, 1978.

131. Connery, J. (S.J.). Abortion: The Development of the Roman Catholic Perspective, p. 304. Loyola University Press, Chicago, Illinois, 1977.

132. Ashley, Benedict, Rev. (O.P.) Chapter in an Ethical Evaluation of Fetal Experimentation, pp. 113-133. Edited by Donald G. McCarthy and Albert S. Moraczewski, O.P. Published by the Pope John XXIII Medical-Moral Research and Education Center, St. Louis, Missouri, 1976.

133. The National Conference of Catholic Bishops. The Challenge of Peace: God's Promise and our Response. Printed in Advent Reflections. Published by The Pope John Paul II Center of Prayer For Peace, Shrine of Saint Elizabeth Ann Seton, 7-8 State Street (South Ferry), New York, N.Y., 1984.

134. Granfield, David. Abortion Decision, Chapter XIX, Number 5, p. 55. Published by Image-Doubleday, Garden City, N.Y., 1969.

135. Ratzinger, Joseph (Cardinal). Interview to the Italian Monthly, Jesus, August 1984. Quoted in Long Island Catholic, Thursday, p. 2, January 10, 1985.

136. Dowd, Dick. We Americans Tend to go by the Rules, Long Island Catholic, Thursday, p. 6, January 10, 1985 .

137. Catholics For Free Choice. Advertisement in the Sunday New York Times, p. E-7, October 7, 1984.

138. Maguire, Marjorie Reiley. Spokesperson for Catholic Committee on Pleuralism and Abortion under the auspices of Catholics for Free Choice. Communication of September 14, 1984 from Washington, D.C. Quoted in Long Island Catholic, Thursday, September 20, 1984.

139. Herbers, John. Catholic Activism; Reasons and Risks. The New York Times, Sunday, September 23, 1984.

140. Lewis, Flora. The Question Is Law. New York Times, September 11, 1984. Quoted in Letters to the Editor under title, A Reversible Ruling.

141. McLees, A.V. (Msgr.). To The Editor: A Reversible Ruling. The New York Times, Thursday, September 20, 1984.

142. Chanin, Bernard. Needless Alarm over U.S. Judiciary's Ideology. The New York Times, Thursday, September 20, 1984.

143. Editorial. ECRASEZ 1'infame! Long Island Catholic, Thursday, November 29, 1984.

144. No author. Cardinal Bernardin Issues Statement Condemning Abortion Clinic Bombings. Long Island Catholic, Thursday, January 24, 1985.

145. MMWR (Morbidity and Mortality Weekly Report). Health Effects on Restricting Federal Funds for Abortion United States. Published by the Center for Disease Control, U.S. Department of Health and Human Services/Public Health Service, Vol. 28, No. 4, February 2, 1979.

146. Davis, Henry (S.J.). Moral and Pastoral Theology. Vol. 1, p. 91, Sheed and Ward Publishers, New York, N.Y., 1919.

147. Tribe, Lawrence H. Religion, Politics Should Speak to, Not Control, Each Other. Speech Prepared at Harvard Law School. Presented in New York at Conference on "Government Intervention in Religious Affairs". Quoted in Long Island Catholic, Thursday, September 20, 1984.

148. Fox, Samuel J. (Rabbi Doctor). Massachusetts Counsel of Rabbis Issues Abortion Statement (by its president). Reported in The Pilot, Vol. 157, No. 34, p. 2, Friday, September 21, 1984. Published by the Archdiocese of Boston, Massachusetts.

149. Bernardin, Joseph (Cardinal). Major address delivered at Georgetown University on "Religion and Politics", October 25, 1984. Reported in Long Island Catholic, Thursday, November 1, 1984.

150. Gumbleton, Thomas (Bishop). Telephone interview on abortion with Auxiliary Bishop of the Archdiocese of Detroit, Michigan. Reported in Long Island Catholic, Thursday, October 18, 1984.

151. Paris Theatre v. Slaton. United States Supreme Court (June 1973).

152. Catoir, John (Rev.). On Pornography and Abortion. Long Island Catholic, p. 7, Thursday, January 24, 1985.

153. Morality in Media. List of Responses in Fight Against Traffic in Pornography and "Cableporn". Quoted in reference 152.

154. Prospect, Wayne. Public Policy and Pornography: A Double Standard. New York Times, Sunday, p. 30, October 14, 1984.

155.   Mirror of Medicine. Equal Rights Amendment. MD Magazine, January 1979.

156.   Hamblin, Dora J. The Etruscans' Day Was Short, But They Have Cast a Long Shadow. Smithsonian Magazine, Vol. 15, No. 1, pp 59-57. February 1985.

157.   Steinharter, Rudolf H. Director of the Venereal Disease Program. Quoted by Stewart Ain in reference 158.

158.   Ain, Stewart. Report on Venereal Disease. Sunday News, July 16, 1972.

159.   Johnson, D. and Cunningham, P.G. E.R.A. and Abortion: Really Separate Issues? Supplement to the Catholic League Newsletter, Vol. 11, No. 8, pp 1-6. Published by Catholic League for Religious and Civil Rights, 1100 West Wells Street, Milwaukee, Wisconsin 53233, 1984.

160.   Alexander, E. and Fiedler, M. The Equal Rights Amendment and Abortion: Separate and Distinct. America, April 12, 1980.

161.   Fisher v. Commonwealth of Pennsylvania. Pa. Commw. Ct. (March 9, 1983).

162.   Balch, Burke J. Mixing Personal Morality and Public Policy. The New York Times, Thursday, p. A31, September 20, 1984.

163.   Editorial. Most Basic Duty. The Long Island Catholic, Thursday, September 13, 1984.

164.   Mitchell, F.E. (Port Jefferson Station). Letter to the Editor: Spread the Good News. Long Island Catholic, Thursday, November 1, 1984.

165.   Kelly, Kathleen (Hofstra Pro-Life Club). Letter to the Editor: Abortion. Long Island Catholic, Thursday, November 1, 1984.

166.   Rasky, Susan F. Reagan Restrictions on Foreign Aid for Abortion Programs Lead to a Fight. The New York Times, Sunday, October 14, 1984.

167.   Combined News Services. Governor Cuomo's Talk Draws a Variety of Reactions. Long Island Catholic, Thursday, September 20, 1984.

168.   Cuomo Addresses St. Francis College Audience on Key Issues. Terrier, St. Francis College Alumni Newsletter, Vol. 1, Winter 1984.

169.   Adams, Robert T. Governor's Call Draws Mixed Views. Long Island Catholic, Thursday, October 11, 1984.

170.   Religious News Service. Governor's Call Draws Mixed Views. Long Island Catholic, Thursday, October 11, 1984. Quotations of Robert T. Adams, Associate Publisher of The Brooklyn Tablet, and Rev. Larry Lossing of the Pope John XXIII Research Center, St. Louis, Missouri.

171.   Herhes, John. Abortion Issue Threatens to Become Profoundly Divisive. The New York Times, Sunday, October 14, 1984.

172.    Perlez, Jane. Ferraro, the Campaigner. The New York Times Magazine, Section 6, September 30, 1984.

173.    Blum, Virgil C. (S.J.). Whatever Happened to the Democratic Party? Long Island Catholic, Thursday, December 6, 1984.

174.    Shields, Mark (Former Harvard Professor). Public Opinion Magazine, October/November 1984.

175.    Editorial. Faulty Reasoning. Long Island Catholic, Thursday, August 9, 1984.

176.    Malone, James W. (Bishop). Catholic Conference Rejects Morality/Policy 'Dichotomy'. Long Island Catholic, Thursday, August 16, 1984.

177.    Callahan, Daniel. Restraint Serves Pleuralism. The New York Times, Thursday, p. A31, September 20, 1984.

178.    Pope John Paul II. Address at the General Audience, January 9, 1985, given in the Paul VI Hall, Vatican City. Reported in the Long Island Catholic, Thursday, January 24, 1985.

179.    Ficarra, B.J. (M.D.) Anti-Catholicism (Letter to Editor), Long Island Catholic, Thursday, November 15, 1984.

180.    Kaufman, Irving R. (Judge of U.S. Circuit Court of Appeals, Second Circuit, 1973-1980). Keeping Politics out of the Court. The New York Times, Sunday, Section 6, p. 72, December 9, 1984.

181.    Statement of the U.S. Catholic Conference Administrative Board on Political Responsibility issued March 22, 1984. Reprinted in Long Island Catholic, Thursday, October 18, 1984.

182.    Editorial. Please Vote. Long Island Catholic, Thursday, November 1, 1984.

183.    Marrin, Wiliam C. (Rev.). Jesus' Words Apply to Us. Long Island Catholic, Thursday, November 1, 1984.

184.    McGann, John R. (Bishop). Election Day, November 6, 1984. Long Island Catholic, Thursday, November 1, 1984.

185.    No author. High Abortion Rates Seen in Eastern Europe. American Medical News, April 15, 1983, p. 21. Publication of the American Medical Association, Chicago, Illinois.

186.    Lauder, Robert E. (Rev.). Integrating Religion and Life. Long Island Catholic, Thursday, p. 7, January 10, 1985.

187.    The Book of History, Vo!. XIV, pp 6071-6082. The Educational Book Co., The Grolier Society, New York and London. Printed by the Colonial Press, Boston, Mass., 1923.

188.    Lorant, Stefan. Presidency. Of Presidential Elections. The Macmillan Co., New York, N.Y. 1952.

189.    Lauder, Robert E. (Rev.) Neopaganism. Long Island Catholic, Thursday, p. 7, September 1, 1983.

190.    Briggs, Kenneth A. Bishop Criticizes Mixing of Church and State. The New York Times, Sunday, p. 59, November 4, 1984.

191. Briggs, Kenneth A. Archbishop of Manila to Visit China to "Promote Harmony". The New York Times, Sunday, p. 4, September 23, 1984.

192. Boothby, Lee (Esq.). Religion, Politics Should Speak to, Not Control Each Other. Quoted in Long Island Catholic. Reference 147.

193. Hamilton, D. (Msgr.) When New York Barred Catholic Priests. Long Island Catholic, Thursday, November 15, 1984.

194. Weekly Digest Column, Long Island Catholic, Thursday, p. 7, February 14, 1985.

195. Ornstein, Franklin H. Interfaith Understanding. Letter to the Editor. From the President, Long Island Chapter, American Jewish Committee, Great Neck, N.Y. Reported in Long Island Catholic, Thursday, January 25, 1985.

196. Malone, James W. (Bishop). Church's Role Exists at Intersection of Public Opinion, Policy. Long Island Catholic, Thursday, November 15, 1984.

197. Blum, Virgil C. (S.J.) Catholics: Do We Belong in America? Long Island Catholic, Thursday, February 7, 1985.

198. Rosenblum, Victor (Law Professor at Northwestern U. Law School) A Legal Scholar Explains Pro-Life Position. American Medical News, February 16, 1979.

199. Editorial. Blurring the Lines. Long Island Catholic, Thursday, August 16, 1984.

200. Editorial. Prophetical Office and Public Office. Long Island Catholic, Thursday, February 7, 1985.

201. Morbidity and Mortality Weekly Report. Published by the Center For Disease Control, U.S. Department of Health and Human Services/Public Health Service, Vol. 26:361, 1977.

202. Morbidity and Mortality Weekly Report. As in reference 201. Vol. 27:71, 1978.

203. Savage, W. and Paterson, I. Abortion: Methods and Sequelae. British Journal of Hospital Medicine, pp 364-369, October 1982.

204. Wulff, G.J. L. and Freiman, S.M. Elective Abortion. Complications Seen in A Free-Standing Clinic. Journal of Obstetrics and Gynecology, Vol. 45, No. 3, pp 351-357, March 1977.

205. Grimes, D. and Techman, T. (R.N.). Legal Abortion ad Placenta Previa. American Journal of Obstetrics and Gynecology, Vol. 149, No. 5, pp. 501-504, July 1, 1984.

206. Hogue, C., Cates, W., Jr. and Tietze, C. The Effects of Induced Abortion on Subsequent Reproduction. Epidemology Review, Vol. 4, No. 6, pp. 66-94, 1984.

207. Le Bolt, S.A., Grimes, D. and Cates, W., Jr. Mortality from Abortion and Childbirth. Journal American Medical Association, Vol. 248, No. 2, pp. 188-196, July 9, 1982.

208. Grimes, D., Flock, J.L., Schulz, K.F., and Cates, W., Jr. Hysterectomy as Treatment for Complications of Legal Abortion. Journal Obstetrics and Gynecology, Vol. 63, No. 4, pp. 457-462, April 1984.

209. King, T.M., Atienza, M.F., Burkman, R.T. The Incidence of Abdominal Surgical Procedures in a Population Undergoing Abortion. American Journal Obstetrics and Gynecolocy, Vol. 137, No. 6, pp. 530-534, 1980.

210. Horsley, Jack E. Abortion: Medically Easy, Medicolegally Risky. Medical Economics, January 8, 1979.

211. In re: The Pennsylvania Abortion Control Act. Majority Decision written by Mr. Justice Harry A. Blackmun, United States Supreme Court, 1974.

212. Kelly, Thomas (Bishop). Statement by Secretary of National Conference of Catholic Bishops, 1974.

213. The Pennsylvania Abortion Control Act written after the U.S. Supreme Court's 1973 ruling.

214. Planned Parenthood v. Danforth (No. 74-1151), Supreme Court of Missouri (1974).

215. Birgitta. Twin Circle, July 21, 1972.

216. Kolos, W.D. Wearing it, Eating it, Having it All Right Now. The New York Times, Sunday, December 16, 1984.

217. O'Connor, Liz. Helping Troubled Couples Rediscover Their Love. Long Island Catholic, Thursday, Februry 14, 1985.

218. Shakespeare, Romeo and Juliet, Act II, Scene 2, Line 21.

219. Cates, W., Jr. and Rochat, R.W. Illegal Abortion in the United States 1972-1974. Family Planning Perspective, Vol. 8, pp. 86-92, 1976.

220. Center For Disease Control. Abortion Surveillance, 1976. Issued August 1978.

221. Cates, W., Jr., Schulz, K.F., Grimes, D.A. and Tyler, C.W., Jr. The Effect of Delay and Method Choice on the Risk of Abortion Morbidity. Family Planning Perspective, Vol. 9. pp 266-274, 1977.

222. Cates, W., Jr. and Tietze, C. Standardized Mortality Rates Associated with Legal Abortion: United States, 1972-1975. Family Planning Perspective, Vol. 10, pp. 109-112, 1978.

223. Editorial. Compassionate and Compelling. Long Island Catholic, Thursday, October 18, 1984.

224. Mahoney, E.J. (Canon). Questions and Answers. Vol. II, Precepts, p. 54. Published by Burns, Oates, and Washbourne, London, England, 1949.

225. O'Connor, Liz. Archbishop O'Connor Speaks on Human Lives, Human Rights. Long Island Catholic, Thursday, October 18, 1984.

226. Donne, John (Rev.). Devotions Upon Emergent Occasions, XVII, 17th Century.

227. Surrago, Edward J. History of the Family Planning Clinic: Growth Amid Controversy. Nassau County Medical Center Proceedings, Summer/Autumn 1984.

228. Davis, J.E. (Professor of Urology). On the Sterilization Series. Medical Tribune, Wednesday, January 11, 1978.

229. Friedman, G.A. Involuntary Sterilization. Medical Tribune, Wednesday, January 11, 1978.

230. Meyer v. Nebraska, 362 U.S. 390 (1923).

231. Skinner v. Oklahoma, 316 U.S. 533, 541 (1942).

232. Relf v. Weinberger, 372 F.Supp. 1196 (D.D.C. 1974).

233. Edwards v. California, 315 U.S. 160 (1941).

234. Population Services International v. Wilson, 398 F.Supp. 321 (S.D.N.Y. 1975).

235. Newsday, August 20, 1982. Editorial based on July-August Family Planning Perspectives, a journal of the Alan Guttmacher Institute - Planned Parenthood Federation. Quoted in Long Island Catholic, Thursday, August 27, 1982.

236. Pope Paul VI's Encyclical: "Of Human Life", 1968, No. 22.

237. Thomas, John L. (SA.J.) Marriage and Rhythm. Newman Press, Westminster, Maryland, 1957.

238. St. Paul's First Letter to the Corinthians 7:3-5.

239. The penitent thief on the right side of Christ Crucified, Good Friday, according to the Gospel of St. Luke, 23, 40-41.

240. Words of St. Peter the Rock upon whom Christ built his Church. Peter 5:17-19.

241. Nikitemko, Alexander V. (Censor). The Diary of a Russian Censor. Edited and translated by Helen Jacobson. Amherst University of Massachusetts Press, 1975. From an entry on page 310 for February 16, 1866. Quoted in Biological Psychology and the Tsarist Censor: The Dilemma of Scientific Development by Daniel P. Todes. Published in Bulletin of the History of Medicine, Vol. 58, No. 4, pp 529-544, Winter Edition 1984.

242. Gospel according to St. Luke 6:36-38.

243. Gospel according to St. Luke 1:41.

244. Handbill Publication of the Knights of Columbus (no date).

245. Holmes, K.K. The Chlamydia Epidemic. JAMA, Vol. 245, pp1718-1723, 1981.

246. Bell, T.A., Kuo, C.C., Stamm, W.E., Tam, M.R., Stephens, R.S., Holmes, K.K. and Grayston, J.T. Direct Fluorescent Monoclonal Antibody Stain for Rapid Detection of Infant Chlamydia Trachomatis Infection. Pediatrics, Vol. 74, No. 5, pp. 224-228, 1984.

247. Smith, T.F. Sexually Transmitted Infections due to Chlamydia Trachomatis: Rapid Detection by Immunofluorescence Microscopy. Mayo Clinic Proceedings, Vol. 60, No. 3, pp. 204-206, 1984.

248. No author. News You Can Use. U.S. News and World Report, p. 61, August 5, 1985.

249. No author. National Weekly Digest, p. 2, The Long Island Catholic, Thursday, August 8, 1985.

250. No author. Working Women and Pregnancy. Under title News You Can Use in Your Personal Planning, p. 61, U.S. News and World Report, August 5, 1985.

251. No author. National Weekly Digest, p. 2, The Long Island Catholic, Thursday, August 8, 1985.

252. Glass, J.C. No-fault Compensation for Human Subjects Injured in Biomedical Research: A Public Policy Conflict. The Pharos, Vol. 48, No. 3, pp. 2-4, Summer Issue 1985.

253. Rawls, J. A Theory of Justice. Belknap Press of Harvard University Press, Cambridge, Massachusetts, 1971.

254. Williams,Robert H. Textbook of Endocrinology. W.B. Saunders Co., Philadelphia and London, 1962.

254A. Walsh, Kenneth T. The Bush administration's modest plans to help prolife backers (Other abortion-related controversies). U.S. News & World Report, Pg. 26, April 24, 1989.

255. Webster v. Reproductive Health Services, Missouri Supreme Court. U.S. Supreme Court Docket Number 88-605, April 26, 1989. Based on Webster v. Reproductive Health Services, probable jurisdiction noted January 9, 1989, 57 U.S.L.W. 3451 (January 10, 1989).

256. George Gallup Poll on abortion, released to the media on April 15, 1989 by American Institute of Public Opinion.

257. The Long Island Catholic, Pg. 4, Thursday, March 30, 1989.

258. O'Connor, John J. and Koch, Edward I. His Eminence And Hizzoner, 366 pp. William Morrow and Company, New York, N.Y. Reviewed by Andrew Hacker in New York Times Book Review Section, Pg. 3, March 26, 1989.

259. Criminalizing First Amendment Rights. Are Prolifers Racketeers? Catholic League Newsletter, Vol. 16, No. 4, Pg. 1, April 1989. Published by the Catholic League for Religious and Civil Rights, 1100 Wells Street, Milwaukee, Wisconsin 53233.

260. Kelly, Tom. The Marcher's new clothes. The Washington Times, Thursday, Pg. F-4, April 27, 1989.

261. No author. Abortion March on April 19, 1989. The Washington Times, Thursday, Pg. F-3, April 20, 1989.

262. Aristotle (384-322 B.C.) The process of change. Treasury of Philosophy, Edited by Dagobert D. Runes, Philosophic Library, publisher, New York, N.Y., 1955.

263. Raine, Harrison. To judge and be judged. U.S. News & World Report, Vol. 106, No. 16 Pg. 12-13, April 24,1989. Editorial Offices 2400 N Street, N.W., Washington, D.C. 20037.

264. Bauer, Gary. Where Roe issues should be decided. The Washington Times, Thursday, Pg. F-4, April 20, 1989.

265. Walsh, Kenneth T. The Bush administration's modest plans to help prolife backers. U.S. News & World Report, Vol. 106, No. 16, Pg. 26, Washington, D.C. 20037, April 24, 1989.

266. Scully, Matthew. Factions brawl on steps of the Supreme Court. The Washington Times, Thursday, Metropolitan Section - Section B, Pages B-1, B-2, and B-3, April 27, 1989.

267. Price, Linda. Court hears arguments on abortion regulation. The Washington Times, Thursday, Front Page, April 27, 1989.

268. Frank, Judy. Taney: Famed Dred Scott Decision marks him in history. The Washington Times, Thursday, Page E-7, October 13, 1988.

269. Editorial. Take a hike, not a walk. The Long Island Catholic, Vol. 28, No. 2, Page 1, Thursday, April 27, 1989. Published by the Diocese of Rockville Centre, Hempstead, New York, 11550.

270. De Celles, Charles, Ph.D. Personal communication to the author. An augmentation of a letter, Reflection on Missouri's Declaration That Human Life Begins At Conception/Fertilization, sent to Attorney General William Webster, Esq. of St. Louis, Missouri. Plaintiff's advocate before U.S. Supreme Court in the matter of Webster v. Reproductive Human Services. Full citation thereof under reference number 255. Date of communication June 1, 1989.

271. Gest, Ted. New abortion fights. Why the Supreme Court probably won't overturn Roe v. Wade. U.S. News & World Report, Vol. 106, No. 16, Pgs. 22, 23, April 24, 1989.

272. Neff v. George, 364, Illinois, 306, 4 N.E. 2d 338,390,391.

273. Moore v. City of Albany, 98 N.Y. 396, 410.

274. State v. Mellenberger, 163 Oregon 233, 95 P 2d 709.719, 720,128 A.L.R. 1506.

275. Anonymous. What price sympathy? ROBINS READER. Published by A.H. Robbins Pharmaceutical Co., Richmond, Virginia, Spring/Summer Edition 1989.

276. Doder, Dusko. The old sexism in the new China. U.S. News & World Report, Vol. 106, No. 16, Pages 36 to 38 inclusive, April 24, 1989.

277. Conversation of John Boswell with Alvin P. Sanoff in Horizons Section of Magazine. U.S. News & World Report, Vol. 106, No. 17, Page 62, May 1, 1989.

278. Boswell, John. The Kindness of Strangers. Pantheon Books, New York, N.Y. 1989.

279. Massell, Theodore B. (M.D.) of Los Angeles, Cal. Letters to the Editor: Female Infanticide in China. The PHAROS OF ALPHA OMEGA ALPHA, Honor Medical Society Magazine, Vol. 52, No. 2, Pg. 36, Spring 1989.

280. Crowley, Daniel F. (M.D.), author of "The Disease of Overpopulation" reply to Dr. Theodore B. Massell. Letters to the Editor. The PHAROS see reference 279, 1989.

281. Innerst, Carol. Group Seeks Probe of Sex-Selection Abortions. The Washington Times, Thursday, pg. A-4, March 30, 1989.

282. National Catholic News. Abortion opponents applaud ban on experiments on aborted fetuses. The Long Island Catholic, Thursday, Page 6, April 21, 1988.

283. Shreibman, David. Better paid and better educated are more apt to favor abortion. The Wall Street Journal, Wednesday, A 10, April 26, 1989.

284. No author. American Baptists 'struggling' with abortion issue. The Long Island Catholic, Thursday, Page 6, April 21, 1988.

285. Nelson, J. Robert (Rev.) The ecumenical challenge of ethical issues. ORIGINS, NC Documentary Service. Vol. 18, No. 45, Page 765, April 20, 1989.

286. Sheehan, Pete. Nat Hentoff, Jewish atheist, writes for life. The Long Island Catholic, Thursday, Page 7, October 22, 1987.

287. National Conference of Catholic Bishops. Campus of The Catholic University of America, Washington, D.C. 20064.

288. Brooks, Barbara. Abortion in England 1900-1967. London: Croom Helm, 1988. Distributed in the USA by Routledge, Chapman, and Hall.

289. Reed, James. Book review of Barbara Brooks textbook listed in reference 288. James Reed, Department of History, Rutgers University, New Brunswick, New Jersey. Book Review Section, Bulletin of the History of Medicine, Vol. 63, No. 1, Pages 162, 163, Spring 1989. Publication of the American Association of the History of Medicine, Johns Hopkins University, Baltimore, Maryland, 1989.

290. Hinshaw, Rick. Nellie Gray: Prolifers urged to 'stick to the basics,' The Long Island Catholic, Thursday, Vol. 28, No. 4, Page 4, May 11, 1989.

291. Leo, John. Baby boys to order. U.S. News & World Report, Vol. 106, No. 1, Page 59, January 9, 1989.

292. Church of Holy Trinity v. United States, 143 U.S. Supreme Court, 457 at 471.

293. Lichtenstein, Stan. 'Christian Nation' concept an affront. Potomac Almanac, Pg. 9, April 26, 1989. Published in Potomac, Maryland, 1989.

294. Griswold v. Connecticut, 381 U.S. Supreme Court, 479, 85 S. Ct. 1678, 14L. Ed. 2d 510, (1965).

295. Roe v. Wade, 410 U.S. Supreme Court, 113 (1973).

296. Noble-Allgire, Alice M. Court ordered Cesarean Sections: A Judicial Standard for resolving the conflict between fetal interest and maternal rights. Journal of Legal Medicine, Vol. 10, No. 11, Pages 211 to 249, 1989, Published by the American College of Legal Medicine, Maple Glen, Pennsylvania, 19002.

297. Melanie Howard. Recalling the years when abortion was a crime. Potomac Almanac, Vol. 13, No. 35, Pg. 10, May 3, 1989.

298. O'Connor, Liz. Project Rachel: To heal abortion's effects. The Long Island Catholic, Vol. 28, No. 1, Pages 1 and 8, Thursday, April 20, 1989. Published by Diocese of Rockville Centre, Hempstead, New York. 11550, 1989.

299. No author. High Court ruling lets stand right to free elective abortions in prison. The Long Island Catholic, Thursday, Page 4, May 26, 1988. Publication of the Diocese of Rockville Centre, Hempstead, L.I., New York, 11550.

300. Castiglioni, Arturo. A History of Medicine. Alfred A. Knopf, publisher, New York, New York, 1941.

301. Williams, Marjorie and Kamen, Al. Sandra Day O'Connor in Control. The Washington Post, Magazine Section, Page 53, June 11, 1989.

302. In The Supreme Court of the United States, No. 88-605, October Term 1988. William L. Webster, et al., Appellants v. Reproductive Health Services, et al., Appellees. On Appeal from the United States Court of Appeals for the Eighth Circuit. Brief Amici Curiae of Focus On The Family And Family Research Council of America, In support of Appellants. H. Robert Showers, Counsel of Record. Richard M. Campanelli, Gammon and Grange 1925 K St. N.W., Suite 300, Washington D.C. 20006. Attorneys for Amici Curiae. Wilson-Epes Printing Co., Inc., Washington, D.C. 20001, 1988.

303. Surgeon General C. Everett Koop (M.D.). Letter to President Ronald Reagan on complications of abortions, January 9, 1989.

304. Speckhard, A. Psycho-Social Aspects of Stress Following Abortion (1987). Quoted in reference 302.

305. Osofsky and Osofsky. The Psychological Reaction of patients to legalized abortion. American Journal of Orthopsychiatry, 42, 48, 1972.

306. Ashton, P. The psychological outcome of induced abortion. British Journal of Obstetrics and Gynecology, Vol. 87, No. 10, Pages 1115-1120, 1980.

307. Franco, K. Dysphoric Reactions in Women After Abortion. Unpublished paper, Medical College of Ohio, 1984. Quoted in reference 302.

308.  Publicized decision in the Webster matter by the Supreme Court of the United States of America. Majority opinion by Chief Justice William Rehnquist, minority opinion by Associate Justice Harry Blackmun rendered on July 3, 1989.

309.  Ponce, Linda. Court chips away at abortion rights. But Roe survives in 5-4 vote. The Washington Times, Tuesday, Front Page, July 4, 1989.

310.  Harvey, Chris. Battle will shift to states. The Washington Times, Tuesday, Front Page, Published in Washington, D.C. Editorial offices, 3600 New York Avenue, N.E. Washington, D.C. 20002. July 4, 1989.

## ABOUT THE AUTHOR

Educated at the Georgetown University School of Medicine and trained in the American tradition of modern surgery, Dr. Ficarra practiced his profession for thirty-nine years in New York City and its suburbs. Although he has retired from the surgical operating theatre, he has neither retreated from life nor has he withdrawn into eremitic confinement.

During his active surgical career he authored more than two hundred published scientific articles, ten books, and many editorials. Still concerned with the medicosurgical profession he serves on the Committee for Legal matters of the American College of Gastroenterology, the Education Committee of the American College of Legal Medicine, as a member of the Medical Specialty Advisory Board of the Journal Medical Malpractice Prevention, and is a member of the Professional Editorial Board of The Journal of Contemporary Health Law and Policy of The Catholic University of America School of Law, Washington, D.C.

Currently he is President of The Catholic Academy of Sciences in the United States of America, and is a writer and lecturer on Legal Medicine and Bioethics. In the field of non-medical literature he has published a book of short stories with the title *Leaf in the Wind*, as well as a novel, *Zappatori*, which translates to mean the ditch diggers. In the autumn of 1989, his book *Feudal Chateau* was published. Under preparation is a manuscript inspired by an ancient Roman church in the vincinage of Vatican City State.

The doctor's non-professional honors include the pontifical title of Knight of St. Gregory the Great, the ecclesiastical dignities of Knight of the Sovereign Military Order of Jerusalem, Rhodes, and Malta, as well as Knight of the Grand Cross in the Equestrian Order of the Holy Sepulchre of Jerusalem, of which he is the Section Representative for Washington, D.C., Northern Virginia and Southern Maryland of the Southeastern Lieutenancy of the United States of America.

In October 1988, Dr. Ficarra was given the Silver Palm of Jerusalem for his twenty-five years of continuous service to the Holy Land. The decoration was bestowed by His Beatitude the Most Reverend Michele Sabbah, the Archbishop of Jerusalem.